Criminal Justice in New York City

Criminal Justice in New York City

by

James R. Davis

McFarland & Company, Inc., Publishers
Jefferson, North Carolina, and London

Acknowledgments It is difficult to thank everyone who influenced me and this book. I would like to thank all the teachers I had in graduate school while I was studying criminal justice as part of my training and education for a Ph.D. degree in sociology. I would like to thank all the authors of books and articles I read in criminal justice for the information that these books and articles conveyed to me. I would like to name all the criminologists and students of criminal justice whom I met at the annual national and state conventions of sociology and criminal justice who have influenced me in their role as chairpersons, presenters, and discussants of sessions, but the list would extend for pages. I certainly have to thank the librarians of the New York Public Library who helped me to locate special documents and reports for New York City.

Most important, I wish to thank my wife Roberta who has put up with a husband who spends most of his spare time in the library. I also wish to thank my typist, Muriel Bennett, who did an excellent job of typing the various drafts of the manuscript.

British Library Cataloguing-in-Publication data are available

Library of Congress Cataloguing-in-Publication Data

Davis, James R., 1928–
    Criminal justice in New York City / by James R. Davis.
        p. cm.
    [Includes index.]
    Includes bibliographical references.
    ISBN 0-89950-486-8 (lib. bdg. : 50# alk. paper) ∞
        1. Criminal justice, Administration of—New York (N.Y.)—
    Handbooks, manuals, etc. I. Title.
    HV9956.N5D38 1990
    364.9747'1–dc20   89-43646
                                                            CIP

Manufactured in the United States of America

McFarland & Company, Inc., Publishers
  Box 611, Jefferson, North Carolina 28640

PREFACE

I thought of writing about criminal justice in New York City for some time. I had many reasons for this. First, I have lived in New York City since February 12, 1968, and I identify this city as my city. Second, I have grown to love this city. Third, I received my education and training in criminal justice in New York City. Fourth, I am a probation officer for the city of New York. Fifth, although other cities are often in the news, this city had some particularly interesting criminal cases: the Bernhard Goetz case, for example, concerning the subway rider who shot four youths on the subway when they allegedly tried to rob him; the Howard Beach incident, in which three black men, one of whom was killed by a passing auto, were the object of a racial attack by white residents; the Larry Davis case, in which an offender shot and wounded several officers, including a female officer; the Robert Chambers case, concerning the white youth who was accused of killing his girlfriend while engaging in sex with her in Central Park; and the Bess Myerson case, concerning the former Miss America accused of influencing a judge to reduce alimony payments for Myerson's racketeer boyfriend in return for giving the judge's daughter a city job. Sixth, since New York City is one of the largest cities in the country, I thought a book about its criminal justice system would interest not only academics, students, researchers, and practitioners in the field, but also laymen who were not trained in criminal justice but who were interested in the topic. Seventh, since what takes place in criminal justice in New York City often becomes a model for the rest of the country, I thought that this book would interest others outside of New York City.

The main problem in writing this book was choosing a focus. Criminal justice can be discussed from many different perspectives. For example, one can discuss the structure and function of the police, courts, and corrections systems; one can discuss the role of the principal legal actors in the system: police, prosecutors, defense attorneys, prison guards, probation and parole officers, judges, etc.; one can discuss the relation of the offenders to the victims; one can discuss and evaluate what takes place in police stations, courts, prisons, etc. And there are many other perspectives.

Although I discuss criminal justice using all these perspectives to some degree, my main emphasis is on the offender in relation to the system. I implicitly pose two main questions: (1) what kind of punishment do defendants receive in the system? (2) is it safe to walk the streets of New York City?

The methodology I used was a review of the relevant literature, mainly concerning New York City, the insights I gained from my 20 years of experience as a probation officer, and the findings of the special research projects I completed for annual meetings in criminology and sociology. My experience as a probation officer brought me into contact with other legal actors: policemen, parole officers, prosecutors, legal defense lawyers, judges, drug representatives, psychiatric social workers, etc. My research projects were never published, but some were cited in journals, and they add information because all the research was confined to New York City and involved various aspects of the system. Many of these projects were based on sophisticated statistical techniques.

A study like this must pass over some important topics. For example, the role of the victim, although discussed, is minimized. The attitudes of the defendants and their families toward the various parts of the criminal justice system are barely touched upon. White-collar crime in New York City is hardly discussed at all. Juvenile offenders, a subject in itself, is barely examined. I attempt to analyze a few of the more important theories, but many others are not even mentioned. A comparison of the system in New York City to systems in other jurisdictions is hardly mentioned. I am certain that there are other important topics that are omitted in this book; some readers will notice these omissions. However, in spite of these shortcomings, I believe that this book is fairly complete in presenting a fairly comprehensive picture of the system in New York City.

The literature seems to focus more on the police than the courts or corrections. Therefore, if I have alluded to the police more than to other aspects of the system, I take full responsibility for this. I also take full responsibility for any errors in this book.

James R. Davis
Spring 1990

TABLE OF CONTENTS

1

NEW YORK CITY
AS A CASE STUDY

Some researchers in criminal justice confine their studies to one jurisdiction, while others focus on several. Neubauer, for example, in his study of prosecution in Middle America,[1] confined his research to Prairie City, a real city hidden behind a fictitious name, and Casper, in his study of the defendants' views on criminal justice,[2] confined his study to one state, Connecticut. Eisenstein and Jacob compared criminal justice among three cities. Baltimore, Detroit, and Chicago.[3] Levin compared the sentencing process in two cities: Minneapolis and Pittsburgh.[4]

Some researchers generalize beyond the particular jurisdiction studied, while other researchers confine their findings to the particular jurisdiction studied. Some researchers use cross-national data to generalize criminal justice findings. Stuart Nagel used cross-national data in his sentencing study.[5] Some researchers cite empirical studies of many different cities to generalize about various aspects of criminal justice. I did this recently to answer the question, "Is criminal justice a science?"[6]

However, I do not know of any one particular intensive study of criminal justice in all its perspectives for one city.[7] Sometimes researchers study criminal justice in one city, but not in all its perspectives; or they emphasize one perspective in one city and only scratch the surface of other perspectives. This book is apparently the first study of its type, that is, an intensive study of one city, New York City, covering all the perspectives of criminal justice.

Intensive case studies of cities have many advantages. First, residents like to know what is happening in their own cities. Second, intensive case studies make it possible to see if generalizations applicable to criminal justice everywhere are applicable to the particular city studied; one can see how much the particular city deviates from what is happening in criminal justice as a whole

1

in other jurisdictions. Third, an intensive case study of one city can sometimes be more thoroughly analyzed than a study of several cities or jurisdictions. Fourth, an intensive case study can sometimes more easily include sociological factors relevant to criminal justice outcomes—for example, population hetero-geneity or the political system—than other types of studies.

Two scientific methods widely used in research are induction and deduc-tion. Induction creates generalizations from known facts, postulates, axioms, theorems, theories, etc. Deduction generates postulates, axioms, theorems, deduced from facts. Although both methods are used here, induction is the principal method. The methodology involves a review of the relevant literature on criminal justice in New York City, including statistical reports and special reports; research projects completed by the author on various aspects of the system; and the author's experiences as a probation officer.

Generalizations

Some generalizations are applicable to criminal justice no matter what jurisdiction is studied. These generalizations apply most of the time, although there are exceptions which deviate from the generalizations. These generaliza-tions are based on a review of the literature, and are derived from theoretical and empirical studies.

1. *Criminal justice includes three main components: the police, the courts, and the corrections system.* These three components can be subdivided into smaller components and aspects for analysis. For example, the police can be studied from the aspects of the police role, or expected behavior; the structure and function of the police organization; public attitudes and expectations re-garding the police; police selection and training; the history of the police; theories of police behavior; police corruption; police-community relations; police promotion within the organization; police brutality and or violence directed against policemen; the police and the media, etc. Usually only some aspects of the police are emphasized in any one study.

The courts can also be studied from many different perspectives: arraign-ment; prosecution and plea bargaining; legal defense; jury selection and out-comes; pretrial status; sentencing; judges' behavior; selection and function of court personnel; felonies, misdemeanors, and violations; juvenile courts; the flow of cases through the court; etc. Again, in only one study some aspects are emphasized while others are minimized or ignored.

Corrections, too, can include many components. Jails and prisons, for ex-ample, are one main component of corrections.[8] Probation and parole are another significant component.[9] The various elements of community corrections—half-way houses, drug facilities, both in- and outpatient, work-release programs,[10] prison furloughs, etc.—seem to expand every year, and thus draw increasing research attention.

The main components of corrections can be subdivided into smaller components. Jails and prisons, for example, can be studied in reference to the inmate social structure; the formal prison structure and administration; the relationship between inmates and prison guards; inmate misbehavior; inmate education and training; classification of prisons and inmates; women's versus men's prisons; co-sex prisons; custody versus rehabilitation; inmate grievances and legal rights; prison services; courts' interference into prison conditions; effects of prison on inmates; jail and prison riots; history of jails and prisons, etc.

Parole can be studied from the aspect of the selection of parole boards; the decisions of parole boards; parole supervision; the selection of parole officers; parole violations; the effects of parole on parolees; legal rights of parolees; etc. Probation can be studied from the perspective of effectiveness of probation supervision; types of probation supervision; presentence function of probation; conditions of probation; selection of probation officers; caseloads; legal aspects; etc. Also, half-way houses, drug facilities, etc., can be studied from the aspect of effectiveness; selection of inmates; supervision of inmates; community service, etc.

2. *Punishment can be subdivided into four main functions: deterrence, incapacitation, retribution, and rehabilitation.* Deterrence is the prevention of crime either by a particular individual offender or by groups of offenders. For example, if offender X receives two years' prison for a crime, offender X is expected to learn to refrain from future crime because of this punishment; others, for example, offender X's friends and fellow criminals, are supposed to learn to refrain from future crime because of the example set by the punishment offender X received. Incapacitation generally implies jail or prison. Offender X is prevented from committing crimes against society while incarcerated, although offender X can still commit crimes against fellow inmates and prison staff while incarcerated. Retribution refers to "an eye for an eye and tooth for a tooth" type of philosophy. If offender X committed a crime, offender X must be punished in a way that exacts a fit retribution. However, offender X's punishment will probably not equal the harm caused to the victim. Rehabilitation refers to the reformation of criminals. If offender X is incarcerated for two years, and learns a trade while in prison, offender X might legitimately obtain gainful employment after release from prison and thereafter refrain from crime.

The four functions of punishment are not mutually exclusive. Each overlaps with the others. For example, although probation is usually considered a kind of rehabilitation, it is also a kind of incapacitation because probationers who violate the terms of their probation—by failure to cooperate in drug treatment; failure to report to their probation officers; failure to abide by any other conditions imposed by the probation officers—can be sent to jail. To abide by these conditions is incapacitating to the probationer. Probation is also retribution because probationers are being punished. It is also a form of deterrence because one goal of probation is the prevention of future crime.

Although philosophies of punishment are discussed separately from the main components of the criminal justice system in the literature, these philosophies are applicable to all aspects of criminal justice. Philosophies of punishment underlie all decisions of the criminal justice system. For example, a police decision to arrest is a form of punishment because the act of arrest makes the arrested individual a part of the criminal justice system. Once accused of committing a crime, he or she becomes subject to a variety of possible consequences, including fine, probation, and incarceration. Even a dismissal does not negate the initial punishment—embarrassment, disruption of employment, expenses caused by hiring a lawyer, lack of privacy, temporary loss of freedom and other individual rights usually taken for granted, etc.—caused by the act of arrest.

3. *Discretion pervades the criminal justice system.* One of the most influential writers on discretion is Kenneth Culp Davis. According to Davis, "A public officer has discretion whenever the effective limits on his power leave him free to make a choice concerning possible causes of action and inaction."[11] Thus, officials make choices or decisions that affect outcomes. Discretion, in Davis' view, cannot be entirely eliminated. Therefore, maintaining the right balance of discretion is one of the most important issues facing the criminal justice system.[12]

Discretion pervades the criminal justice system. The police have a great deal of discretion in deciding whom to arrest; they also have discretion when charging an offender with a crime. The prosecutors have discretion in charging and recommending a sentence, and even in dismissing a case. Judges have discretion in setting bail, in deciding the pretrial status of the defendant, and in sentencing. Correction officials have discretion to decide when an offender is ready for release from prison. Parole boards have discretion to decide who shall be placed on parole. Probation officers decide who shall be violated.

However, although public officials do have discretion, discretion is structured by rules and regulations. For example, New York state law mandates that every inmate in corrections must get one day off of his or her jail or prison time for every three days of jail or prison time served. Probation officers in New York City must initiate a violation of probation when a probationer commits a felony while under probation supervision. The police of New York state must not use bodily force except to defend their own lives or the lives of others, or to apprehend a fleeing felon who threatens to use force. However, many of these rules and regulations can be interpreted flexibly by the officials who enforce the decisions.

4. *Plea bargaining pervades the criminal justice system.* This fact is supported by numerous studies. It has been true for at least 100 years. It may also be strictly an American practice. If a defendant pleads guilty to a crime, his original charge will be reduced and hence he will receive some punishment—some jail or prison time, or probation—but not the full punishment he would have received if the original charges were proved in court. For example, if a defendant pleads guilty to selling drugs he can be given a reduction of charge to criminal possession of drugs, a misdemeanor, instead of criminal sale of drugs, a felony. In this example of plea bargaining the defendant would receive one year in jail or three years of probation instead of two to four years in prison for selling drugs.

Many theories have been proposed to justify plea bargaining. One of the strongest theories argues that if all defendants were allowed to take their cases to trial by not pleading guilty, the courts would be overloaded and the legal system would collapse. Other theorists argue that plea bargaining serves the function of mitigating harsh punishment. Still others believe that plea bargaining serves to individualize punishment.[13] Even legal defense lawyers, a much neglected group in criminal justice research, very often are influential in persuading defendants to plea bargain their cases.[14]

5. *Many defendants receive individual attention in the processing of their cases.* This is difficult to prove or disprove, but empirical evidence reveals that very often legal actors take special interest in an individual's case. For example, probation officers often devote considerable attention to the supervision process of a particular probationer, in spite of heavy caseloads. Legal defense lawyers, both public and private, try to individualize certain cases. Even prosecutors try to individualize each case, by accumulating legal facts and following other criteria, in order to prove guilt or innocence.

Sometimes individual attention is defined subjectively by defendants. Some defendants believe that the mitigating circumstances surrounding their cases do not receive enough attention; they believe that justice follows an "assembly-line" process, in which almost all cases are treated alike regardless of the circumstances. Very often it is difficult to determine the benefits and disadvantages of assembly-line justice versus individual attention for certain cases.

6. *The seriousness of the crime and the prior record of the defendant are the most important factors affecting punishment.* Empirical studies of all aspects of criminal justice support this generalization. Some of the factors affecting prosecutors' decisions and probation officers' and judges' recommendations for

sentencing support this conclusion. The more serious the crime, and the more severe the prior record of the defendant, the more severe the punishment imposed for the present crime. Determining the seriousness of the prior record and the seriousness of the present offense are sometimes a matter of discretion. No set rules are applicable in every jurisdiction, but some regulations do exist. Moreover, these two factors are decisive in setting bail and the pretrial status of the defendant. The severity of the prior record and the seriousness of the present offense very often determine if a defendant will be remanded or released before sentencing.

7. *Defendants in remand before sentencing will suffer a more severe disposition than those who are not in remand before sentencing.* This outcome has been verified by a number of studies. Offenders in jail do not have the resources necessary to fight their cases, and thus must suffer the consequences of a severe disposition. These resources include private lawyers, money for bail, and employment, all of which are directly and indirectly important for fighting one's case. Private lawyers sometimes, although not always, will devote extra time and effort to fight for an accused individual, especially if the lawyer believes that his/her client is innocent. Also, a private lawyer might well decide to take the client's case to trial, if he/she believes it is worthwhile. Very often offenders who are in remand before sentencing have bail amounts that are too high for them to meet, and as a result must suffer the consequences. Moreover, if an offender is in remand, he or she is usually unemployed and thus the ability to find the money to pay for bail and a private attorney are curtailed.[15]

Other researchers suggest that offenders who are in remand sometimes are there because prosecutors and judges want to sentence them to a prison term. These offenders might be considered dangerous to the public, or the prosecutors and judges believe that these offenders will abscond before sentencing. An offender accused of killing a police officer, for example, is always considered dangerous. In other words, prosecutors and judges do not want certain kinds of offenders on the street. (Should these offenders be given prison sentences, they usually will be given credit for the time they served in remand.)

8. *Judges usually sentence defendants with the aid of other legal actors.* The other legal actors include prosecutors or district attorneys, legal defense lawyers, and probation officers. Prosecutors, or district attorneys, represent the people or the state. Therefore, they generally are oriented toward exacting some type of punishment. Many factors contribute to prosecutors' decisions. Already mentioned was the seriousness of the crime and the defendant's record: number of prior arrests, prior felony convictions, number of prior periods of probation and parole, parole or probation adjustment, drug treatment adjustment, etc. The "strength of the case," how strong or weak the evidence is, also contributes to the prosecutor's decision. Are there witnesses who have strong

evidence concerning the offender's guilt? Will the complainant testify against the defendant? Some complainants make weak witnesses. If, as often happens, the defendant and victim are related in some way—husband and wife, boyfriend and girlfriend, mother and son, etc.—the victim often drops the charges during prosecution. Many other factors, however, go into prosecutors' decisions.

Legal defense lawyers usually attempt to defend the offenders in some way. The lawyer will sometimes try to influence the defendant to plead guilty in order to mitigate punishment. The lawyer may believe that the defendant is guilty, or even if he/she does not know if the defendant is guilty, the lawyer may believe that the punishment the defendant will receive through plea bargaining will be lighter than if the defendant pleads "not guilty" and goes to trial. Studies have shown that generally, but certainly not always, defendants who take their cases to trial and lose are usually given more severe dispositions than others. This is because the state has to expend more resources on a trial than on plea bargaining. However, lawyers often do legitimately try to defend their clients without influencing them to plea bargain.

Very often, probation officers make a sentencing recommendation after interviewing a defendant. Studies have shown that the seriousness of the crime and the prior record are important factors in probation officers' decisions. Also important are employment status, adjustment on prior probation and parole, and pretrial status. Judges take probation officers' recommendations seriously. They are particularly influential in cases where the prosecutor does not make a recommendation, as with some misdemeanors.

The legal defense lawyers and the prosecutors represent the main components of our adversary system. Under the law, both felons and misdemeanants, even if indigent, are entitled to legal representation. Judges do not have to follow prosecutors' recommendations but usually do. In addition, defense lawyers confer with judges and prosecutors in order to plea bargain their cases. Often, too, judges can be influenced by relatives, friends, and employers of the convicted person. These influences can be negative or positive. And, of course, judges themselves are influential in the sentencing decisions.

9. *Disparity exists in the criminal justice system.* Disparity can loosely be defined as "unequal sentences for similar cases." Two offenders can commit identical crimes, can have similar criminal histories, and yet one defendant receives three years in prison while the other receives five years' probation. Very often disparity results from extralegal factors, including employment, age, status in the community, etc. Sometimes disparity in sentencing is the object of appeals in which defendants claim that their constitutional rights have been violated. Disparity is also one of the political forces behind the movement for determinate sentencing.

10. *Many offenders commit crimes against their own racial or ethnic group.* This situation is generally true. Whites tend to commit crimes against whites; blacks tend to commit crimes against blacks; Hispanics tend to commit crimes against Hispanics; Italians tend to commit crimes against Italians; Jews tend to commit crimes against Jews; etc. Crime is usually intraracial and intra-ethnic.

One reason for this is that criminals and victims often know each other, and, therefore, are of the same ethnic or racial group. Another reason why offenders sometimes commit crimes against their own ethnic or racial group is that offenders tend to live in the neighborhood where the crime is committed, and neighborhoods are somewhat homogenous in race and ethnicity. However, in certain street crimes this situation might not apply; muggers, burglars, and car thieves, for example, often leave their own ethnic neighborhoods to commit crimes against more affluent strangers in another neighborhood. Therefore, crime can also be interracial or interethnic.

11. *Sometimes the effects of punishment are positive and sometimes the effects of punishment are negative.* As mentioned earlier, in generalization 2, the four functions of punishment are deterrence, incapacitation, retribution, and rehabiliation. Empirical studies have verified that deterrence sometimes deters offenders and sometimes does not deter offenders. For example, the recidivism rate of criminals is sometimes high, in spite of long prison sentences combined with parole; many parolees violate their parole and return to prison. The same is true of rehabilitation. In spite of probation, parole supervision, employment training, and drug therapy, many offenders commit more crimes. The same is true of retribution or incapacitation. One can question if the punishment is severe enough.

The question in empirical research is whether recidivism would be even higher without the prison sentences and rehabilitative measures employed in an offender's case. Much money has been spent on research—on before and after experimental studies, for example—to determine the influence of deter-rence and rehabiliation. Researchers do not always agree on what outcomes are decisive. Besides recidivism, employment, attitudes and behavior, stability in the community, drug dependency, and other factors are used to determine outcomes in rehabilitation.

12. *The criminal justice system is disunified.* This means that the different parts of the criminal justice system each have their own bureaucracy and management system, and one part of the system is not necessarily accountable to another part of the system. What probation does might have nothing to do with what prosecution does, and vice versa. If probation officers are punitive, this does not mean that the prosecutors have to be punitive, and vice versa. Probation officers do not have to follow prosecutors' recommendations.

Prosecutors very often side with the police, but they do not have to support them. Each part or component of the criminal justice system has its own rules, regulations, norms, mores, workgroups, and personnel. The personnel in each part of the system do not have to reveal their policies to other personnel in other parts of the system.

Many critics believe that the criminal justice system should be unified. They believe that there should be more cooperation among the parts. However, although personnel in the various parts of the system do not have to cooperate, informal cooperation among the various parts and subsystems usually does exist.

These twelve generalizations certainly do not exhaust all possibilities, but they are, in the author's opinion, the main ones found in the literature. These generalizations do not *always* apply in *every* case in *every* jurisdiction. For example, occasionally defendants with heavy prior records obtain lenient dispositions because of a good defense lawyer. Many organized crime figures fall into this category. Although many defendants receive individual attention in their cases, defendants coming before a magistrate or judge for motor vehicle violations might receive assembly-line justice, with hundreds of cases decided in a very short period of time. Although much crime is intraracial, some black offenders do assault and rape white victims, just as some white offenders assault and rape black victims. Exceptions abound but they do not violate the generalizations.

These generalizations are interrelated. For example, disparity, individual attention, and discretion are all interrelated. If a judge shows discretion in sentencing a defendant, it might be because he or she wants to individualize the defendant's case. In other words, individualization, generally considered a good, can cause disparity, generally considered an evil. Different factors can combine positively or negatively to effect the defendant.

Critics of the criminal justice system believe that the system is pervaded with too much discretion, and have fought for some type of determinate sentencing. But even in states where determinate sentences exist, there are many critics of the new laws. Some believe that the new laws are confusing and conflicting; some believe that power has shifted from the judge to the prosecutor; and some believe that sentences are longer under determinate than indeterminate sentencing.

The fact that the four functions of punishment are not mutually exclusive, and the fact that the outcomes of punishment are sometimes positive and sometimes negative, are related to discretion, disparity, and individual attention. Legal actors must have discretion to impose punishment, and thus to individualize each case. The seriousness of prior record and present offense are related to pretrial status, which in turn is related to an outcome influenced by disparity, discretion, and individual attention. Mitigating circumstances are sometimes influential. Therefore, any type of punishment is possible.

The fact that the various parts of the system are disunified can affect an offender's fate. This occurs, for example, when one part of the system, the prosecution, for example, recommends a severe disposition, and another part, legal defense, for example, recommends a lenient disposition. The conflict must be resolved by our adversary system. Again, the generalizations of discretion, disparity, individual attention, the effects of punishment, the seriousness of prior record and present offense, etc., are all interrelated.

Unique Facts in Criminal Justice for New York City

Although every city is unique, and thus has unique facts associated with its criminal justice system, it is important to emphasize some of these facts concerning New York City. These facts are emphasized here to draw a general picture of the city in relation to its criminal justice system.

New York City

Puerto Ricans in New York City are poorer than blacks.[16] During the period 1970 to 1972 63 percent of the people arrested for violent crime were black and 15.3 percent were Hispanic.[17] In 1971, 65 percent of the city's arrested murderers, muggers, and armed robbers were black, 15 percent were Hispanic, and about 20 percent were white. Of 1,466 criminal homicides recorded in that year, 784 victims, or more than half, were black; 370 were white; 306 were Hispanic; and 6 were miscellaneous.[18] An analysis of the violent crimes of murder, forcible rape, robbery, and aggravated assault indicates that young black or Hispanic males predominately commit these crimes. In 1977 arrests for murder, rape, and robbery indicated that blacks and Hispanics represented 84, 86, and 87 percent, respectively, of those arrested for these three crimes.[19] The largest share of those homicide offenders are black, and the second largest share of homicide offenders are Hispanic.[20]

These facts indicate that blacks and Hispanics represent the largest number of offenders and possibly even victims for certain violent crimes.[21] The fact that the Puerto Ricans are poorer than blacks in the city is not reflected in their crime rate; that is, they do not necessarily have the highest rate of crime even though they are one of the most economically disadvantaged groups in the city. In 1977 the city's population was about 25 percent black and 16 percent Hispanic.[22]

The incarceration rate reflects similar ethnic distributions. In a random sample of felons sentenced to state prison in 1973, 58.3 percent were black, and 15.3 percent were Puerto Rican.[23] Between 1971 and 1977 black male inmates accounted for the largest percentage of new admissions to state prison; white males the second largest percentage; and Puerto Rican males the smallest percentage of the three groups.[24] In city jails, however, the largest proportion of inmates seems to be blacks and Hispanics, with whites the smallest of the three groups.[25]

Although New York City has a high crime rate, it does not suffer from the highest rate in the country. In 1971 New York City ranked ninth among the ten largest cities in murder rates.[26] In the early 1980s the number of nonviolent crimes reported to the police, when adjusted to the size of its population, revealed that New York City ranked seventh among the largest cities.[27] New York City is the biggest market for drugs and narcotics;[28] in 1970 the city had about 41,266 narcotics arrests.[29] In 1971 nearly 100,000 cars were stolen on the streets of New York City, or about 300 a day.[30] For years the New York City homicide rate was well over 1,000 a year, and it has now risen to close to 2,000 per year.[31] New York City may not have the highest crime rate in the country, but it does suffer from a great deal of crime.

New York City, particularly Manhattan, has a high-out-of-town population. This group is vulnerable to victimization, and also might include some offenders. A report revealed that more than half of the robberies in New York City had been committed by either juveniles or youthful offenders.[32] During Governor Rockefeller's administration, New York state allocated more money for the treatment of drug users than any other jurisdiction in the country.[33] In 1970–1971 New York City employed approximately 50,000 persons in criminal justice work.[34] Contrary to popular impression, New York City subways are relatively safe.[35]

New York City has a huge drug problem, and many resources have been committed to fighting that drug problem. Although all state drug facilities have closed, many half-way houses and methadone treatment centers are still available for drug users. Juveniles also represent a big crime problem. Many personnel are involved in criminal justice. Although crime pervades all ethnic groups, blacks and Puerto Ricans are heavily represented as both victims and offenders. New York City is a big city with a big crime problem.

The Police

The New York City Police Department is considered a model of enlightened police-community relations.[36] The New York City Police Department has long had a reputation for being one of the best departments in the country.[37] The New York City police are considered one of the most civilized peacekeeping agencies in the world.[38] Commissioner Murphy, police commissioner in the 1970s, instituted hostage negotiations that became a model for the world.[39] The police of New York City have always been considered courageous.[40] Many police officers have given their lives in the line of duty.[41]

In New York City a person with a criminal record can be appointed as a policeman; however, this record usually consists of a conviction for one misdemeanor. That a policeman himself has had an earlier brush with the law can moderate relations with crime suspects.[42] New York City lagged behind other police departments in initiating reform,[43] but from 1972 to 1982 the police department of New York City evolved from one of the most corrupt and brutal departments to one of the cleanest and most judicious departments.[44]

No city has larger crowds to control than New York City.[45] In 1981 the police department numbered 22,286,[46] but in the late sixties it numbered about 30,000. In the early eighties, there were about 23,000 policemen in the city.[47] Unlike some other cities, where police are instructed to shoot first, and ask questions afterward, the police in New York City are restricted in their use of deadly force.[48] Indeed, for many years the police in New York City had the toughest procedures in the country concerning the use of force.[49] The police of New York City in the 1970s were considered less violent than the police of the 1940s or 1950s.[50]

Although the Taylor Law in New York City prohibits strikes by public workers, including police, in the fall of 1976 police officers demonstrated and threatened strikes and job actions over contract negotiations with the city.[51] During Mayor Beame's administration, firemen, sanitation men, and police officers demonstrated and brought traffic to a halt.[52] On January 13, 1971, 40 patrolmen on the 4 P.M. to 12 P.M. shift in the 42nd Precinct in the Bronx went out on a weekend strike and brought with them at least 75 percent of the patrolmen on duty.[53] In the early seventies, possibly due to riots in prison, some 200 sympathizers of prison riots threw bricks and bottles at police and fire department officials. The crowd totaled 3,000.[54]

In the early seventies the police received 24,000 calls per day for help or service.[55] In 1971, 55 police officers were shot, and 10 were killed; the police made a quarter of a million arrests; and 120,000 people passed through the city's 13 jails.[56] In 1971 there were between 94,000 and 102,148 felony arrests in New York City. About 510,000 felonies were reported in 1971.[57] In 1974 there were about 260,750 arrests in New York City, with 43,831 for violent crimes.[58] In 1977 New Yorkers reported about 1,083,500 major offenses to the police; fewer than 150,000, or about 16.5 percent, resulted in an arrest; of these, about 20,200 arrests led to a felony conviction.[59] About 500,000 felony offenses occur each year in New York City, and about 100,000 felony arrests occur annually.[60] There are about 30,000 arrests per year for prostitution alone.[61] In one year, police made 237,311 arrests.[62] The number of arrests in New York City practically doubled between 1968 and 1977.[63] About 58 percent of the arrests for New York State came from New York City.[64] The police barely cleared over half of the murders in 1976.[65]

From 1950 to 1967 assaults on the police increased from 137 to 803.[66] In a typical year in New York City 7 police officers die in the line of duty; 29 are wounded; and 8 commit suicide; in the same typical year 7 black or Hispanic youths are killed by white policemen under questionable circumstances.[67] From 1970 to 1975 28 police officers took their own lives; most of them shot themselves with their own revolver. Divorce, mental illness, and alcoholism are high among the police of New York City.[68]

New York City police have gigantic crowds to control, have high numbers of arrests to make, and can be assaulted or even killed. There are both favorable and unfavorable reports on the reputation of the police. The price the police might have to pay involves suicide, alcoholism, mental illness, marital discord, or other deviant behavior. There are also many complaints initiated against the police annually.

The Courts

Annually, nearly 100,000 defendants pass through Manhattan's different court rooms.[69] Manhattan's Criminal Court is the world's largest criminal court. In 1977, 90,746 arrests were handled in Manhattan Criminal Court.[70] In 1969, 83,348 cases were heard in the criminal division.[71] In 1964 officials of the New York City Criminal Court reported a total of 442,840 nontraffic felony, misdemeanor, and summary offense arraignments in its five branches, an increase of 91,123 from 1968.[72] In the mid–1970s, in one year, defendants were found guilty of 200,000 charges of misdemeanors and violations; 20,000 of these defendants received jail sentences.[73] In 1967, 4,530,000 traffic and nontraffic cases faced arraignment.[74]

New York's first degree murder rule, which legalized the death penalty for the murder of a police officer or a prison guard, was declared unconstitutional by the state court of appeals in the 1970s.[75] Criminal court judges are appointed by the mayor of New York City for fixed terms; supreme court judges in New York City are elected by the various judicial districts for 14-year periods.[76] Defendants under warrant are expected to remain free until rearrested because the warrant squad of the police department is too busy to process warrants for bail jumpers.[77] Juvenile sentences in New York City are considered the toughest in the nation.[78]

The courts suffer from heavy volumes. The election and appointment of judges can involve politics. Since not all warrants are cleared, many defendants are walking the streets of New York City. Defendants who kill policemen or prison guards can escape the death penalty.

Corrections

Annually, about 60,000 men and women are housed in the 18 facilities of Riker's Island.[79] New York City experiences more deaths per 100,000 inmates than any other major city.[80] There were 17 suicides in 24 months in jails in New York City.[81] There were 8 suicides in 1970, 11 in 1971, 11 in 1972, and 13 in 1973.[82] In 1971 there were 32 deaths in city prisons, 11 of them suicides.[83] There were more than 8,000 inmates awaiting trial in New York City in one week.[84] About 60 percent of the prison population is in detention awaiting trial.[85] The mean time between admission and sentencing for misdemeanants is 2.3 days and for felons 20.1 days. Two-thirds of the incoming population stay in detention no more than 8 days; the mean is 35.2 days and the median is 4.9 days.[86] New York state law requires one day off for every three days of time. In 1985 the New York state prison population was 34,317.[87] About 67 percent of the state's prison population comes from New York City.[88]

Under law, convicts cannot be discriminated against in licensing unless the license is related to the crime.[89] In 1977 approximately 55,000 offenders were under probation supervision.[90]

It can be seen that the majority of inmates in jail are awaiting trial. New York state gets its largest share of prisoners from New York City. Huge numbers of inmates live in jails, prisons, and under court supervision.

Summary

The review of the literature revealed that the greatest proportion of the literature was on the police with relatively smaller proportions on the courts and corrections. Nationally, there is much literature on the police, courts, and corrections, but in New York City most of the literature centers on the police. There probably is a need for more research on courts and corrections in New York City. There is also a need for more research on court dispositions, probation, and community corrections in New York City.

We see that the consequences for New York City center on the huge volume of cases that pass through the criminal justice system. How the city handles this huge number of cases in all the components of the system is open to empirical investigation. Some of these answers will be provided in the following pages. This author will try to create a coherent picture of criminal justice in New York City.

2

THEORETICAL PERSPECTIVES

A theory can be loosely defined as a number of interrelated facts, axioms, propositions, theorems, generalizations, laws, etc. *Webster's Dictionary* defines a theory as "a supposition put forward to explain something; speculation; exposition of general principles as distinct from practice and execution; (colloq.) general idea; notion."[1] The *Random House Dictionary* defines a theory as: "(1) a coherent group of general propositions used as principles of explanation for a class of phenomena; (2) the branch of a science or art that deals with its principles rather than practice; (3) an explanation that has not yet been proved true; (4) a guess or conjecture."[2]

In this chapter various theories or theoretical perspectives will be put forward in an attempt to explain the criminal justice system and the behavior of criminals and victims. I will not try to offer formal theories with a comprehensive description and explanation of each theory. While some theories will be discussed at length, others will be covered in a few sentences; still others will have to be ignored due to space limitations.[3]

The classification of the functions of punishment, namely, deterrence, incapacitation, retribution, and punishment, discussed in chapter 1, were theoretical. The concepts of discretion, individual attention, assembly-line justice, and disparity are also theoretical. These concepts can be the starting point of inequality based on race, ethnicity, class, age, and other extralegal characteristics of the criminal justice system. These variables can also be the starting point for the conflict theory of criminal justice, in which the factors of class, race, and occupation can determine outcomes in criminal justice directly or indirectly. This, in turn, can lead to theories of discrimination. As mentioned in chapter 1, plea bargaining can be the result of mitigation of punishment, individualizing defendants, or excessive case loads; this also is theoretical.

The fact that crime is both inter- and intraracial can have theoretical implications. Some officials in criminal justice and some members of the public may believe that as long as crime is restricted to the neighborhoods of the black and Hispanic offenders and does not spread into the areas where the whites live, then whites need not be concerned. This belief leads to a double standard of criminal justice, with one kind of law for minority groups, and another kind of law for whites. Thus the offender-victim category is important. According to this theory, blacks or Hispanics who commit crimes against fellow blacks or Hispanics in black or Hispanic neighborhoods will usually receive lenient treatment, while whites who commit crimes against whites in white neighborhoods will usually receive severe treatment. The point is, according to the theory, that blacks and Hispanics who commit crimes against other blacks or Hispanics in black or Hispanic neighborhoods are dealt with in a non-serious fashion.

Cultural Theories

Two general theories of culture will be presented. One involves Hispanic culture, and the other involves the subculture of violence. This latter theory is attributed to Wolfgang and Ferracuti. I will then discuss a study I conducted that indirectly relates to cultural theory.

Hispanic Culture

Hispanic culture is identified as a minority-group culture, whose norms conflict with the larger national culture. A conflict exists between the Hispanic culture and the larger culture because some behaviors that are accepted in Hispanic culture are considered deviant or illegal in the larger society. The Hispanic people living in the United States have a legal tradition derived from Spanish colonial law; however, Americans have a legal tradition derived from English common law. The Latin-American countries, such as Puerto Rico and the Philippines, are civil-law countries, while the Anglo-American countries are common-law countries. The differences between these two legal systems are significant.

Civil law is based on the rationality of the human will. It is characterized by codification, the separation of public and private law, which restricts equity in legal proceedings involving the state, and the historical acceptance of closed proceedings in which the judge plays an investigatory role. Common law, however, is based on the assumption that social control is dependent less upon a state-imposed rationality than upon the legal order that exists in nature. In common law the doctrine of stare decisis (precedent), the adversary system in criminal justice, habeas corpus (the writ against illegal imprisonment), and trial by jury testify to a fundamental legal restriction upon the power and authority of the state and serve as a contrast with civil law.

The two traditions represent different views on the place of power and authority within society and different cultural responses to social control. The important point is that civil law establishes its codes on the basis of legal principles, while common law bases its principles on the complexity of the case. Residual elements of civil law remain lodged in the Puerto Rican legal system even though Americans gained control of Puerto Rico in the last century. Most importantly, many cultural expectations of the law possessed by Puerto Ricans today remain rooted in civil law tradition.

The commission of crimes by Hispanic persons in the United States cannot be separated from other forms of social deviance that appear to be related to the stress induced by culture shock. It must also be remembered that some of the crimes committed in the Hispanic culture might not be considered unlawful in Hispanic culture but are considered unlawful in American culture.

Although Hispanic family ties are strong, evidence suggests that the support provided by the family and culture which is so vital to its members may be abruptly cut off when transitional responses are labeled as "criminal" by the host society and the individual is imprisoned. Imprisonment of an Hispanic, especially in the early stages, contributes to the disappearance of cultural forms. Lawbreaking and the resultant incarceration are associated with stigma in Hispanic families; the Hispanic lawbreaker may find that he is effectively expelled from his social group through exclusion from the parental home.

Upon admission to the correctional system, the Hispanic inmate is separated both physically and psychologically from his culture. Temporarily housed in a detention center or reception unit, and bearing the stigma of criminal charges, the Hispanic inmate exists in a cultural vacuum that poses a serious threat to his mental health as well as to the structure of the family network to which he belongs. Deprived of cultural support systems, because of his family's humiliation at his imprisonment, it is no great surprise that the Hispanic inmate constitutes a major suicide threat during the early days of his detention.

Research indicates that when a new Hispanic inmate is assigned to his permanent housing in the correctional system, the new inmate is received into an Hispanic subculture that provides him with immediate reference points as he is socialized into the institution.

Violence as part of the Hispanic subculture is seen not as an outgrowth or adaptation of a culture in transition but as normative to the original culture. A study of Puerto Rican male offenders who had committed violent crimes found that almost 70 percent of them belonged to a subculture in which aggression was a common form of behavior. A significant debate continues about whether violence is a reflection of the initial subculture or whether it is a result of the breakdown of the initial culture and its gradual replacement by the structure associated with modern, urban civilization.

There is general recognition that agencies should employ more Hispanic people in both law enforcement and treatment capacities. Social investigations conducted by probation officers that may contain value assumptions about certain social groups or certain life-styles, although not evidence for consideration by the court, clearly provides extralegal information that may be used by the judge in determining the disposition and length of the sentence. Hispanics constitute such a small percentage of offenders being processed by the system that they are classified as "other" in official statistics. They do not appear as an identifiable ethnic group. Government agencies fail to achieve a uniform statistical definition of the composition of the Hispanic population.

There may be a greater proportion of Hispanics on probation than was originally arrested, reflecting a greater percentage of Hispanic prosecutions following arrest than that of other arrested groups. The proportion of Hispanics who are finally incarcerated appears to be greater than the proportion sentenced to probation. The percentage of Hispanics released on parole may be disproportionately small. Data on the involvement of Hispanics in the criminal justice system is spotty and incomplete; most of this data comes from a variety of uncoordinated sources and from inconsistent reports on ethnicity. The many different ethnic groups comprising the Hispanic culture contributes to our data problems. Although prison statistics are the most complete, they are not always consistent in reporting ethnicity and sometimes omit descriptions of ethnic compositions of the prison population.

In 1979, in New York state, 19.8 percent of the 20,122 prisoners of both sexes were Puerto Rican, and 19.9 percent of the 19,568 male inmates incarcerated by the state were identified as Puerto Ricans. From 1973 to 1979 there has been a gradual increase in the percentage of Puerto Rican inmates in New York state prisons. During the same period in New York state, the proportion of white inmates has remained relatively stable and the proportion of black inmates has decreased slightly. Between 1971 and 1977, in New York state prisons, the absolute numbers of Puerto Ricans admitted increased by 14.4 percent, and the percentage of Puerto Ricans in the total inmate population also increased. Although blacks and whites accounted for the largest percentages of new inmates during this period, it is possible that Puerto Ricans will eventually become the second largest group of inmates in state facilities.

The percentage of New York City Puerto Ricans newly incarcerated in state facilities is greater than the proportion of new Puerto Rican inmates from the state as a whole. The proportion of new Puerto Rican inmates from New York City is twice as high as the estimated percentage of Puerto Ricans in the city's male population. The educational level of Puerto Rican inmates is lower than that of blacks or whites. In 1975 and 1976 Puerto Ricans had higher percentages of inmates newly admitted as a result of an action in which someone died, whether these actions were classified as murder, negligent homicide, or non-negligent homicide. There is a high proportion of crimes involving death among Hispanics. The Puerto Ricans are second to blacks in the proportion of homicide offenses. Many Hispanics also commit drug-related offenses.

A study of 505 federal cases revealed that Hispanics were less likely to be placed on probation and received longer sentences than those in a non–Hispanic control group.

Knowledge of the Hispanic experience in criminal justice is sparse.[4]

Subculture of Violence

A subculture, as proposed by Wolfgang and Ferracuti, implies that there are value judgments or a social value system that stands apart from but is also a part of a larger or central value system. Subcultural values are learned, adopted, and exhibited by participants in the subculture, and differ in quantity and quality from those of the dominant culture. No subculture can be totally different from, or completely in conflict with, the society of which it is a part; to be a part of the larger culture implies that some values related to the ends or means of the whole are shared by the part. Any group in a subculture will have formal and informal sets of sanctions to apply to members who violate the major subcultural themes. The intensity or strength of the subcultural values can be measured either by a scaling analysis of individual attitudes of allegiance to the subcultural values or by a scaling analysis of penalties for deviation from subcultural norms.

Wolfgang and Ferracuti offer two examples of a subculture of violence. They indicate that almost all the brutal and senseless paraphernalia of slaying known to history have been exhibited in Columbia. Frequently, homicide is carried out against whole families, and especially in the past has followed a pattern of extermination and genocide. Nowhere in the Western world since the end of World War II has senseless brutality been so prevalent as in Columbia.

Mexico, too, has experienced extremely high rates of homicide for years. The high rates of criminal homicide existing in Mexico, the emergence of social factors such as male sex, membership in the working class, and a tradition of employing physical aggression, suggest that there exist in Mexico subcultural areas of violence.

Wolfgang and Ferracuti point out that one study found that two-thirds of homicide offenders had prior police records; of these two-thirds, three-fourths had prior records of aggravated assaults. Thus, many homicide offenders have prior records involving assault. For several decades the rates of homicide have steadily decreased while rates of aggravated assault have steadily increased. The decline in violent deaths may well be due to improved medical facilities that can treat the victim better and save his or her life. Once in a hospital, the assault victim has a better chance of recovery and survival today than in earlier decades.

Wolfgang and Ferracuti suggest why crime is so prevalent in urban areas. Some of the reasons are victims are depersonalized and anonymous; property is insured; and consumer goods exist in greater abundance, are vividly displayed, and are more portable now than previously.

Sometimes families are involved in subcultures of violence. Wolfgang and Ferracuti suggest that about one-fifth of all police killings result from responding to family disturbance calls.

The authors emphasize repeatedly that no subculture can be totally different from or totally in conflict with the society of which it is a part. However, acts of violence in a subculture are not necessarily viewed as illicit conduct and those who commit violent acts often do not have to deal with feelings of guilt about their aggression.

Wolfgang and Ferracuti repeat a generalization that is known about killings. They say that probably less than 5 percent of all known killings are premeditated. Individuals who kill are more likely to be episodic offenders who have never had serious personal contact with the police or with the criminal courts. As an example of the subculture of violence, the authors cite the case of the epidemic of indirect suicides that took place in Norway and Denmark in the seventeenth and eighteenth centuries, when depressed people committed murder, presumably to court arrest, trial, and execution, because they would not commit suicide for religious reasons. Because of this problem, a special law had to be passed to bar these individuals from receiving the death penalty, in order to stop homicides committed by would-be suicides.

The authors do not deny some psychological explanations for homicide. They say that, in general, the less clearly motivated a murder is, in the sense that it is difficult to comprehend its motives, the higher is the probability that the homicidal offender is abnormal. Rorschach tests of murderers, when compared with normal subjects, yield a personality characterized by egocentrism and a lack of emotional control. He or she can also be described as an explosive, immature, hyperthymic person who is unable to establish social control. He or she displays a deficit of conscious control and a strong need for the immediate gratification of impulses. But supporting cultural evidence for a consistent personality pattern for the homicidal offender is scarce and unreliable.

Whites in Southern United States have homicide rates four to five times higher than whites in New England. In England, one-third to one-half of the homicide offenders are classified as legally insane, whereas in the United States only 2 to 4 percent of homicide offenders are classified as insane. The authors claim that the label of insanity is difficult to explain.

Thus, according to Wolfgang and Ferracuti, killings and aggression in the subculture of violence are both sociological and psychological.[5]

Empirical Study

I did some research in the Bronx, New York City, on how the families of defendants placed on probation were affected by the probation status of their relatives. I interviewed 35 probationers and 8 relatives of these probationers, all but one of whom were black or Hispanic, to ascertain how probation affected their lives and the lives of their families.

First, reviewing the literature on families of prisoners, I found that many marriages before or after separation by incarceration were characterized as happy, and that wives did not necessarily leave their husbands because of the latters' imprisonment. Adjustment before separation sometimes correlated positively and sometimes negatively with adjustment during the incarceration of the husband. Many relatives helped the families during separation. Feelings of shame and stigma were not universal. Generally, the families of those incarcerated suffered emotional and financial problems.

The results of the interviews with the 35 probationers and their relatives revealed that there was a subculture among probationers in which some relatives and friends had been in trouble with the law. At least 20 of the respondents admitted that they had either relatives or friends who had been in trouble with the law. At least 19 of the 35 admitted that although they had told their probation status to their immediate relatives, they did not reveal their probation status to their distant relatives or to some friends. Six of the eight relatives interviewed felt embarrassed by or ashamed of their relatives' probation status. However, ten of the respondents were undecided as to whether they were ashamed.

I concluded that although some feelings of shame and stigma existed among the respondents, a subculture among probationers in which some friends and relatives have been in trouble with the law helps to mitigate feelings of shame and stigma that would be stronger among other groups.

At least 24 respondents, including relatives, stated that they either were helped by their relatives or as relatives helped the probationers. The help involved advice, counseling, financial aid, food, shelter, clothing, legal aid, and employment. Only two of the respondents admitted that some people avoided them because of their probation, but virtually no one admitted that their peer groups avoided them.

I also concluded that since many probationers received help of some type during probation, there was a strong support system that helped to mitigate the stigma that had been placed on probationers and helped the probationers to redirect their deviant lives into law-abiding behavior. Not many probationers felt isolated. This conclusion coincides with prior research on prisoners' families. The fact that no peer group avoided the probationers also coincided with prior research on prisoners' families.[6]

This research seems to support a subculture in which deviant norms are somewhat acceptable among the families, friends, and peer groups of both prisoners and probationers. This subculture does not necessarily prove the existence of a subculture of violence, and this subculture does not necessarily mean that probationers and their families do not want to redirect their lives or their relatives' lives into the norms of the dominant culture, for many do. It means that there is some evidence for a subculture of deviant behavior among some groups, which supports the subcultural theories of deviant behavior presented here.

Theories of the Offender

The great majority of muggers and strong-armed robbers are "opportunist robbers." The members of this group are usually impulsive, highly disorganized, lower-class adolescents and young adults, who rarely plan their crimes. Instead, they select such targets as the disabled or elderly people because of their availability and vulnerability, rather than because of the value of the money and jewelry they have on their person.[7] As mentioned previously, probably less than 5 percent of all known killings are premeditated. The individuals who commit these crimes are more likely to be episodic offenders who never had serious contact with the police or the criminal courts.[8]

Almost everyone who persists in crime gets caught sooner or later. This fact explains why prison is the criminal's alma mater. Many criminals drink or use drugs before or during a crime in order to reduce their tension and to control their fear. Tension, combined with drugs and alcohol, causes some of the blunders criminals commit during a crime.[9] Many, if not most, offenders do not commit crimes in a social vacuum or because of a random, reckless desire to do evil; they are frequently responding to a set of circumstances and personal problems that make breaking the law a likely or viable act. If the motivating circumstances were removed or the problems resolved, many of these people would have little difficulty following society's rules.[10] A relatively small number of offenders account for a large proportion of all serious offenses.[11]

Perhaps theories of counseling, when applied to criminals or potential criminals, can help solve some crime problems. For example, offenders who show a pattern of assault or sexual crimes might be amenable to psychotherapy. This is the medical model in criminal justice, in which offenders are considered sick and in need of medical help, such as pyschotherapy, to cure them. Although this model is somewhat out of fashion these days, there are still some strong believers in this model.

Theories of the Police

Police attitudes are deeply rooted in the requirements of their job and of society. Education alone cannot change them. Anyone who defies the police is likely to be arrested, but a black or Puerto Rican is more likely to be clubbed during their arrest. The police reflect with surprising sensitivity the attitudes of the larger society. Where society is fearful and repressive, the police are fearful and repressive. When society is ambivalent, as in attitudes regarding prostitution and gambling, the behavior of the police reflects that feeling as well. The mores of the police department itself also form police attitudes. Sometimes the police do provoke violence in order to make an arrest. Police sometimes manufacture evidence if they believe that someone is guilty, either in fact or in intent. The police sometimes use psychological persuasion.[12] The closer the police officers' relationship with the people in his beat, the more people he knows, and the more these people trust him, the greater his chances of reducing crime.[13] However, some believe that the public does not want the police to change.[14]

The police have to make a decision to shoot in a split second. If a policeman overacts by firing his gun, it is generally because he is scared, not because he is sadist or a psychopath.[15] The police are upset when they kill.[16] The police believe that the dangers of their job cause them to use illegal methods in their work.[17] Methods that made the police heroes in the past now can make them criminals because of society's changing mores.[18]

Therefore, role theory as it applies to the police and the police hierarchy— patrolmen, sergeants, lieutenants, captains, commanders, detectives, chiefs, deputy chiefs, etc.—is important. It is also important to study the role aspects of the police over time to see what, if any, changes have taken place.[19]

Theories of the Victim

The victim is a very important person in the criminal justice system. Victims who do not report a crime right away give the offender, and even potential witnesses to the crime, time to get away. But most victims do not report the crime right away. First they call a spouse, a parent, or a friend, someone who can provide sympathy or advice. It is only after victims recover from the immediate trauma that they remember to call the police.[20]

Very often victims and offenders are not strangers; many victims and offenders have a prior relationship. A Vera Institute study verified that this was true for nearly half of the cases brought to court. The study revealed that the proportion who were acquaintances ranged from 21 percent in auto theft, to 69 percent in assault, to 83 percent in rape cases. Even in robbery and burglary, the victim and offender were acquaintances in 36 percent and 39 percent of the cases, respectively.[21]

It is known that prosecutors and other criminal justice actors distinguish between people who are acquaintances and people who are strangers. Very often offenders who commit crimes against acquaintances are treated more leniently in criminal justice than offenders who commit crimes against strangers.

Silberman states that when the victims know offenders, they often refuse to press charges, or to cooperate with the prosecutor in other ways. Complainant noncooperation accounted for more than two-thirds of the dismissals of victim felonies in New York City, and well over one-half in Washington, D.C.[22] Silberman, referring to the Vera Institute study, states that when crimes are serious, evidence is strong, and victims are willing to prosecute, felons with previous criminal histories ended up with relatively heavy sentences.[23] In New York City, a study revealed that 87 percent of case dismissals were due to complainant noncooperation, usually because the complainant had had a prior relationship with the defendant.[24]

Some researchers believe that the victim in criminal justice has been neglected. Some believe that the victim does not have a chance to speak his or her opinion about sentencing recommendations. Very often, the victim is used as a means to clear cases, and has no real input into the system. Perhaps if victims were treated with more respect and attempts were made to alleviate some of their fears, victims of crimes would be more cooperative. Victims and their part in the criminal justice system deserve far more study.

Other Perspectives

Most prosecutors in the United States have chosen to side uncritically with the police. This situation exists because prosecutors depend on the police to a great extent. However, good prosecutors will dismiss cases if they believe that the police arrested under unjustifiable circumstances.[25]

Much of the tension and misunderstanding between the police on one hand, and defense lawyers and judges on the other hand, stems from the latter groups' failure to understand the degree to which police action is rooted in the exigencies of the moment, when reflection is not only impossible but also may be terribly dangerous to the police officer himself and to other parties involved.[26] Legal actors have different perceptions of the criminal justice system than do police officers. This difference can cause conflict and misunderstandings.

Respect for the law and belief in its legitimacy are more effective instruments of social control than fear of punishment.[27] Many juveniles are charged for offenses that would not be crimes at all if committed by adults, incorrigibility, truancy, running away from home, and many other types of behavior that do not appear as direct threats to the public safety.[28] Perhaps theories of social control applicable to juvenile offenders are important.

For years, the police have concentrated on violations of gambling laws. However, for years the police also knew that the public did not want the gambling laws enforced.[29] Perhaps this is one reason why the police often give in to corruption in their dealings with gamblers.

These latter examples illustrate that theories of criminal law are important in criminal justice. The factors that are responsible for criminal law, the power behind the scenes, the meaning of the law, the enforcement of the law, deviations and flexibility of the law, etc., are all relevant theoretical perspectives in criminal justice.

Summary

Some of the relevent theories in criminal justice were presented in this chapter. These serve as a theoretical basis for the study of criminal justice in New York City. There are many other theories and theoretical perspectives omitted in this chapter. Some other theories and theoretical perspectives will be discussed in the following chapters in reference to relevant topics.

3

THE POLICE OF
NEW YORK CITY

History of the New York City Police

The 1844 Municipal Police Act abolished the night watch and created the police department of New York City. The mayor was given the power to select 200 men to protect the city. In 1845 a full-time police department was created; the police now numbered 800 men. In the first years of operation a force of 1,000 men made some 144,364 arrests. There was a notable absence of arrests for property crime during this period.

In 1853 requirements for joining the force were simple. A candidate had to be a citizen of the United States; be able to read and write; and know the first four rules of arithmetic. A candidate had to obtain a doctor's certificate to attest to his physical fitness, and had to secure 25 character references from citizens. During the first few years the police in New York City wore civilian clothes, but they did have badges. The police began to wear uniforms starting in 1854.

During the first six months of 1854 the police made 25,000 arrests, 2,800 more than during the previous half-year. The increase was attributed to greater pride in the new uniform. Around 1857 the department obtained a police commissioner appointed by the governor.

From the 1840s to the 1860s the population of New York City increased from 350,000 to 820,000, but in the 1860s the police numbered 1,000, only 150 more than the 1840s.

During the early period shootings and knifings went on regularly within the shadow of the station houses. All types of savagery continued unabated near police headquarters. Although the police department was a fully functioning municipal service, it continued to lag behind the needs of the city and its residents.

In 1860 some 71,000 crimes were recorded, of which 11,294 were crimes against property and 59,836 were crimes against people. In 1863 one-tenth of all New Yorkers had police records. However, even with this new figure, few criminals were caught. There were continuous complaints that the police as well as the judges were responsible for crime, perhaps because of corrupt activities.

In 1877 candidates for the police force had to be under age 30, stand at least 5'½" tall, weigh at least 138 pounds, be in good health, and demonstrate good moral character. The candidates needed ten appointment petitioners to recommend appointment. Within a few years the purchase of admission to the force and to promotion became a scandal.

The responsible citizens during that period were aware that the police had opportunities for blackmail, graft, and other abuses. The police did engage in various acts of corruption. Resorts in which laws were violated had been allowed to flourish. The police took from $20 to $100 per year from fruit merchants for the latter's right to pile produce on the sidewalk. The police harassed honest businessmen, conspired with dishonest men, and were partners in open gambling. Police brutality was rampant. Police assaulted private citizens with their clubs, broke bones, and bloodied heads.

The Lexow Committee was initiated on March 9, 1894 to investigate police abuses. Between 1892 and 1894, 108 police were indicted for crimes, 48 for felonies. However, only four policemen were actually expelled from the department; other officers got off with fines of from 2 to 30 days' pay. Out of 56 assaults in the third degree, 55 in the second degree, and one attempted assault, only one officer was dismissed for clubbing a private citizen.

The Lexow Committee resulted in reduced police attacks upon respectable citizens and peaceful strikers. However, no one expressed any disapproval of police brutality directed against criminals. It was accepted that abuses of power against social outcasts would incur no restraint.

In 1895, Theodore Roosevelt was appointed police commissioner of New York City. Disguised, he lurked in the streets, hoping to catch police who were sleeping, socializing, or dishonest. Roosevelt adhered to the letter of the law. He recommended the arrest of both the prostitute and her male customer. Roosevelt had the power to fire men without legal proof of inefficiency or dishonesty. Roosevelt gave the police a taste of honest administration. The rank and file of the police discovered that one could earn advancement without political pull. Roosevelt hired the first female secretary and recruited strong, young Jews. Roosevelt imposed strict discipline from above. Men had to accept responsibility for their own actions. However, he incurred opposition within the administration.

New York City has a long tradition of discrimination against black people. Toward the close of the 1800s blacks were systematically excluded from churches, schools, and other institutions. During the draft riots in 1900 the police inflicted barbarous measures upon Negroes. The whites seemed to support these brutal police measures. During the 1900 riot gangs of young toughs began hunting down Negroes and thrashing them. Some officers stood idly by, benignly observing the punishment meted out to blacks; other police officers joined in the attacks against blacks.

General Theodore A. Bingham was police commissioner from 1906 to 1909. He cleaned out areas of Manhattan and Brooklyn that were corrupt. He used his power to remove objectional inspectors. However, he was ousted from office and corruption and abuse prevailed.

In 1913 Arthur Woods was appointed commissioner of police. He initiated play streets for children, talks by policemen in school, improved training for the police, and took a hard line against graft.

The prohibition period during the 1920s made more work for policemen. In 1931 the police invaded 6,217 speakeasies, 306 nightclubs, 171 breweries, 94 plants, and 64 drugstores. The police arrested 17,513 people, destroyed 459 stills, and seized 400,000 gallons of whiskey and 122,150 wine bottles. The Prohibition era was a time of unparalleled criminality. During Prohibition crime became big business, and the police began to get rich by protecting murderers and kidnappers.

In 1929 Commissioner Grover Whalen created a secret force of 50 men who were to live in the underworld. Due to this force, illegal immigrants were caught, a $200,000 bond robbery was solved, and members of the Communist party were identified.

Police were involved in extorting money from innocent women. Twenty-eight police were suspended for this type of crime. Two detectives who shook down a woman and attempted to rape her went to prison as a result of this crime.

Gambling was a big source of police arrests. In 1935, in Brooklyn, there were 2,275 arrests for gambling. In 1936 there were 3,368 arrests for gambling in the same borough. In 1938 there were 3,373 arrests for gambling in Brooklyn. But in 1939 there were 21,181 gambling arrests in Brooklyn. The huge jump in arrests indicates that police must have been accepting bribes to ignore gambling in Brooklyn before 1939.

In the period from 1924 to 1930, 61 police officers were killed in the line of duty.

During the Great Depression of the 1930s the police helped the destitute and the hungry. They contributed $35,522 a month to various relief programs. They located jobs for the destitute. Police records show that 71,155 people received help in a two-week period.

From 1954 to 1960 under Mayor Robert Wagner, the police reached new levels of professionalism. Patrolmen were assigned to work with juveniles.

Police received better training. Wagner added 7,000 men to the force; men were distributed more efficiently. Political influence was removed from the department. Corruption was reduced. Some police tactics were improved.

John Lindsay, who succeeded Wagner as mayor, continued to reform the police department. Discipline was enforced. Written instructions permeated the police. Lindsay sought better educated, more devoted police, and he was attuned to modern problems. In 1966 he appointed a Jewish chief inspector. He also created the Civilian Review Complaint Board in 1966.

Men of Irish descent dominated the department from the 1900s to about 1966. During World War II some police participated in right-wing pro–Nazi activities. During the 1950s and 1960s complaints mounted against alleged abuses by the police.[1]

During the years from 1895 to 1936, called the Progressive period, the police department as well as the prosecutor's office and city courts, offered a rich source of employment for political party members who were faithful and in need of work.[2] The police, along with court officials, bail bondsmen, and lawyers, framed innocent women on charges of prostitution and extorted money from them in exchange for promises to fix their cases. Between 1895 and 1936 police arrested many older New Yorkers and the native-born, because the women during this period only amounted to 4 percent of the work docket; defendants under the age of 20 and the foreign-born accounted for less than their number in the city population.[3]

During the period from 1895 to 1936 the newspapers told of illegal and frivolous arrests, and the extortion of women by police officers and bondsmen, mainly of prostitutes.[4]

From 1900 to about 1930 the rate of violent crime in New York City increased faster than the growth in the general population of the city. However, the crimes committed by aliens during this period mostly concerned minor local ordinances.[5] During the Prohibition era there were 180,000 complaints of liquor-law violations annually in New York City. However, violators waited two, three, or even four years for their cases to appear in court, and as a result their cases were dismissed.[6] For at least 100 years, since the police organization started, gambling has been a major source of police arrests in New York City.[7]

Minority Relations Within the Department

From 1900 when blacks first joined the police force until fairly recently whites have maintained a position of dominance in the police force, relegating blacks to subordinate roles, denying them access to job opportunities and advancement. Black policemen were denied the opportunity of working in white neighborhoods, a common situation in all northern cities. In New York City black police complained of the difficulties they encountered when they attempted to enter the detective bureau in the early 1960s, and had difficulty in obtaining positions in other plainclothes commands.

Mayor Lindsay recruited 1,000 black and Hispanic police officers. By 1973 there were over 3,000 black and Hispanic police in the department. Judge Robert Carter, a federal judge, in 1980, deemed that one of every three new recruits should be a minority. However, several months later, a federal appellate judge reduced the quota of minority police to one in four.

The New York State Division of Human Rights recently ruled that grammar questions on exams for advancement to captain in New York City discriminated against black lieutenants. Between 1974 and 1982 the number of black sergeants increased by 30 percent, and the number of white sergeants decreased by 13 percent. However, the percentage of ranks above sergeants held by blacks between 1974 and 1982 remained the same, namely 3 percent. There is evidence that black officers were beaten up by white officers in the past, and the newspapers would not print the story.[8]

Statistics show that minority police are more likely to be seriously wounded or killed on the line of duty than white policemen.[9]

Although there was one black policeman in the department in 1865, blacks as a group did not enter the department until the early 1890s. Wiley G. Overton, a black policeman hired in March 1891, was ignored by the other officers. As a result, Overton suffered physical and emotional trauma. He served one year and eight months before resigning on January 11, 1893.

On June 28, 1911, Samuel Jesse Battle was the first black policeman appointed under the consolidation of Greater New York. For more than two years not one white policeman spoke a word to Battle. However, Battle was transferred to the Harlem police station and finally earned the respect of the white officers on the force.

On May 21, 1926, the first black sergeant was appointed, although there were a few temporary black sergeants on the force prior to this date. On January 7, 1935, Battle was promoted to full lieutenant, the first black to obtain this position. On January 23, 1947, the first black acting captain was appointed. In 1920 Wesley C. Redding became the first black detective in New York City. In 1921 Reuben Carter became the first black officer in the city assigned to traffic duty. In 1930 Redding became the second black sergeant and the first black sergeant to supervise precinct patrol units of all races. On January 30, 1953, Redding was the first black appointed captain with permanent civil service title.

One complaint of black officers in the past concerned the fact that they were assigned exclusively to work in black communities while white officers were allowed to work in black and white communities. The majority of black officers were supervised by white supervisors, and blacks received disproportionate amounts of departmental disciplinary action. Black officers also received the most distasteful working assignments.

On November 23, 1963, Lloyd Sealy became the third black captain in New York City. Less than a year later he became the first black to command a Harlem precinct. Shortly afterwards, Sealy was promoted to assistant chief inspector, the first time that a black officer was given a borough command in New York City. In 1955 Robert Johnson became the first black supervisor in the 43rd police precinct when he was made sergeant. He was promoted to lieutenant and was the first black officer assigned to the 42nd precinct in the Bronx, and was the first black commanding officer in the Bronx. Johnson was made inspector and was in charge of the 16th Division, the first black officer in this position. In 1966 a black lieutenant was made the first black officer in the 32nd police precinct.

In 1947 William R. Bracy was the first black officer assigned to a youth squad in Brooklyn. He was also the first black sergeant to supervise Queens uniform personnel. In 1959 Bracy was promoted to lieutenant and became the first black assigned to the 19th precinct. He was reassigned in 1967 to the 101st division squad as a commanding officer, becoming the first black detective commander in Queens. In 1977 Bracy was promoted to assistant chief inspector of the Brooklyn North area, thus making him at that time the highest ranking black officer in the department.

In 1959 the first black patrol supervisor served in the 81st police precinct. In 1974 the first black officer was made chief of uniform services. On July 7, 1955, the first black sergeant was assigned to the 40th precinct in Bronx as a patrol supervisor. In 1961 the first black officer to command the 28th precinct and the second to command a Harlem precinct was appointed.

The black police in the late 1940s became increasingly embittered and distraught over the mistreatment which they received from the white police officers. White officers in the detective bureau were assigned to sensitive positions, but black officers in that bureau would often be assigned to some spectacular arrest in which the officers risked their lives.

In 1950 there were 368 black police officers in New York City. In 1935 there were 125, and in 1938 there were 147. However, blacks were still underrepresented on the force. In those days, many black officers who applied for higher positions in the police department were ruled medically unfit by the medical staff of the department. After the landmark Supreme Court antidiscrimination decision of 1954, blacks were finally advanced in rank and placed in command positions. By 1956 there were 1,031 black police officers; by 1958 there were 31 black police sergeants. Federal funding for New York City police can be withheld if there is not a comprehensive program for recruitment and upgrading of women, blacks, and Hispanic police officers.

By 1969 there were approximately 2,000 black and Hispanic police officers on the force. In 1974 there were 2,508 blacks in the department. However, the layoffs in 1975 disproportionately affected black, Hispanic, and female officers, since they had been the most recently hired. Eight black officers have been shot by white officers in recent years, but there is not one instance of a white officer shot by a black officer.[10]

The first police women in New York City were matrons. They were used mainly as social workers to deal with children and prostitutes. The first real police position in New York City for women was established in 1921. Women in the 1950s were denied the right to take the civil service exams for promotion. It was not until 1964 that women through court order were allowed to take the civil service exam for sergeant. The first unisex exam that included both men and women was given in 1973.

In 1974 there were only 700 women in the department. Now women are assigned to all departments and have opportunities to be promoted to high ranks. However, there might still be a significant amount of prejudice in the police department. In 1979 the department consisted of 2.2 percent women.[11]

This brief history of the police reveals several things. First, the police grew in number from hundreds in 1845 to about 23,000 in the 1980s. Second, police dishonesty and corruption pervaded the department from the beginning of its history. Third, police brutality pervaded the department throughout its history, and police brutality still is a news item occasionally. The police were particularly brutal against blacks, prostitutes, and immigrant whites. Fourth, police periodically were suspended and tried, and even imprisoned for corrupt activities. Fifth, the police department discriminated against blacks in appointments, promotions, and assignments throughout its history. Sixth, liberal and reform-minded mayors, not the police department itself, were responsible for initiating reform.

These characteristics of the police may be true of other jurisdictions in the United States. Police corruption and brutality are not necessarily restricted to New York City. The following pages will reveal whether these characteristics of the police hold today, and to what degree, if any, there has been improvement.

It should be emphasized that the police very often follow the norms and mores of the dominant culture in society. Throughout police history the public was not concerned about illegal treatment meted out to criminals and public outcasts; thus, it should come as no surprise that the police regularly abused these groups. However, brutality against honest, upright citizens was resisted and criticized, and reform was initiated. Politics was a way of life in early America, and political favoritism and patronage pervaded the police force, most notably regarding police appointments and promotions. Gambling has always been tolerated in America, so it is no wonder that police failed to eradicate gambling completely in New York City. The police department reflected American society at large by discriminating against blacks and other minorities both within its ranks and in the community.

The Police Bureaucracy

In the old days one monolithic culture permeated the department. But Reuss-Ianni, after studying two police precincts, one in the Bronx and one in Manhattan, concluded that now there exists two distinct cultures, a street cop culture and a management cop culture. The management culture is positively oriented toward public administration and looks to life management and its associated technologies for guidance on how to run the department. These people forgot about being police officers and are now professional managers. The mangement culture is antithetical to the values of the precinct cop culture.

The police desire a return to the good old days. The police believe that their bosses in management give their loyalties to the social and political networks that embody management but not to them.

Reuss-Ianni believes that there is some uneasy accommodation between these two cultures, but they are increasingly in conflict. This conflict isolates the precinct functionally, but not structurally, from headquarters. The isolation of the police from management produces disaffection, strong stress reaction, increasing attrition of personnel, and growing problems of integrity. The street cop culture resists attempts by headquarters to introduce organizational change. Therefore, the precinct as a social organization becomes the major reference structure of the men rather than loyalty to the department. Police believe that managers want to control them.

The police believe that in the good old days the department was a cohesive home for the commonly shared ethos of the street cop culture. There was a code of shared understanding and conventions of behavior binding on everyone, from the top brass to the newest recruits. The results were predictable. Mutual dependence stimulated morale and esprit de corps.

The police no longer demonstrate complete solidarity. Increased education made alternative job possibilities and careers outside of the department available, which reduced solidarity, since one's career was no longer necessarily tied to the job or to relations with fellow officers. Minority recruitment led to new criteria for promotional advancement, and this further eroded the traditional solidarity supported by similarity of socioeconomic, cultural, religious, and ethnic backgrounds.

Management now does away with the organic and nonrational bounds among people as the basis for organization and decision making, and substitutes a system of abstract rules and departmental operations and applies these rules to particular cases.

The street cop culture sees immediate local police response as more important than preplanned and packaged solutions to problems that may never occur during day-to-day police work. Management is concerned with crime on a city-wide basis, but the police are concerned with the happenings on the immediate precinct level. The police try to maneuver around, outwit, and nullify policy decisions from headquarters. Management culture consists of several, frequently competing authority-power systems or networks, which can be called into operation in decision making, control, and accountability.

Certain values and behaviors particular to street cop culture are shared to some extent by all police officers, including many managers, but these values and behaviors differ among subunits and between ranks.

Promotions above captain are made by the police commissioner. This includes appointments from captain to deputy inspector to inspector to deputy chief to assistant chief, and from there to three-star chiefs who command the five major bureaus, namely, field service, detectives, organized crime control, personnel, and inspectional services, and the four-star chiefs of operation, the highest uniform rank. The commissioner also has the power to jump someone up more than one rank at a time.

Directly beneath the police commissioner are seven deputy commissioners: the first deputy commissioner, who is acting head of the department in the police commissioner's absence, and the deputy commissioners of administration, community affairs, trials, public information, criminal justice, and legal matters. The deputy commissioners are civilians, but the first deputy and the police commissioner are police officers who have come up through the ranks.

The police can not trust everyone now because of changes on the job, including conflict between management and street cops, minority hiring, and corruption. The police at the precinct level tend to sort themselves on the basis of age, sex, length of service, race, ethnicity, specialized expertise, connections, and behavior under fire. Connections are the only way to be promoted at the top. The police do not band together in mutual support all the time.

Management is divorced from the street; it is involved in making political decisions rather than policing decisions. The street cop culture of the good old days is working class in origin and temperament, and its members see themselves as career cops.

The management cop culture is more middle class. Its members' education and mobility have made them eligible for jobs totally outside of policing, which makes them less dependent on and less loyal to the street cop culture. The management cop culture represents those police who have decided that the old way of running a police department is finished for a variety of reasons — including social pressures, economic realities of the city, increased visibility, minority recruitment, and growth in size — so that the department cannot be managed easily in the informal fashion of the old days. They do not like the street cops, and they have a low regard for community relations, but consider it as something that must be done for politically expedient reasons if not for social ones. The managing cop is sensitive to public opinion and will not support a policeman who assaults someone in custody without probable cause.

The street cops are still into the old ways of doing things and are confused and often enraged at the apparent change in the rules of the system. They fight back in the only way they have at their disposal, by foot dragging, absenteeism, and a host of similar coping mechanisms and defensive techniques. Well-intentioned but overeager police managers have sought to intervene in police work through replacement rather than through adaptation. In the replacement method, management cops attempt to replace inefficient or outmoded techniques with new and more efficient ones. Adaptation as a technique is more gradual and involves redefining or modifying existing practices.

If relatively permanent structural changes are to be brought about, police officer perspectives in policy must be changed, first to introduce appropriate change in attitudes and behavior and then to maintain support for the changes once they are introduced. These changes and attitudes are essential, but they will not be sustained unless the ideas or techniques are incorporated in the value systems of the department or become items of the agenda of both precinct and headquarters.

Managers do not care about the effects of their policy on the daily lives of street cops. They do not have to live with these situations. The policy and decision making at higher levels of administration are perceived by precinct level personnel as arbitrary and unrelated to local needs and conditions. To the extent that precinct level personnel are not part of the planning of management and have no stake in the success of planning, precinct level cops will not exert much effort toward the realization of these goals or objectives.

Reuss-Ianni based her conclusions on observation and interviews during 15 months in one precinct and three months in another precinct. One of the precincts was in Manhattan and the other one was in Bronx. She concluded that the two precincts were more alike than unlike.[12]

Some police officers are thoughtful and articulate, but much of this thoughtfulness is wasted by the way the police departments tend to be organized and run. Departments use only a minute fraction of the knowledge that is at their disposal.[13] The PCCIU is the police commissioner's confidential investigating unit, and its primary function is to investigate wrongdoing by the police. No cop ignores talk of this unit. Its members are feared and despised. The slightest rumor that the PCCIU shoo-fly is around is enough to clear a coup, a resting place for cops while on duty, quickly and with panic.[14]

A qualified commissioner can be recruited from outside the department, but all uniformed commanders have to be named from within the ranks. Everyone who becomes a New York City police commander has to begin as a patrolman after completing police academy training.[15] According to the city charter, a police commissioner can be dismissed by either the mayor or the governor, and it is sufficient for either to announce only that this dismissal is in the city's best interest. The police commissioner can be dismissed at any time with a wave of the hand.[16] It is not necessary in the police department to have performed distinguished acts in order to be promoted to high ranks; promotion would come from the two-star chiefs and the deputy chiefs. For the most part, all it took was a friend at headquarters and keeping one's mouth shut.[17] Thus, political appointments were still being made during the last two decades.

Police Role, Police-Community Relations, and Civilian Complaints

The police role, police-community relations, and civilian complaints against the police are interrelated. Certainly the expected behavior of the police involves police-community relations. How the police relate to minority groups such as blacks, Hispanics, hippies, and the elderly, is important news for the public. Minorities have won legal, political, and social rights in the last few decades, and some of these involve the arrest process either directly or indirectly. The quantity and quality of civilian complaints against the police are an indication of how well the public believes that the police are performing their role.

Police Role

The police have a lot of discretion in their role; however, this discretion is sometimes structured by commands, formal or informal, from higher authority. For example, in 1968, in Grand Central Station, in response to charges of people defacing the clocks, police formed a column of twos, and with night sticks out, charged the information booth. People who were standing quietly by as much as 60 to 70 feet away from the information booth, and who had nothing to do with the defacing of the clocks, were slammed into unmercifully and without warning by the sheer force of the police charge. People who had no idea of what was happening felt the crack of clubs on their heads as the police made for their objective. On the first charge at least a dozen people went crashing to the marble floor of the station. In the melee that followed, people were thrown, or clubbed to the ground, trampled upon, and brutalized. The police did not use a public address system or bullhorn to get the crowd to peacefully leave the station. Word circulated from the mayor's Urban Action Task Force that the police should "take it easy on the blacks but beat the crap out of the hippies."[18]

Discretion means that the police act according to the dictates of the individual officer. However, although the police have discretion in deciding whether or not to make an arrest, their decisions are made uniform when they have reason to suspect that someone has committed a serious offense.[19]

Complaints of police brutality are hard to verify. Charges of resisting arrest or assault may be included against the citizen when there are no injuries in order to increase the bargaining power of the police. Police assault against citizens is usually the punishment for some open and flagrant defiance of authority. Prosecutors often insist on a waiver to dismiss damages against the police for a dismissal of the defendant's case without a trial, although such a waiver's legality is doubtful.

John H. McNamara found that the results of a test on recruits and new policemen resulted in most officers agreeing that some force was necessary and justified when a citizen unjustly insulted and cursed a police officer, and that respect in tough neighborhoods depended on the willingness to use force frequently and effectively.

The genesis of nearly all street abuse is defiance of authority, real or imagined, regardless of whether the action is arrest alone or arrest and summary punishment. Criticism of a policeman's handling of a situation, for example, is interpreted as an extremely offensive challenge to the officer personally as well as to his authority. Typically, such an arrest is made using the charge of interfering with an officer, although in some cases the charge may be disorderly conduct.

Police resent citizens taking down police shield numbers. The problem of identification of police officers is exacerbated by the fact that all policemen wear the same blue uniform. Taking down the shield number is one of the most threatening actions to a policeman, not only because he interprets it as an act of defiance, but also because his behavior is about to come to the attention of his superiors. Although verbal criticism is not such a direct threat, many policemen feel that this, too, deserves punishment.

Bohemians, homosexuals, political activists, particularly of the left, derelicts, prostitutes, and narcotics users all invite police action. There is no more embittering experience in the legal system than to be abused by the police and then to be tried and convicted on false evidence. Patrolmen believe that the facts of an arrest are commonly distorted in order to advance.

The Mapp decision in the U.S. Supreme Court resulted in the fact that a defendant now cannot be convicted upon evidence obtained without probable cause to make an arrest or a search. If a policeman does not witness a crime being committed, he can enter a house only with the use of a warrant, or in the course of making an arrest for a felony. But police sometimes invade private premises without obtaining the permission of the occupant or without obtaining a warrant.

The Revised Penal Law of New York state effective September 1, 1967, provided that an officer could not justifiably use deadly force except to defend his own life or the life of other persons against deadly force, or to apprehend a felon who had used or threatened to use deadly force. This means that an officer cannot shoot a felon unless the felon has a weapon and has made some attempt to use it. It is no longer justifiable to kill the driver of a stolen car.

Twenty-five of 27 justifiable homicides of the police for the year 1964 were considered justifiable because the killings were made in response to an immediate threat under the terms of the law.[20]

One of Police Commissioner Murphy's most significant reforms was directed toward brutality at its most extreme. In 1972 he set up an intense watchdog group called the Firearms Discharged Review Board, which met regularly to question every shot fired from a cop's gun. Everyone, including the chiefs, had to qualify as marksmen twice a year, once indoors at headquarters and once on the outdoor range in the Bronx.[21] Murphy also introduced the "model precinct" concept, but it eventually foundered. He believed in efficient management. He increased supervision of the police. He wanted to decentralize the police.[22]

There is some evidence that exposure to college education tends to soften hardline or primitive attitudes toward others by enhancing the officer's self-image and esteem.[23] There is a division in the police between the old and the young. The older group believes that the young officers take the job too seriously, and the young officers believe that the older police do not take the job seriously enough.[24] Many young police make good arrests, but often they are stolen by detectives in their own precincts.[25]

The police do not enforce all the laws in the lower-income neighborhoods that they would in middle-class areas. One reason is the sheer volume of business which makes it difficult to police all except major infractions.[26] All policemen who kill a citizen go before a grand jury.[27] Contrary to opinion, most police have not fired their guns on duty, and most New Yorkers have never in their lives seen a uniformed policeman with a gun drawn.[28]

A police officer named Kelly in the mid–1970s was charged with murder because he had beaten an Hispanic drug dealer suspect who had died of a ruptured spleen several hours after the beating. Two years after the incident, Kelly was dismissed from the department. He was convicted of criminally negligent homicide and sentenced to four years in prison. He was the first New York City police officer to be tried for the murder of a prisoner while in police custody. The allegations were that the arresting officer had beaten the suspect while in police custody and subsequently had beaten him in the second floor squad room of the precinct, causing his death. Seven police officers eventually testified against Kelly, admitting that they had lied during the initial grand jury investigation, attempting to protect Kelly, explaining it was an acceptable practice to commit perjury to help a fellow officer. Some officers believe the job has changed because "you don't know who you can trust anymore."[29]

There is evidence that officers deliberately make arrests at the end of the tour in order to make overtime money. However, the officers' overtime payments are losing their attractiveness because more efficient court processing systems have eliminated much of the overtime that officers spend on overtime work. Some officers are actively avoiding making arrests that might tie them up after work on a day that was now committed to another job, or even leaving them tired from the arrest-related overwork.[30] Before July 1, 1969, police were not paid for working overtime.[31] However, in the mid–1970s, a policy change substituted time off for money in making overtime arrests.[32] No overtime was permitted in the early eighties.[33] In the 1960s police were forbidden to engage in outside work.[34]

During 1977 about 100 officers were forced to work without guns on non-patrol assignment. Their weapons were removed because they were found to be suffering from psychiatric problems and were considered potentially dangerous.[35] In the late 1970s Commissioner McGuire weeded out misfits. By the end of 1978, 173 police officers were arrested, suspended, or placed on modified assignment. In 1977, 139 officers were weeded out.[36]

Although the police will not admit that they abide by quotas in making arrests, many police will admit that they have priorities they must meet. There is evidence that the precinct sets objectives—for example, percentage increases, decreases, and current number of robberies, civilian complaints, number of warrants, etc.—and they use these objectives to satisfy the precinct and the higher echelon. They also consider the rate of civilian complaints to the number of arrests and the number of radio runs as objectives.[37]

The lower-middle-class policeman often seeks to establish his manliness with his nightstick and his gun, two of the few prestige symbols within his reach.

The police believe that changes in the rules for use of firearms are a depressing symbol of the decline of police autonomy. Men might select police work because it means freedom from constricting restraint and routine, but the reality of police work reflects an increasingly constricting world. Many police resist the decline in police standards. The police hate all the paper work that they are required to handle in the course of a day.[38]

Police officers believe that they have little effect on the crime rate. They believe that most crimes are committed by blacks and that any attempt to solve black violence and crime must come from police repression of blacks rather than from attempts to solve the economic, social, and racial problems facing many blacks. The police criticize the criminal justice system because they too often see charges they made in a legitimate arrest reduced through plea bargaining or thrown out of court.[39]

The police are in conflict not only with the criminal, but also with each other. The police no longer put their major energy, skill, and courage into making arrests. They put it into not being caught while committing their own crimes.[40]

The turnover in the department in the late 1960s amounted to 1,000 men a year, mostly consisting of men who retired, who left to take other jobs, or who were dismissed for various reasons. Most policemen hate the guns and wish they did not have to carry it. In the late 1960s there were 3,000 detectives in New York City.[41]

According to law, a man cannot be convicted of an offense for disobeying an unlawful police order, or for disturbing the public peace that results from arguing with a policeman over an unlawful order. Moreover, according to a law of the early seventies, a man has the right to resist an unlawful arrest.[42]

The new bullet-proof vests obtained by the police force in the early eighties turned out to be too heavy. The police who wore them developed back problems.[43]

In the 1960s the police believed that compared to any other sector of the city, Central Park was safer. The police felt that there was less crime in Central Park and police apprehended criminals at higher rates there than in other sections of the city. The police seemed to be in the right place at the right time in Central Park. Witnesses to crimes, however, are more numerous in other parts of the city than in Central Park.[44]

Police engage in service work as well as work involving law enforcement. The police, for example, protect foreign missions and consulates on an ongoing basis.[45] The average response time for a police officer is 25 minutes, but in a real emergency the response time is five to ten minutes.[46]

Ten policemen died in the line of duty in 1968 and ten more died in 1971.[47] In 1971, however, according to another source, seven police were killed, 242 were injured, 19 police had their guns taken away from them and were assaulted with their own weapons, and the police shot and killed 50 criminals and wounded 212.[48] Another source stated that in 1971 ten policemen were killed by black militants; five of these police officers were black.[49] Assaults on the police have increased since 1950, when there were 137 assaults upon the police. In 1960 there were 444 assaults upon the police; in 1966 there were 544 assaults upon the police; and in 1967 there were 803 assaults upon the police.[50] Almost one-fifth of all policemen killed on duty are those who responded to disturbance cases which included family quarrels.[51]

Police-Community Relations

Insults and racial slurs rather than arrests make ghetto people most antagonistic to the police.[52] During the Lindsay administration under police commissioners Howard Leary and Patrick Murphy, the perception of the police as a military type of organization changed because of the police commissioners' fundamental changes in police nomenclature, equipment, and dress. Police-community relations were expanded, police-citizen dialogue was encouraged, citizen liaison and advisory boards were enlarged, and human relations training for members of the police service were emphasized. Family crisis intervention was introduced to make the police more responsive to the concept of team policing.[53]

During Police Commissioner Murphy's term, a campaign against prostitutes was begun.[54] However, in 1975, prostitutes were fined rather than imprisoned.[55] In the early seventies, police expended more energy and used greater sensitivity while investigating sexual assaults because of the public effort generated by groups concerned with the rights of women and victims of rape.[56] This shows that the police department through its top command is sensitive to public issues.

The police look suspiciously and with antagonism at anything that involves community members in precinct operations. As one officer said, "They ought to keep the hell out of our business. They just get in the way." Police resent civilians in police jobs. They resent them because they believe that civilians really do not understand a policeman's job, and because to civilians their job is just a job, but to the police themselves their job is a career. Police resent civilians because civilians replace fellow officers on jobs previously reserved for officers who had finished their time or were burned-out. Sometimes civilians lodge complaints against precinct officers, which arouses considerable police resentment. Police resent that civilians have holidays off and police resent that civilians are not as dependent upon their job as the police are. Many civilians keep to themselves, but some civilians and police officers are friendly. Civilians also create social class and ethnic tension.[57]

Some believe that police prejudice in Harlem is so extreme that residents would rather not have white police working there.[58] However, the majority of blacks, while they may resent white policemen, need them and they know that they need them. In Harlem, a year after the racial riots in the 1960s, public opinion surveys indicated both widespread hostility against the police and widespread desire for more and better police protection.[59]

As mentioned, the police perform many nonpolice functions, for example by calling ambulances for the sick, or giving directions, etc. Some of these functions are unrelated to crime prevention. As mentioned earlier, one function is protecting foreign missions and consulates.[60] These functions, however, may improve police-community relations.

Blackout—1977

Two researchers interviewed people in 1977 concerning the July 13, 1977, blackout in New York City. Both financially and socially the blackout was costly to New York, although New York was already shaken by fiscal crisis. Looters were unconcerned with the race of their victims; there was stealing from Jews, Puerto Ricans, and blacks. However, white merchants were overwhelmingly their victims. The looters consisted of both the poorer members of the community who were caught up in the hysteria of the street, and the better-off employed residents who seemed to be motivated solely by greed. These persons had little or no experience in crime, and were likely to have family and community ties. In addition to the criminal types, alienated youth, and the unemployed, badly educated ghetto poor under 35 years old were among the looters.

In all, 1,616 stores suffered damage during the blackout. Food markets and apparel stores were included in the looting. The most frequently looted item was sneakers. Racial issues appeared second to economic issues. Much credit for the lack of racial fighting was given to patrolmen for "keeping their cool."

The spontaneity in the outbreak of looting together with the absence of strong mutual police action created a feeling among the looters and would-be looters that they were immune from arrest. They sensed that they would suffer few or no consequences as a result of their actions. This was responsible in large part for the build-up of a tremendous momentum in the looting, to the point where the looting could only have been stopped by huge masses of men.

Police action was criticized as "being soft." However, in the racial riots in 1967 in New York City, minority group leaders labeled police actions as "brutality" because they had felt that the police had overacted in many instances during the riots. During the 1977 blackout not one rioter was shot by the police, although two looters were killed by store merchants. The departmental policy was strict on not firing aimlessly into the air or into people.

This was the first time in New York City's history that all five boroughs were simultaneously involved in a civil disorder, and it was alarming to see how police had to stretch their protection in such a vast area. Some precincts did not have sufficient men to make arrests at all; they feared that the bookkeeping involved in making arrests would strip the streets of the police.

By the time the blackout was over 3,076 people had been arrested and charged with a variety of offenses, including assault and criminal trespassing in the first, second, and third degree. They also were charged with possession of a weapon, criminal mischief, larceny, robbery, possession of stolen property, arson, and inciting a riot. Of those arrested, only 6.7 percent were women; nearly 1,600, or more than half of the group, were between the ages of 16 and 25. Juveniles accounted for 173 of the arrestees. Conversely, 232, or 8 percent of the arrestees, were over the age of 40. Blacks comprised 65.3 percent of the arrestees; 30.3 percent were Hispanics; 4 percent were whites. About 56.1 percent of the arrestees had prior criminal records. The arrestees on the night of the looting had unemployment rates almost three times as high as the arrestees during the 1960 riots.

Extensive and destructive looting occurred in neighborhoods not generally associated with dense ghetto-like poverty. This was surprising. The looting and stealing were at a minimum in the Lower East Side; this might have been the result of a genuine community spirit existing in this area.[61]

Civilian Complaints

Middle-class people are more likely to register complaints than the poor, and cases involving middle-class citizens are easier to authenticate. Police complaints tend to be made by people who never had any conflict with the law and have no reason to fear the police. The poor have a rough life anyhow, and they accept police roughness as part of the game.

A project was initiated to accept police complaints, and from March 1, 1966, to June 31, 1967, the project received a total of 441 complaints. Of these 441 complaints, 123 were accepted for further investigation and litigation because corroborating evidence was available. Seventy-one complaints were finally authenticated, that is, corroborating evidence was found and no conviction was obtained to cover the abuse. These 71 complaints constituted 57 percent of the complaints accepted and 16 percent of all those received. Seven police trials resulted and eight police officers were disciplined. Some accepted a reprimand without a trial. The complainants in 59 percent of the 71 complaints were arrested.[62]

On November 5, 1977, Thomas Ryan was found guilty of criminally negligent homicide in the killing of Israel Rodriquez. He was also acquitted in the assault charge of Luis Santiago. Earlier, police officer Thomas J. Shea had shot and killed a 2-year-old boy in Queens, but he was acquitted. However, Shea was dismissed from the force after a departmental hearing. Earlier that year another police officer, William Walker, was acquitted in the shooting of a college student in Brooklyn. Walker, too, was dismissed from the force. Another police officer, Robert Torsney, was acquitted on grounds of insanity for murdering a 15-year-old Brooklyn boy.

Police officers Dennis Greene and Patrick Halligan were tried for assault in the first degree, but the evidence against them was not specific enough to convince a jury. In February, 1978, while still awaiting departmental trial, both Greene and Halligan were restored to active duty and assigned to precincts in Manhattan. The police officer who had been arrested with them, Joseph Chiney, was completely cleared of all charges; however, he had lost pay while suspended. In 1982, having passed the civil service examination, Chiney was made a sergeant. No charges were brought against the police who had lied under oath to the grand jury and later changed their stories in the case of Thomas Ryan.

Thomas Ryan, however, was the first New York City policeman convicted of committing homicide while on duty. On October, 1978, Ryan was arrested again and indicted on an assault charge for running down a postal worker and leaving the scene of an accident. He was sentenced to four years prison but did not show up on the day he was scheduled to begin his prison term for killing Israel Rodriquez, and a bench warrant was issued. He finally gave himself up on November, 1981, still proclaiming his innocence.[63]

The police are far more careful today than previously when they take official action against blacks.[64] This might be due to the racial riots of the 1960s, the legal and social rights of blacks, the vast number of complaints against the police initiated by the blacks, the gradual increase of the number of blacks in the police department, and other social changes. The colored community would accept abuse from a Negro policeman, but would become hostile when abused by a white policeman.[65]

Police who are brought up on departmental charges have several choices of defense. They may represent themselves, retain outside legal counsel, or select the services of the defense counsel of the department.[66]

Civilian Review Board

The Civilian Complaint Review Board was established in July, 1966, by Mayor Lindsay and it was abolished by majority vote in the referendum of November, 1966.[67] On July 1, 1966, the police commissioner appointed four civilians unconnected with the police department to act with the three existing members of the Civilian Complaint Review Board drawn from the department. This created a nonpolice majority on the board. The police criticized the Civilian Complaint Review Board because they believed it was a threat to their authority.[68] The Patrolmen's Benevolent Association mounted an effective financial compaign against the board which included allusion to the specter of black violence; this spearheaded the board's defeat.[69]

Approximately 90 to 92 percent of the complaints during the short life of the Civilian Complaint Review Board were found to be unsubstantiated. The complaints started to come in at the rate of 90 to 110 per month. The total number of complaints in 1966 was about 1,000. The total number of complaints for 1967 was about 1,300. The increase in complaints was probably due to the widespread publicity the board received, which for the first time gave knowledge and information to the people that there was an agency and a place where complaints could be made.

Of the complaints brought to the Review Board, "unnecessary force" was the most frequent; allegations of "discourtesy and derogatory treatment" came second; "abuse of authority" came third; "racial slurs and insulting language" came last. In some instances, the complainant withdrew the complaint.[70]

Other Complaints

Of 2,409 cases submitted to the board during 1977, 73.3 percent were unsubstantiated, 11.6 percent were substantiated, and 15.1 percent were classified as other dispositions. Of those unsubstantiated, 41.8 percent lacked sufficient evidence to prove or disprove the allegations, while 31.5 percent were unsubstantiated due to noncooperation from the complainants. Of the 11.6 percent substantiated, 68.6 percent involved excessive use of force, 25.7 percent involved abuse of authority, and 4.5 percent involved discourtesy.[71]

The incidence of class A complaints, the most serious complaints, decreased from 642 in 1981 to 191 in 1982.[72]

In 1985 there were 7,073 complaints of police misconduct; in 1986 there were 5,128 complaints of police misconduct, a reduction of 27.5 percent. The most important allegations of police misconduct involved, in rank order from first to last, unnecessary and excessive use of force, abuse of authority, discourtesy, and ethnic slurs. Now all commanding officers are held accountable for the civilian complaints filed against their precinct.

The new Civilian Complaint Review Board, which was created by a legislative act of February 22, 1987, will consist of six members appointed by the police commissioner and six public representatives appointed by the mayor with the consent of the city council. However, the Policeman's Benevolent Association brought a civil action seeking to prevent the implementation of the legislation, and it was still pending as of the writing of this book. The Review

Board now has a conciliation unit, and as a result, in 1986, 96 percent of all investigations were completed within 90 days.[73]

Police Corruption

Although corruption has always existed in the police department, an inquiry into police corruption was initiated during Mayor Lindsay's administration. The Knapp Commission, created in 1970, consisting of five private citizens appointed by the mayor, five commissioners, and eight lawyers, many of whom were former prosecutors, was established to investigate charges of police corruption that had been reported in the *New York Times*. The Knapp Commission investigated corruption over a two-and-one-half-year period, and then submitted its report to Mayor Lindsay. Police officers objected because too little attention was paid to the good work they had done and because they had been singled out when corruption had existed elsewhere. The Knapp Commission did not indict all police officers, however.

Patrick Murphy was appointed police commissioner in October, 1970. He waged a tough and persistent campaign against police corruption. The formation of the Knapp Commission under Mayor Lindsay was the first time in the history of New York City that a mayor had created an independent commission to investigate corruption. In effect, Serpico, a New York City plainclothesman, began the process of investigating police corruption in 1967 when he was used as an informant to report on active police corruption. His allegations led to indictments against 19 plainclothesmen in the Bronx for involvement in an illegal payoff which had netted $800. Also, an investigation by the Brooklyn district attorney resulted in indictments against 37 Brooklyn plainclothesmen who had netted $1,200.

Four of the investigations were conducted by the Bureau of Internal Affairs, one by the Bureau of Narcotics and Dangerous Drugs, and one by the Post Office Department. Also, the services of exmembers of the F.B.I., Army Intelligence, and the Immigration Service were used. The commission also received a promise of a grant to continue its work.[74]

The policemen despised Commissioner Murphy because of his constant talk of corruption, since they believed that they were already despised enough and shot at enough already. Two top policemen, who themselves engaged in corruption and acted as informants, were rewarded for their allegations against other officers.[75]

Corruption in the police department was investigated even before the Knapp Commission had been formed. In the 1940s, because of gambling corruption, 45 policemen, several of high rank, were convicted in criminal court or departmental trials, and approximately 150 others either retired or resigned. Plainclothesmen falsified records of gambling arrests even before the formation of the Knapp Commission. The Police Commission's Confidential Investigation Unit (PCCIU) was created partly as the result of an inquiry into police corruption. The entire force fears the unit because of its policy of aggressive investigation.[76]

There were other instances of police corruption before the era of the Knapp Commission. In 1965 an eight-year grand jury study indicted 37 members of a gambling ring, including 16 former policemen and 3 still on the force. In 1970 District Attorney Hogan estimated that as many as 1,000 police were on the take.[77] The police extorted money from prostitutes in return for promises to fix their cases.[78] The police also accepted Christmas gratuities from businessmen.[79]

Examples of Corruption

The Knapp Commission revealed many types of police corruption. Narcotics corruption lacked the organization for illegal payoffs from gambling, but individual payments could be as high as many thousands of dollars; one investigation revealed an $80,000 payoff. There were a large number of small payoffs. The policemen assigned to radio patrol cars participated in illegal activity from gambling which yielded payoffs more modest than those received by plainclothesmen.

The corrupt police also received payments from construction sites, bars, grocery stores, and other business establishments. The police received payments from bottle clubs, after-hour bars, tow trucks, motorists, cab drivers, parking lots, prostitutes, and defendants wanting to buy dismissal of their cases. It was found that bars, especially unlicensed bars, and construction sites were the most common sources of illegal income to the police. Payoffs were made to policemen assigned to the Property Clerk's Office and to the Police Department's Automobile Storage Yards by field representatives of one of the nation's largest automobile finance companies. Favors in the police department would be routinely bought and sold; appointments to the rank of detective could be brought for $500 to $2,000.

Police paid other policemen a couple of dollars for typing arrest reports and hundreds of dollars for choice assignments. Police surgeons were bribed to certify that policemen were permanently disabled, making it possible for policemen to retire early and receive all or part of their pensions.

The most widespread form of misconduct in the police department was the acceptance by police officers of gratuities, free meals, free goods, and cash payments. Almost all policemen either solicited or accepted such favors in one form or another. This practice was widely accepted by both the police and the citizenry, who felt that this was not corruption but a natural benefit of the job. The public did not regard gratuities as a serious matter.

When called to a house or an apartment when someone had died, the police have been known to burglarize the premises if the deceased had been living alone. Police would plant phony betting slips on gamblers and then collect $25 or $50 in order not to arrest them.

Police were either "grass eaters" or "meat eaters." The former, comprising the majority of the police, accepted gratuities of $5, $10, and $20, but did not aggressively pursue corruption payments. The vast majority of the police did not deal with large amounts of money. The latter comprised a small percentage of the police, and spent a great deal of their working hours aggressively seeking out situations they could exploit for financial gain, which yielded payments of thousands of dollars. The acceptance of a gratuity by a police officer was classified as a Class A misdemeanor punishable by a year in jail.[80]

Cooperation and Prevalence

The laws against gambling, prostitution, and the conduct of certain business activities on the Sabbath all contributed to the prevalence of police corruption in different degrees of seriousness. Many laws are difficult to enforce because the "victims" of the crimes are willing participants and seldom complain to the police. Some of the laws police officers are called upon to enforce in relation to licensed premises are so vague and ill-defined that they are subject to abuses in practice.[81]

The police were absolutely terrified by the Knapp Commission.[82] Although not all policemen were corrupt, the police who were not corrupt took no steps to prevent or to punish known corrupt activity. There was a serious refusal at all levels of the police department to acknowledge that a serious problem existed. Corruption to some degree infected a majority of policemen on the force. However, corrupt officers were protected by a code of silence by those who remained honest. The Knapp Commission persuaded only four officers to assist in the investigation.

The Knapp Commission recorded 1,700 written or telephone complaints, 375 of which had been forwarded by the Rankin Committee. Most of the complaints coming from the public were not appropriate for investigation by the commission's limited staff, and many of them were either crank complaints or too vague to be of any use. The public believed that corruption was prevalent and widespread, and many, particularly ghetto residents, had personal experience with this. However, practically no one was willing to testify personally, for fear of reprisals by the police. Bar owners, construction supervisors, hotel managers, and other similarly situated businessmen refused to cooperate until the Knapp Commission subpoenaed records that reflected illegal payments.

Only then did representatives of the hospitality and construction industries decide to cooperate more fully.

One hundred and thirteen police officers were subpoenaed, of whom 79 testified. In addition, 116 subpoenaed witnesses—104 civilians and 12 policemen—testified informally before commission staff members. One police officer, named Phillips, participated in 69 operations in which tape-recorded conversations involving corruption were obtained. Other officers, including plainclothesmen and detectives, who had been involved in corrupt activities, spoke to the commission staff on a confidential basis.[83]

Although police corruption involved more than 60 percent of the police officers in the department, the police themselves believed that too little attention was paid to corruption in other branches of the city government. A sample of police respondents believed that those who were critical of police corruption failed to make allowances for the social pressures, contingencies, collusions, and compromises that forced some policemen to break the law. They also believed that the critics had failed to take account of individual differences among police in committing corrupt acts. They also believed that the Knapp Commission did more than anything in the history of the police department to destroy public trust in the police. The Knapp Commission and the Civilian Review Board, said the respondents, had made them scapegoats for the ills of society.[84]

Arrests and Punishment

The statistics on arrests and punishments are somewhat fragmented, but they do give some general idea of the punishment for corruption. In Brooklyn, 36 current and former plainclothesmen were charged with corruption, of whom 24 were indicted. Federal indictments were returned against a lieutenant, two gamblers, and eight sector patrolmen. One patrolman was sentenced to ten years in prison for selling narcotics and to a five-year prison sentence for possession of a large quantity of narcotics.

Twenty-six police officers and 14 civilians were indicted by various federal and state prosecutors in cases originated by the commission. Thirty-four police officers, including 24 of those indicted, were suspended and 57, including the indicted or suspended, were brought up on departmental charges.

The commission uncovered 164 individuals who were engaged in criminal behavior, 66 of whom were police officials, and 98 of whom were civilians. Witnesses uncovered incidents of corruption amounting to criminal violation involving 301 individuals, but the commission did not confirm this. Witnesses condemned 31 officers who violated department rules and regulations, but this again was not confirmed by the commission. In addition, alleged incidents involving 810 individuals, 286 of whom were police officers, were reported by credible witnesses, but the commission was not able to evaluate them.

A considerable number of high-ranking officers were demoted or transferred during the first year and a half of Commissioner Murphy's tenure. Out
of 58 convicted officers, 17 were dismissed from the force, 5 were placed on
one year's probation, 24 officers were fined an average of 48 vacation days,
8 were fined an average of 13 days' pay, and 4 officers were reprimanded.
Several of the police commissioner's decisions on penalties were subject to
judicial review and were actually reversed in several cases because of pension
forfeiture upon dismissal for cause from the force.

During the period 1968–1972, of 218 defendants, 158 were patrolmen, 39
were detectives, 9 were sergeants, 11 were lieutenants, and 1 was an associate
chief inspector. Sixty-three of the defendants pleaded guilty, 28 were convicted
after trial, 46 were acquitted or dismissed, and 81 were still awaiting trial. Of
the 91 officers who were convicted, 80 were sentenced. Forty-nine were either
set free or given suspended sentences, and 31 received jail terms, 14 of whom
received less than one year. It appeared to the commission that the risk of
severe punishment for corruption was slight.[85]

In the first ten months of 1973 more than 80 policemen were arrested on
corruption charges, and 31 police were suspended for suspected graft and
receiving payoffs. Departmental trials met most standards of due process and
followed procedures similar to those in criminal court. The defendant was
represented by an attorney either of his own choice or provided by the department, and had a right to cross-examine witnesses. However, a system of informal sanctions was applied to the plainclothes forces for discipline.[86]

The Knapp Commission discovered that corruption reached the most sophis-
ticated level among plainclothesmen assigned to enforce gambling laws.[87]
Police were known to take gifts willingly contributed. However, district attorneys were unwilling to prosecute the few police who were caught taking
them. Businessmen were told to refrain from giving gifts, but refused to do so.
Units were set up to catch police with trunks of loot, given to them at Christmas.
Radio cars operated by off-duty police were seen cruising business districts at
Christmas time, and they were followed by the corruption units. This took a
lot of time and very few police were caught. In addition, Murphy granted
amnesty around Christmas time to all police facing minor disciplinary charges.[88]

Results of Corruption Campaign

During the Knapp Commission's campaign, a *New York Times* reporter
believed that policemen of all ranks had become apprehensive about being
caught taking payoffs, and that nearly all forms of corruption had decreased.
Also, in precinct houses located in black neighborhoods, for the most part, the
residents were treated with more courtesy and understanding than in the past,
even when they entered to complain about a policeman.[89]

The department has managed to make organized corruption more difficult and to make general institutional corruption less prevalent. After the Knapp Commission, in 1974, there was a significant increase in the number of complaints against police officers. This was probably due to a greater willingness on the part of civilians and police officers to turn in corrupt police. In addition, in the years following the Knapp Commission, there was a significant decrease in the number of officers taking bribes related to gambling. However, after the Knapp Commission, there was a significant increase in the number of officers involved in taking bribes from narcotic sources. Officers are required to attend integrity and ethics workshops, but these are viewed as a mechanism by which officers are to be pressured to turn in fellow officers or to report corruption. In general, the department has been successful in eliminating large-scale system-wide organized "illegal payoffs," but has been less successful in combating individual problems of corruption.[90]

The Knapp Commission recommended that the police be taken off duties at bars, restaurants, and building sites, to perform their principal job of protecting lives and property. In January, 1972, the department specified that anti-gambling enforcement efforts would be concentrated on high-level figures in gambling combines, and that low-level runners would no longer be arrested except when complaints were received. The department also specified that uniform policemen may no longer make gambling arrests unless a supervisor is present. The Knapp Commission in 1972 also indicated that numbers and bookmaking should be legalized and that their regulation should become a civil rather than a criminal matter.

Sergeants are now required to accompany their men in initiating narcotics arrests and to take custody of the seized narcotics. The department also ordered that no uniformed men were to enter bars except in emergencies or to obtain meals. However, this ruling apparently had little effect in combating bar corruption: four detectives shook down a West Side bar almost immediately after the ruling. In 1970 the department ordered all police officers not to enforce the Sabbath Laws unless a specific complaint was received or a flagrant violation was observed. Incidents of shake-down by officers have decreased since this ruling went into effect.

Now all patrol borough commanders and the heads of all the specialized units are required to submit at regular intervals anticorruption plans identifying the chief corruption hazards within their commands, and to detail the measures taken to reduce these hazards. New recruit training now includes 20 hours of discussion and lectures on police crime and corruption.[91] There is evidence, however, that arrests for bookmaking and numbers have decreased from 11,467 in 1965 to 1,394 in 1975.[92]

The police have complained that too little attention was being paid to corruption in other departments, such as the fire department, the sanitation department, and the upper reaches of city government. They felt that they were being singled out.[93] Now, all commanding officers are accountable for the civilian complaints filed against their personnel.[94] In the early eighties, the United States attorney for a district in New York City announced that there was no evidence of widespread corruption in the police department. However, in the early eighties, nine police officers, one of them retired, were charged with taking bribes ranging from $300 to $5,100 from illegal after-hour clubs. In 1979 many charges against police involved bribe-taking and narcotic use. Many of the charges were unsubstantiated, but 35 police officers and detectives were arrested, 96 were suspended, and 22 were placed on modified assignment.[95]

Minority Relations Within the Department

As of January, 1982, the proportion of nonwhites in the police department was 17 percent. In the early 1900s a former member of the New York City Police Department interviewed a sample of 46 black policemen. Not all respondents shared the view that prejudice, discrimination, and especially inequality were things of the past. Only about a quarter of the respondents believed that black officers were treated on an equal basis with white officers.

Nine of the policemen in the study denied that the New York City Police Department and its supervisory staff treated black officers in the same way as whites. Friendships outside of the job, which excluded blacks, could carry into the job in the distribution of rewards and favors.

The systematic assignment of black police officers to black precincts in the city was another area of concern to some respondents. However, the department, in making these assignments, believed that this would lead to easing of tensions in the community. However, the respondents did not believe that racial discrimination in discipline existed in the department. The younger respondents appeared more disenchanted with conditions on the job than the older men, possibly due to the lack of experience and appreciation of the more overt forms of racial discrimination characteristic of earlier years. The older, more experienced officers were perhaps better equipped to evaluate and recognize changes that have been made in recent years.

All respondents agreed that Commissioner Murphy had done more to eliminate racial problems in the department than any other administrator before him. In order to reduce racial tension, the department in 1971 instituted a series of human relations training programs for patrol officers.

There seemed to be a positive feeling among most of the black officers toward white policemen they had worked with regularly in the past. However, both occasional acts of violence, and remarks that assigned negative characteristics to all blacks living in the ghetto, disturbed the respondents and sometimes hurt black-white relations. The most frequent charge by respondents against white officers in their dealings with blacks was brutality.

A number of the black respondents believed that it was a good idea to assign blacks to black precincts. One black respondent believed that this policy effectively reduced the discriminatory behavior of prejudiced white policemen. Many respondents believed that white policemen exaggerated the prevalence of danger in slum communities and took unnecessary steps to avoid contact with blacks. Black policemen in black communities were accused of "selling out," and were susceptible to the charge of being an "Uncle Tom."

The majority of men supported an "integrated precinct," the policy of a black and white officer working together. The black respondents did not believe that they were more effective crime fighters in the black community than white policemen. However, a few respondents believed that black policemen provided more effective service to ghetto clientele than white policemen. A little less than half of the respondents believed that the black offenders gave black officers a more difficult time than they gave white policemen. Some respondents believed that black officers tended to resort to more extreme measures than the white officers.[96]

Pressures for minority recruitment and redress of past discrimination led to new criteria for promotional advancement, and these helped to further erode the sense of solidarity supported by the similarity of socioeconomic, cultural, religious, and ethnic backgrounds.[97]

Alex conducted a study in which he interviewed 42 white policemen chosen randomly. He found that black policemen were competent professionals who used police work as one of the few channels available to them for social mobility. He also found that the new black policemen were subject to racial prejudice, isolation, and segregation. The black policemen were not trusted as partners, and at times they were required to do the most dangerous work to prove to their white colleagues that they were real professionals, trustworthy, and competent. Black policemen were rejected by both white society and the black community they had to police. The motives for joining the police force were the same for blacks and whites, mainly job security and good income. However, 18 white respondents joined for status, prestige, tradition, self-realization, and autonomy, while the majority of blacks joined for economic reasons.

Alex found that white policemen in his sample were hostile toward integration because blacks and Puerto Ricans threatened not only their established claims to the job, but also their social mobility. All the respondents felt that the test standards had been simplified or modified so that the police department could recruit more black and Puerto Rican policemen.

Black policemen assigned to white neighborhoods were perceived as a threat because this encroached on the territory thought to belong to white officers. Almost all the respondents believed that racial factors gave rise to tension and conflict on the job. Some blacks refused to ride with whites in integrated patrol cars. Many of the respondents believed that blacks should do more plainclothes and undercover work because they could infiltrate black extremist groups.

Alex stated that the militant black policemen who identified with the black community might be more reluctant than white policemen to arrest a black. White-black conflict was exacerbated when a black policeman refused to accept the white policeman's judgment in arresting blacks. Black policemen might refuse to support or aid a white arresting a black. Black officers might even release a black prisoner arrested by a white officer. White policemen longed for the older black policeman who was civilized and disciplined, and was servile to the whites. White policemen resented blacks deviating from uniform standards, although allowed by the department, and some refused to work with blacks who wore nonstandard dress and hair cuts.[98]

As mentioned, Klein in the late sixties stated that the black community would take considerable abuse from a black policeman but often would not permit a white policeman to perform his duty in an orderly, acceptable, and civil manner.[99] However, as mentioned, Alex and Leinen found that sometimes blacks were rejected in their own community.

There probably is some subtle discrimination in the department concerning female officers. In 1982 there were 1,300 female police officers in the department, only 30 of whom were sergeants.[100]

Police Recruitment and Training

One of the most comprehensive studies of police personality was undertaken by Niederhoffer in New York City. Niederhoffer stated that the desire for security was the most frequent reason for becoming a policeman. He also mentioned that during the depression, in the 1930s, many college graduates entered the police force. He claimed that the typical policeman was a high school graduate with less than average intelligence, a curious personality, and above average endowment. Many police from lower-class backgrounds considered the job of policeman a stepping-stone to success. However, whatever their original socioeconomic status, the police must display middle-class values because they enforce the laws.

Niederhoffer stated that the police system itself turns the policeman into an authoritarian personality. This authoritarian personality caused police to emphasize male sexuality, to condemn homosexual offenders, and to show ambivalence toward women. Niederhoffer believed that police officers were by nature no more authoritarian than the rest of the population; they were not self-selected in authoritarianism. The most authoritarian policemen were at the bottom of the occupational pyramid on the street.

Niederhoffer found in interviews that the police believed that academy training was a waste of time. Two-thirds of the police force had a cynical attitude toward education. The majority of the police believed that they would be found guilty of departmental charges even when they had a good defense. Less than 10 percent believed that the rules were fair and sensible. Seventy-five percent of the sample believed that they could not trust the public to cooperate with the police. They had a cynical attitude toward the press and the courts.

Niederhoffer believed that the typical police recruit started his career without a trace of cynicism. A high arrest record enforced his cynicism, but also made him feel superior to other men because of his constant dealing with crime. Although Niederhoffer confined his study to New York City, he believed his findings were generally applicable. He concluded that the police personality was entirely the result of the constraints of the police role.[101]

McNamara conducted a study for the New York City police based on questionnaires, interviews, and tests. He used an F test to measure authoritarianism. He concluded that the scores on the F test were surprisingly low, and within the expected range for the policemen's socioeconomic origins, but still exceeded those of a cross-section of authoritarianism measured by Adorno. McNamara believed that men were attracted to police work mainly for the civil service security and economic benefits associated with the job. He believed that recruits on the job were nonpunitive.

The recruits in McNamara's sample themselves believed that police work was prestigious, but did not believe that the public perceived the work as prestigious. After years of experience, police did not believe that there was enough legal authority attached to their job. There was an increase in authoritarianism as evidenced by scores on the F test. Police recruits at the end of their training believed that more force was necessary. Some police believed that they must instill fear into citizens as part of their work. McNamara concluded that uncertainty was responsible for the difficulties police feared in their role, and that police were unaware of different citizen values.[102]

In the 1970s some 6,500 members of the police department were attending institutions of higher learning on their own, and of these nearly 2,000 had already obtained degrees.[103] At the police academy, where new recruits are trained, the police received a workload that was fully equivalent to a university curriculum. The curriculum included courses in police science, English, math, history, psychology, political science, business law, state law, and city law. Grades were considered part of the procedure.[104]

Some believed that police join the force to help their fellow men, although few would admit this.[105] It is unknown if the police are allowed to obtain overtime, since the literature is conflicting on this. However, police might informally obtain overtime on second jobs.

Men select police work because of freedom from constriction, restraints, and work routines, but this is not borne out in reality. The realities of police work fall short of recruits' expectations. Men are sometimes appointed with at least one misdemeanor conviction.[106]

Empirical Studies

A study was conducted on 356 men appointed in 1965, 281 of whom had been approved and 75 of whom had not been approved by background investigators. The results showed that after 18 months, better performance was not associated with favorable judgment during the background investigation. In a second study in New York City, 1,000 recruits were tested in 1962 and 1963 and evaluated in the first quarter of 1964. The results showed that prediction tests were unrelated to high and low rank performance.[107]

A study on 2,000 officers appointed in 1957 in New York City was conducted to study police background characteristics and performance in 1968. The active sample was 1,608 men. In addition, 307 men appointed in 1957 whose employment was terminated prior to 1968 constituted the inactive sample of the study. The methodology used was regression analysis and analysis of records. The men who were terminated from the department, the inactives, did not possess any characteristics that might be considered possible indicators of future bad performance. Few of them were rated low by the background investigators compared with the active sample. The men who left the department tended to be younger than those who stayed, and single; if married, they had fewer children and fewer family responsibilities. They had a greater history of job mobility and more education than those who stayed, and many had received military commendations.

Of the 1,608 men in the active sample, 883 had one or more complaints, and 451, or 51 percent of the 883, had one or more substantiated complaints. Among black officers, 50, or 61.7 percent out of 81, had at least one substantiated complaint. Only 4 percent of civilian complaints resulted in any sanction or punishment against the officers. Some 71 percent of the remaining types of departmental complaints were brought to trial, and over 75 percent of these were substantiated; however, only 15 percent of criminal allegations were handled by departmental trial. Officers with some college education were significantly less likely to receive civilian complaints than officers with less education.

The study also revealed that black subjects were rated lower than white subjects. The officers who completed their college education before or during the service advanced more rapidly than others. Those who served in the military performed no better or worse than others. However, bad performance in the military was related to bad performance in the police department.

The study also revealed that those who had an arrest history performed just as well as those who did not. The men with previous psychological disorders achieved promotion as frequently as other men but had more incidents of departmental complaints and more absenteeism than others.

The study revealed that officers with a history of court appearances might have had difficulty in interacting with citizens. Only seven of the nearly 2,000 recruits were dismissed from the force. However, 30 percent of the subjects received negative ratings while on probation. Subjects termed "excellent" by the background investigation had the lowest incident of misconduct while those termed "poor" had the highest incident of misconduct. The men with the high recruit training scores were much better performers than those with low scores. High recruit training scores were associated with rapid career advancement.

The recruit scores were significantly related to departmental charges. Subjects with poor probationary ratings had more allegations of misconduct, of which more were brought to trial and substantiated than subjects with good ratings. Subjects with poor probationary ratings tended to be absent more frequently than average. White officers with high I.Q.s won more awards than average, while black officers with high I.Q.s tended to be brought to trial for misconduct—more frequently than lower-scoring counterparts.

For white officers, military discipline and employment discipline were found to be consistent predictors of the pattern of the departmental discipline problem. Multiple appearances in civil court were the strongest predictor of the harassment pattern of white officers, although differences between those with and without multiple appearances were not large. The authors concluded that a history of court appearances might reflect difficulty in getting along with people. Arrest for violent crimes, multiple summons, and debts were weakly related to the ineffective performance among white officers. White officers with a prior arrest for a nonviolent crime were found to have a lower incidence of the harassment problem. High I.Q.s among white officers were viewed as a positive attribute.

The data showed that the ratings of blacks tended to be lower in general than those of whites, and that more background characteristics were found to correlate negatively for blacks than for whites. This occurred in spite of the fact that they were better educated than the whites and did not differ from the whites in employment history, arrests or summons history, or the number of times they appeared in civil court.

In 1957 less than 1 percent of the recruits were dropped from the academy or dropped during probation. This figure was not substantially higher in recent years. For the detectives, the variables were not valid for prediction of performance, probably because promotion of detectives depends less on standard performance than on who may influence appointments.

The authors concluded that the department might not be meeting the needs of the most intelligent black officers. The results of the study indicated that it was not possible to develop a single equation for weighing the background variables and early performance scores of recruits to obtain a single predictor of overall later performance that would be valid for both black and white officers.

The authors concluded that the performance of officers in the academy training program was a strong predictor of departmental performance measures, such as career advancement, departmental disciplinary action, and absenteeism, but it was not predictive of those aspects of performance that generally involved police interaction with citizens, such as civilian complaints. The authors also concluded that those recruits whose scores in examinations in the police academy were below passing should be dropped rather than given an additional opportunity to pass. In addition, they concluded that those recruits whose probationary evaluation was unsatisfactory on several dimensions of performance should be terminated if their recruit scores were also low.[108]

In another study, I interviewed 61 defendants, only one of whom was female, in the spring of 1982; most were in remand in Brooklyn criminal court, essentially a misdemeanor court; the respondents were mainly black or Hispanic. I administered a questionnaire to the defendants consisting of both open-ended and closed-ended questions. I also analyzed 44 cases in the district attorney's office corresponding to the respondents' cases, and interviewed 11 complainants and 10 police officers pertaining to the defendants' cases. The questionnaire included details of the actions in the crimes, the respondents' interaction with the police, the respondents' attitudes toward the crime, and their relationship with the complainant.

The results showed that about 60 percent of the respondents denied their guilt, and 40 percent admitted their guilt. In practically every arrest, there was some definite evidence to link the defendant to the crime, for example, a license check of a stolen vehicle, witness identification, codefendant "ratting" on the respondent, police officer observation, etc. About a third of the respondents stated that the police had observed the crime; about a third stated that the victim or complainant had called the police; and a third did not know who had called the police. Time estimates for police arrest were between "right away" to "two months." Virtually no defendant admitted that he or she had been hostile to the police or had resisted arrest.

Ten stated that the police had hit them or had pulled a gun on them, although the respondents said that they had done nothing. A few, however, admitted they had run. The majority of the arrests were performed peacefully without incident. About one-half of the respondents told the police they were innocent, and another half of the respondents did not have a chance to say anything. About 13 respondents admitted that they had committed a crime in the past for which they had not been arrested or the police had let them go. About 29 of the respondents thought that the police would let them go because of innocence or lack of evidence. Only two admitted that they had planned the crime in question, the vast majority committing the crime because of opportunity.

I concluded that in many cases the arrest process was routine. This was particularly true in department store arrests. The police officer gathered evidence in a routine way. The defendants' responses in the crime in most instances were routine. The defendants also calculated their chances of being caught. Although much of the arrest process was routine, there was still much discretion in the arrest process.[109]

In another study in the fall of 1985 and winter of 1986, I interviewed 305 black and Hispanic respondents chosen nonrandomly, who were living in four areas of the Bronx, to determine their attitudes toward the police. The results showed 119 believed that the police were doing a good job, 65 believed that the police were doing a poor job, and 105 believed that the police were doing a fair job; 15 had no opinion, and one refused to respond. One hundred and sixty-one did not believe that there were enough policemen in their neighborhood.

One hundred and twenty-seven were victims of crimes in their neighborhood. Nineteen of these victims did not call the police because of fear, because the offender got away, or because they believed that the police would not or could not do anything. Most respondents mentioned that the police had come in less than a half-hour. However, 27 thought that the response time was reasonable, and 43 thought it was not reasonable. Fifty-five were satisfied with the way the police handled their case and 48 were dissatisfied.

One hundred and eleven called the police for something other than a crime, such as illness. Sixty-four were satisfied with the way the police handled their call for service for something other than a crime, and 31 were dissatisfied. Eighty-four respondents thought that their neighborhood was good, 84 thought that it was poor, and 117 thought that it was fair. Seventy-three respondents had one or more family members who had been arrested for a crime. Eighteen revealed that police harassment or brutality occurred during the arrest of the family member.

A chi-square analysis revealed that attitudes were related to ethnicity, to employment, to whether or not the respondent believed that there were enough policemen in their neighborhood, to evaluation of police service, to whether or not someone was arrested in the family and to whether or not this arrest was accompanied by perceived harassment or brutality by the police, and to attitudes toward one's neighborhood.

The results also showed that attitudes were related to police response time, visibility of police, and to role performance. Attitudes toward one's neighborhood were related to people in the neighborhood, housing, crime, unemployment, poverty, and drugs.

I concluded that the response time and role performance of the police were the most important factors associated with attitudes toward the police. Therefore, the police should try to improve these aspects of their job. Since the respondents generally had a more positive attitude toward the service aspects of the police job compared with the crime aspects of the job, this role should be continued to improve police-community relations. I also concluded that the results implied that the respondents thought that the police were a vital and necessary institution in their neighborhood.[110]

Summary

Although the literature reveals some changes in the police since its early history, it is difficult to ascertain how much they have changed and what are the consequences of the changes, since no empirical tests were employed to measure these changes. Two types of changes are revealed in the literature. First, the police are becoming more bureaucratized, and there is much alienation between the street cop and the bureaucrat. This bureaucratization and possible rationalization of the street police system can have profound effects for the future.[111] It can affect the police arrest process and police-community relations. However, no attempt is made here to evaluate such changes.

Second, although police solidarity certainly still exists, there is some evidence that this is eroding due to the increase of nonwhites joining the police, investigations of corruption, civilian complaints, changes in the legal and social rights of minorities, black solidarity against abuses of police practices, greater education for police officers, outside intervention, etc. Some policemen seem to be more careful today in dealing with minorities. This erosion of solidarity is related to the bureaucratization of the police. Again, no attempt is made here to evaluate such change.

There are some who do not believe the policy system has changed at all. The system is still characterized by politics, corruption, and brutality. However, empirical research is needed to ascertain how much change, if any, has actually taken place. Also, the informal social system of the police, not reviewed here, should be studied to ascertain policies formally prohibited but practiced informally.

THE COURTS OF NEW YORK CITY

In this chapter I will attempt to integrate the various aspects of the courts in New York City into a coherent, complete picture of what takes place in criminal justice. After all, it is in the courts where an offender is arraigned, bail is set, the people and the defense argue their cases, various other individuals plead for or against the offender, and sentencing and punishment are imposed. This is where the public and the media concentrate their evaluation of the system. One cannot deny the importance of the courts in criminal justice.

Theories

Several theories of the court deserve attention, including organization and bureaucratic theory. Eisenstein and Jacob do not see the courts as bureaucracies. Courts lack the hierarchy of a bureaucratic organization. However, they believe that the courts are organizations. They introduce the term "work group" as the focus of interaction among the principal legal actors, namely, prosecutors, defense attorneys, and judges. The principal actors in these work groups develop norms that make behavior predictable in criminal justice.[1]

Laurence Mohr does not believe that organizational theory applies to the courts. He considers courts to be like "decision-making systems" rather than like organizations. In certain respects, however, Mohr states that courts are like organizations, as, for example, in the details of case assignment and the management of personnel such as clerks and stenographers. Mohr states that organizational effectiveness depends upon the correct manipulation of a hierarchy, rules, specialization, spans of control, qualifications for office, and other bureaucratic characteristics. Courts do not have what organizational theorists mean by "management."

Mohr believes that courts have goals and structure. Mohr concludes that although the fit between courts and organizations is not perfect, many themes of organizational theory can apply to the courts.[2]

Joseph Hoane doubts that courts can be called "organizations." They cannot be called "bureaucracies" either because they lack a hierarchy of offices, strict and systematic discipline, and a contractual method of employment. The court is a system of interrelated parts that is sometimes centralized. The court is never a true system of divided labor because courtrooms are autonomous and each performs a ritual task of clarifying statuses. This ritual role in courtrooms prevents them from being defined as a "bureaucracy" or as an "organization." However, courts do have bureaucratic power, as in the process of plea bargaining.[3]

Roberta Rovner-Pieczenik believes that courts can be viewed as large-scale organizations in which there is interaction among various subgroups concerning specific interests and a meeting of these interests. She introduces three models to explain court organization, namely, the "Rational Actor Model," or how court actions are reasonable; the "Organizational Model"; and the "Bureaucratic Model."[4]

Feeley states that although there are elements of bureaucratic organization within the courts, discretion has more in common with decentralized, nonhierarchical forms of bargain and decision than with bureaucracies. Although there is a superficial resemblance to bureaucratic control in the adversary process, the criminal justice system is more like a market than a bureaucracy. Efficient solutions are arrived at because of shared goals, not because of conflicting interests.[5]

Thus, we see that there is a division of opinion on whether courts can be called "organizations" or "bureaucracies," mainly due to the conflicting interests in the various parts of the system. However, there seems to be some informal cooperation among the various actors in the system.[6]

One of the most important functions of the court is sentencing. Not only do judges sentence defendants, but prosecutors, legal representatives, and probation officers participate in sentencing decisions. Prosecutors make sentencing recommendations upon which legal representatives and judges confer. Probation officers very often make sentencing recommendations subject to approval by their supervisors, and studies have shown that probation recommendations are often influential in judges' decisions. Very often all the legal actors use the same factors, prior record and seriousness of the offense, in arriving at a sentencing decision.

Theories of sentencing involve disparity. Disparity has already been defined as "unequal sentences for similar crimes or cases." If two defendants commit one crime with equal involvement, and both have no prior record, and both are employed and are the same age, ideally both should receive identical sentences. This is one reason why political agents are lobbying for determinate sentencing.

In addition, according to conflict theory, defendants are sometimes sentenced on the basis of occupation, race, and social class, so-called extralegal variables. This can be a case of disparity and discrimination, the latter defined as "preferential treatment based on race, class, and occupation."

As mentioned in Chapter 1, legal defense very often influences defendants to plead guilty in order to mitigate punishment. Prosecutors represent the state and the people, and they try to induce plea bargaining, offering a lesser sentence than the original charge in order to speedily process cases and to mitigate and individualize punishment. Very often bail is set by judges in consultation with prosecutors and legal defense in order to keep defendants in remand so that they will return for sentencing, or because judges are going to impose a prison sentence anyway.[7]

History of the Court

Fishman collected data on 3,618 felony prosecutions in New York City for the time period 1895–1932, the so-called "Progressive Era." In 1900, 93,389 cases appeared before the city magistrates for either preliminary or summary dispositions. Petty violators had their cases heard by one judge, until 1910 without a district attorney present. In 1930 over 400,000 cases were heard, an increase of 300 percent from the previous year; this increase was well beyond the growth of the general population in the same period. In 1900, for every 100,000 persons in New York City, there were 4,554 prosecutions, but by 1930, this figure climbed to 12,984 per 100,000 of the population. Many of these crimes were minor, local ordinances.

During the period 1895–1932 the efficiency of the courts seemed to be declining at an alarming pace, with rates of conviction dropping, delay increasing, and recidivism growing at a perilous rate. Critics declared that city courts and prosecutors encouraged greater criminality by their very shortcomings.

The average amount of time it took most felony cases to go through city courts was 89.5 days, or nearly three months. For misdemeanors, the time was only a day or two. For those defendants who held unskilled occupations and could not afford bail or counsel, the courts were efficient, but for those who had higher positions and could afford privileges, the system worked more slowly and inefficiently, possibly because they were more particular.

It appears that defendants who had a prior relationship with the victims had a low conviction rate. Roughly one-half of the felony cases appearing before the magistrates were dismissed. The majority of the remainder of the felons pleaded guilty and chose to forego their right to a jury trial. Even without guilty pleas, and after dismissals, conviction rates were less than 50 percent.

Most citizens placed under arrest, roughly 75 percent, eventually went free because magistrates, grand juries, prosecutors, and judges found the evidence against them insufficient to warrant prosecution.

The system did not affect all defendants equally. Some believed the breakdown of the system was evidenced by court delay, convictions, and crime. Women constituted only about 4 percent of the dockets. Also, defendants under the age of 25 accounted for a small proportion of the dockets. The foreign-born accounted for a small number of the dockets compared to the general population. The older and the native-born offenders seemed to contribute their fair share of the dockets. However, 43.5 percent of the recidivists, the young, ages 16–25, and 48.3 percent of the defendants who committed crimes against strangers had a difficult time in court, since bail rates for them were set high. For those who failed to raise bail, confinement in the Tombs was a horrible experience, since it was filthy, overcrowded, and characterized by corruption and mismanagement.

The incidence of bail-release increased steadily through the early twentieth century. Grand juries during this period took no more than a few minutes to hand down either a dismissal or an indictment that conformed with the prosecutor's counsel. Grand juries dismissed about 24.5 percent of the cases which appeared before them during "Progressive Era," far higher than the dismissal rate today.

Harsher sentences were given to recidivists, young offenders, and those who committed offender-stranger crimes, especially robberies and burglaries, because most citizens thought that these groups posed a serious threat to the social order. On the other hand, first offenders, women, older criminals, and prisoners who had prior relationships with their victims usually received a second chance. Offenders who had a prior relationship with the victim committed crimes that posed a greater danger to friends and relatives than to the community at large.

Prior to an indictment, most defendants who went through the criminal justice system during the early twentieth century did so without the benefit of legal counsel. However, according to New York law, in the early twentieth century, all criminal defendants in felony prosecutions had a right to legal counsel. Starting in 1917 free legal counsel was provided from the Legal Aid Society to all prisoners who proved themselves "worthy."

Criminal defense attorneys, like professional bail bondsmen, were easy to locate. These attorneys attracted lower-class clients. These lawyers, to many, were corrupt. According to many observers, the defense that criminal attorneys gave their clients was perfunctory, incompetent, and negligent. Some lawyers extorted money from their clients, failed to serve their interests, and even failed to appear for them when their cases came to trial.

However, few prisoners were willing to go through the criminal justice system without a lawyer. Once indicted, defendants faced conviction and punishment. A prisoner could avoid the punishment his crime legally warranted in a number of ways, such as by winning an acquittal, by winning a judicial discharge, by plea bargaining, etc. About 25 percent of all defendants escaped prosecution.

Only a minority, less than 14 percent, of criminal cases during this period went to jury trial, and this number decreased with time. About half of those who went to trial received acquittals. For many years the acquittal rate was even higher (78 percent in 1896; 70 percent in 1900; 58.7 percent in 1904; 52.5 percent in 1908; 56.3 percent in 1920, 56.3 percent in 1924; 57.5 percent in 1928; 53.6 percent in 1932). Many cases, about 19.2 percent, ended in a judicial discharge because the court decided that the existing evidence could not legally support the conviction of a defendant. Trial by jury took time and money, and as a result, only those who could afford it were likely to go to trial.

By all accounts, however, most courts relied on the prosecutor's recommendations completely and accepted their motions without scrutiny. The benefit of a plea bargain in the form of a lighter sentence for a lesser plea was irresistible, and was practiced. The poor could not afford trial and therefore pleaded guilty. Many district attorneys exploited the poor in this way.

However, the defendants whom prosecutors recommended for discharge were those who posed little threat to the social order. About 28.3 percent of defendants who had prior relationships with their victims were recommended and given discharges; about 29.9 percent of women defendants received discharges; defendants over the age of 26 were likely to receive dismissals; prisoners charged with crimes against the person (assault 24 percent, homicide 27.2 percent, and rape 23.2 percent) were more likely to receive dismissals than those charged with property crimes (burglary 10.6 percent and robbery 20.7 percent). Defendants who could afford bail (39.4 percent) and an attorney (20.7 percent), and those who went to trial consistently had higher dismissal rates than indigent defendants who had no trial.

The first probation law was passed in Albany in 1901; it gave judges the authority to set conditions of supervision on defendants with suspended sentences. Sentencing practices among judges followed certain patterns. The most severe sentences were imposed on those whom the judges and prosecutors believed represented the greatest threat to the urban community; those

defendants whom the judges, prosecutors, and the public regarded more benignly received lighter sentences.

Younger defendants were more likely to receive lighter sentences than
older defendants. About 30.5 percent of the younger prisoners, as compared
to 4.5 percent of the older defendants, received reformatory; 26.4 percent of
the younger prisoners versus 17.8 percent of the older defendants received
suspended sentences. The court and the public held ambivalent attitudes
toward the younger offender. Although the younger offender was considered
more dangerous than the older offender, he was also considered to be less in-
grained in his criminal ways, and therefore more salvageable.

Judges were more inclined to grant suspended sentences and probation to
wealthy defendants and to those who managed to raise bail than to those who
could not raise bail. On the whole, legal representation made little difference;
prisoners who could afford an attorney received roughly the same punishment
as those who could not afford one. For certain offenses, however, the presence
of an attorney was more decisive, but not always beneficial.

Defendants who pleaded guilty were far more likely than those who went
to trial to receive suspended sentences (26.4 percent versus 4.3 percent).
Guilty pleas accounted for 95.4 percent of all probation dispositions. Defendants who pleaded guilty were less likely to receive indeterminate sentences
compared with others (23.6 percent versus 27.8 percent), or to receive prison
of more than a year compared with others (11.8 percent versus 16.4 percent).

The trend of the period from 1898 to 1936 was to move from a determinate, fixed, relatively moderate system of sentencing to a more open-ended
and harsher one. Indeterminate sentencing became mandatory for a number
of crimes, and determinate prison sentences correspondingly declined. Now
determinate sentencing is again being considered, legislatively and politically.

Extralegal considerations, including wealth, bail, and counsel, influenced
both prosecutors and judges, and helped to determine outcomes or dispositions. The perception of criminal justice officials regarding the seriousness of
the prisoners' offense and their dangerousness to the community might have
carried more weight than the legal issue of guilt or innocence.

In 1901 New York state enacted probation legislation. In 1901 Manhattan
became the first city in the state to have its own court for children. By the turn
of the century, however, juvenile crime seemed to be increasing at an alarming
rate and growing more serious. New York City was one of the first cities to
establish Children's Court.

The establishment of Children's Court was followed by the creation of
Night Court (1907), Family Court (1910), Women's Court (1910)–which later
specialized in prostitution-related offenses–Term Court (1914), Traffic Court
(1917), Probation Court (1919), Homicide Court (1922), and Commercial

Frauds Court (1923). New York City's criminal justice system had entered the age of specialization.

Trial by jury consumed more time than did plea bargaining; the former resulted in a lower overall conviction rate. Those who benefited most from the jury system were not the most dangerous offenders, but financially comfortable offenders who represented little immediate threat to the social order. Now, however, trials, whether by jury or by judges, generally result in more severe dispositions than plea bargaining.[8]

In colonial New York, death was the prescribed punishment for more than 200 offenses including a petty offense like pickpocketing. Colonial American judges and juries acquitted large numbers of defendants, or found them guilty of less serious offenses, in order to avoid pronouncing the death penalty.[9]

Presentence reports can be traced to 1915.[10] Today the Probation Department of New York City is responsible for preparing the presentence reports on defendants.

Juvenile Courts

Researchers at the New York State Office of Children's Service made a study on what happened to every juvenile arrested for violent crime during the 12 months preceding June 30, 1974. They were able to track 90 percent of the arrests, 5,666 in all. Some 3,032 cases (53.5 percent) were adjudicated at intake; charges were dismissed or withdrawn on 1,401 cases in which petitions were filed; there were 143 acquittals. Convictions were obtained in 521 cases, representing 9 percent of the total and 20 percent of those who were actually charged with a crime. Forty-three percent of those convicted, or 3.7 percent of those arrested, and 8.5 percent of those actually charged with a crime, were punished with incarceration in a training school, prison, group home, or other institution.

In its study of New York City Family Court, the Office of Children's Service found that fully one-half of the cases that were adjusted at intake, and nearly half of those that were dismissed at a later stage, were dropped because the victim, complainant, or key witnesses did not show up or were unwilling to proceed. Some of the complainants might have been afraid of reprisal from the offenders or their friends. Other victims refused to cooperate because of a prior relationship with the offender.

One reason juvenile sentences are so lenient in New York is that the jurisdiction of New York State Family Court for juveniles ends at age 16. However, in spite of its leniency, New York state has the toughest juvenile sentencing policies of any state in the nation. It incarcerates comparatively few youngsters in juvenile facilities, but it jails large numbers of 16- and 17-year-olds. One reason for the tough juvenile punishment is reflected in the higher rate of robbery by young offenders, and another reason is the freer use of punishment by the adult system, since offenders 16 or 17 are sentenced in adult courts.

Since February 1, 1977, 14- and 15-year-olds in New York charged with committing a designated felony such as murder, armed robbery, aggravated assault, and rape, have been tried in a special section of Family Court. If convicted of a Class A felony, the juvenile offender must be committed to the State Department of Youth for five years, with a minimum of one year in a secure facility and a second year in an open residential setting. In the first eleven months of 1977, 608 such petitions were filed.[11]

The Family Court offers a miserable example of turnstile justice. Children, often 8 to 10 years of age, come before judges either unrepresented by counsel or represented by a legal aid lawyer who does not even know the child's name. Many juvenile cases are disposed of in three minutes.[12]

In Juvenile Court, for the most part, sentences bear no relation to the seriousness of the offense or to the offender's culpability. Sentences are often arbitrary and capricious. However, probation is the most frequently used disposition in juvenile court. Juveniles have no right to appeal. Juvenile courts are not required to keep transcripts. Juvenile proceedings are closed to outsiders. The juvenile system gives out far more punishment and less treatment than is acknowledged.[13]

Arraignment, Bail, Prosecution, Legal Defense

In this section I will present empirical data on arraignment, bail, prosecution, and legal defense in the New York City courtroom. Everything that happens to the defendant from their first court appearance to the time of sentencing will be analyzed here. Sentencing will be discussed in a later section.

Arraignment

In arraignment, where cases are first heard, cases are often disposed of very quickly. In AR1, in Manhattan Criminal Court, so many cases come in daily that the judges, prosecutors, and legal defense attorneys are hard-pressed to dispose of them quickly. Even in arraignment, except for heinous crimes, lawyers try to plea bargain with judges and prosecutors. Most defendants plead quickly to a reduced charge and minimum sentences are imposed. This is especially true for misdemeanors, since incarcerating a misdemeanant in the overcrowded jails might force the release of a hardened criminal. Therefore, first offenders can expect their cases to be A.C.D., adjournment contemplating dismissal, and even prostitutes, pickpockets, and bookies are released with a fine or time served.[14]

In 1977, 63 percent of all cases were disposed of at the initial arraignment. This number would have been higher, but the prosecutors prescreen cases before they go to arraignment. For example, many classes of cases, such as college kids caught smoking a joint or teenagers arrested for trespassing in abandoned buildings, are thrown out before they go to court.[15]

In 1969 a felony prearraignment processing was introduced into the Bronx and the Queens felony arraignment processes by the New York City Police Department. This project was initiated to reduce police costs and increase productivity. Harper, a researcher at John Jay College, conducted the study. As already mentioned in chapter 1, in 1969 there were 442,840 nontraffic felony, misdemeanant, and summary offense arraignments in all five branches, an increase of 91,163 over the calendar year of 1968.

The Lacey study, a study of the prearraignment process, was conducted during a 12-day period on a sample of 1,118 arraignments. The study disclosed that excusing victims and police officers from the formal arraignment was of limited significance. The study revealed that arraignment was, for the most part, a brief bail setting in which the absence of the officer and victim had had no discernible impact; the arraignment process itself did not have an impact on case dispositions.

Harper, in his study, noted that all felony arrests are screened in the Manhattan Criminal Court by assistant district attorneys to determine which felony arrests qualify for prearraignment processing. The New York City District Attorneys, however, were dissatisfied with the felony prearraignment processing because it reduced the number of felony arrests that could be disposed of at the formal arraignment. Moreover, felony prearraignment threatens the percentage of potential disposable felony arrests at the formal arraignment because the arresting officer and the complaining witnesses are not present.

Harper concluded that felony prearraignment processing saved the New York City Police Department hundreds of thousands of dollars in overtime costs resulting from new arrests and also permitted more efficient utilization of police personnel. However, the negative findings were that prearraignment processing under certain conditions jeopardized the alleged felony offenders' constitutional rights and violated the New York City Administration Code.[16]

The Rand Corporation studied the flow of cases in the city's court system from arraignment to final disposition. The results showed that in 1967 there were approximately 4,530,000 traffic and nontraffic cases in the arraignment section of Manhattan Criminal Court. This included 330,000 nontraffic cases and 4,200,000 traffic cases. The great majority of the nontraffic cases involved police and departmental summons. Of those nontraffic cases, 195,000 were found guilty, 181,000 by plea, and 14,000 by conviction. Of the 195,000 found guilty, 20,000 were committed, 152,000 paid fines, and 23,000 received treatment (probation, drug therapy) or unconditional discharge.[17] About 59 percent of the defendants were found guilty at arraignment; about 10 percent were incarcerated; about 78 percent paid fines; and about 12 percent were given probation, discharges, or other forms of treatment. These percentages probably offer an accurate representation of arraignment as it works today.

Bail

Judges have a great deal of discretion in setting bail. Bruce Wright, a black judge, was transferred from Criminal Court to Civil Court because of his policy of setting no bail or very little bail for offenders accused of committing very serious crimes. He incurred the wrath of the Patrolmen's Benevolent Association and the *Daily News,* and off-duty officers in 1974 picketed his home.[18] Conversely, Judge Rinaldi, in Brooklyn in the early 1970s, always gave blacks and Puerto Ricans high bail and long sentences.[19]

Most bail jumpers face only modest charges and have either no record or only a minor record. They have relatively little to fear from the court, because the worst they face is a small jail sentence. In 1973 more defendants jumped bail than were eventually sent to prison, 6.2 percent and 5.4 percent, respectively.[20]

A study involving 14,439 Manhattan Criminal Court defendants, all scheduled for a postarraignment appearance between January 1 and March 30, 1967, was conducted to determine bail practices in New York City. Of the 14,439 defendants, 10,462, or 72.5 percent, obtained some form of pretrial release. Of those released, 25.6 percent were charged with felonies, 49.8 percent with misdemeanors, and 23.9 percent with violations. Of those released, 51.2 percent were released on recognizance or parole, 21.4 percent were released on bond, and 25.4 percent were released on cash bail. The conditions of release are unknown for the remainder.

Of the 5,538 defendants released on recognizance, only 1,543, or about 28.8 percent, had been investigated by the Office of Probation's Release on Recognizance Division. Of all those released on recognizance, only 905, or 16.9 percent, had been recommended by the Office of Probation for R.O.R. (release or recognizance). In felony cases, 55.9 percent had been investigated and 31 percent had been recommended for release.

The overall rate of willful nonappearance for 1967 was 13.9 percent, breaking down to 16.5 percent for felony cases, 11.0 percent for misdemeanors, and 23.6 percent for violations. In general, rates of nonappearance did not increase with the seriousness of the crime charged. Thus, the practice of permitting the crime charged to be the primary determinant of the condition of release or amount of bail for the deterrence of flight is open to debate. The rates of nonappearance increased as the amount of cash bail increased. This situation, too, calls into question the effectiveness of the present bail system as a deterrent for nonappearance.

The enforcement policy with nonappearance is almost nonexistent. The most reasonable alternatives for nonappearance seem to be a major expansion and improvement of the R.O.R. screening procedures, including a system of postarraignment bail reevaluation, extensive computerized notification procedures for all released defendants, and a more rigorous enforcement policy with respect to jumpers by the police, the prosecutors, and the courts.

A sample of 1,497 jumpers and 1,562 nonjumpers were selected for further study. This study was compared to a study in 1960 involving felony cases. Significant differences between the findings of the 1960 study and the more recent study were noted. First, the overall percentage of accused felons who achieved pretrial release rose from 45 percent to 55 percent. Second, the percentage of felons released on recognizance rose from 2 percent to 22 percent. Third, the percentage of felony cases in which no bail was set fell from 29 percent in 1960 to 3 percent. Fourth, there was a sharp downward shift in the levels of bail set from 1960 to 1967. Fifth, from 1960 to 1967 there was a decrease in the ability to post bail at any given level.

The total number of jumpers in the released group of 10,462 was 1,819, or 17.4 percent. Of the 1,819, 361 voluntarily returned to court, leaving a total of 1,458, or 13.9 percent, jumpers. A substantial proportion of jumpers were charged with relatively minor crimes. For example, persons charged with violations accounted for 40.5 percent of all jumpers. Over a quarter of all nonappearances were attributed to persons charged with the crime of prostitution.

The relatively low rates of nonappearance for serious crimes, such as robbery, compared with nonserious crimes might be attributed to a more selective release policy with respect to those charged with serious offenses.

Jump rates were 9.1 percent for those recommended for release by the judge, 15 percent for those not recommended for release by the judge, and 14.6 percent for those not investigated. In every crime category the jump rate was lower for those recommended for release than for those not recommended for release.

The most important factor in releasing those without bail was the influence of "roots in the community." However, the rate of nonappearance has risen from the 1.6 percent rate of 1961–1964.

The most important conclusion of this study was that there is little justification in the bail-jumping statistics for generating bail amounts primarily by the seriousness of the charge.[21]

The most important part of arraignment is the determination of bail. It is possible that although racial prejudice is not overt, it is still prevalent in other ways.[22] Bail is important for the indirect effects it can have in sentencing. Those not released before sentencing because of excessive bail generally do not have the financial resources to fight their cases.

Prosecution

Prosecutors have a great deal of power and discretion. For example, prosecutors have the power to correct police abuses—indeed, more power than the courts themselves have because they can refuse to prosecute when they believe police testimony is doubtful, or when the defendant's defense is overwhelmingly strong. But most district attorneys are concerned primarily with getting convictions, and they exercise their discretion to control the police even less often than the courts do. The Manhattan office in 1965 was an exception because its prosecutors were concerned with police abuses and exercised their discretion creatively.[23]

In Manhattan, Robert Morris Morganthau, the borough district attorney, made some significant changes. He switched to a vertical system, merging Indictment, Criminal Court, and Supreme Court into six trial bureaus. Under the new system, one assistant prosecutor followed a case from the initial complaint to the final disposition. According to Morganthau, the switch significantly reduced the backlog of pending cases, cut the medium time from indictment to final disposition from 44 weeks to 14½ weeks, and increased the conviction rate to 85.5 percent. He boasted that more defendants had been sent to state prison. He also claimed that 70 percent of felony cases went directly to a grand jury without a hearing in the criminal court; this figure compares to 10 percent to 15 percent in the past. The percentage of cases sent back to criminal court was cut from 10 percent to less than 1 percent. The percentage of dismissals after indictments was cut from 20 percent to 13 percent, and the conviction rate after trial rose from 65 percent to 70 percent.[24]

One of the important functions of prosecution is conviction. In 1977, out of 150,000 arrests, 20,197 led to a felony conviction. One of the most important factors for prosecutorial dismissal is the prior relation of the defendant with the victim. In New York City a study revealed that 87 percent of dismissals had occurred because the victim failed to cooperate in cases in which the victim and the defendant had had a prior relationship; this figure compares with 29 percent of dismissals in cases in which defendant and victim had been strangers.[25]

In misdemeanor cases, in 1977, out of 83,348 cases heard in criminal part, only 153 went to trial; of these, 70 resulted in conviction and 83 in acquittals.[26] Comparing 1973 with 1978 in Manhattan, the proportion of dismissals declined from 40 percent to 30 percent, and the proportion of convictions rose from 59 percent to 69 percent.[27]

For the most part, prosecutors drop charges, or reduce a felony charge to a misdemeanor, because they doubt that the defendants are guilty, because they lack the evidence needed to prove guilt, or because they feel that the crime is not serious enough or the defendant not culpable enough to warrant the stigma of a felony conviction. The more serious the offense, the larger the proportion of cases that are settled by trial.[28]

Two-thirds of the officials in prosecutors' offices in New York state indicated that they had some form of supervisory review of plea-bargaining decisions. In addition, more than half of the officials in these offices indicated that they had official guidelines concerning plea bargaining.[29] The recommendations are for guidelines in plea bargaining.[30]

Plea bargaining is a peculiarly American institution, without parallel anywhere in the world. In a study in New York City, in 85 percent of the cases the prosecutors accepted the police charges without change. However, this is not always true.[31]

A study revealed that many plea bargains were decided based on inadequate information, and without the intensive investigation required to make intelligent, knowledgeable decisions.[32]

Legal Defense

The Legal Aid Society, which represents nearly all indigent defendants, is only one of a hundred or more effective legal aid organizations in this country. However, it was the first to be founded and is still the largest and one of the best administered.[33] Custom dictates that the cases of private counsel usually receive priority over those of the salaried legal aid lawyers.[34] Legal aid lawyers defend as many as 50 cases a day, which leaves no time for preparation.[35]

In misdemeanor cases, the quality of defense in New York City is better than in many other cities — if only by default. Some of the largest cities in this country, including Baltimore, Detroit, and Chicago, conduct most of their misdemeanor trials without defense counsel, and even without a prosecutor.[36]

It has been already mentioned that legal defense itself very often counsels defendants to plead guilty. Legal defense confers with prosecutors and judges to determine pretrial status, bail, and sentencing dispositions. In New York City, an indigent defendant can obtain the services of a Legal Aid lawyer or an 18-B lawyer; the latter is assigned by the court on a per diem basis to defend indigent defendants.

A study of factors found to be important in sentencing dispositions revealed that defendants represented by Legal Aid lawyers received more serious dispositions than defendants represented by private counsel. However, the statistical path model revealed that Legal Aid defense only affected dispositions indirectly, since it was associated with probation officers' recommendations, and only explained about 7 percent of the variance. However, Legal Aid might defend only certain types of defendants; in addition, the study might indicate that Legal Aid was used only to obtain guilty pleas.[37]

Prosecutors estimate that false arrests average about 5 percent; defense attorneys estimate that false arrests average about 8 percent. From these data, evaluators concluded that about 7 percent (2 percent more or less) of those arrested actually did not engage in a criminal activity.[38]

A questionnaire was administered to respondents in New York City to discern their satisfaction with legal defense. The results showed that females were more satisfied with public defenders than males were. Those represented by public defenders blamed their lawyers for the outcomes of their cases. The young, the black, and the lower-income groups were most dissatisfied with the present legal system. Blacks had more negative feelings about Legal Aid than whites and Hispanics. About 18 percent of the sample did not know how to initiate a complaint against a lawyer.[39]

Amazingly, there is little research in the literature of New York City on legal defense. This is an area, obviously, where more research is needed. An empirical study of legal defense will be discussed at the end of this chapter.

Sentencing

Sentencing is probably the most important function of the court. This is where defendants receive the punishment for their crimes.

The Vera Institute of Justice analyzed the records from arrests through disposition of a representative sample of 1,888 people arrested on felony charges in 1971. The conviction rate was 56 percent, with one convicted offender in two sentenced to jail or prison. The study also revealed that 84 percent of convicted defendants who had a prior criminal record as an adult were sent to prison, while only 22 percent of those without an adult record were sent to prison. The Vera Institute study concluded that when crimes were serious, evidence was strong, and victims were willing to prosecute, felons with previous criminal histories ended up with relatively heavy sentences.[40]

Out of 2,520 felons arrested for homicide, robbery, narcotics crimes, sex crimes, hijacking, and bribery during 1972–1974, 460, or 18 percent, were incarcerated.[41]

Career criminals, those who spend a lifetime in crime, only sometimes receive heavy sentences. In the first three months of 1982, 47 out of every 100 arrests of identified career criminals resulted in sentences to state prisons. This relatively high rate of incarcerating can be traced to the New York City police department's concern that the criminal justice system was not dealing adequately with career criminals. The police have made a special effort to find and arrest career criminals. In years past as few as 7 out of 100 arrests of career criminals resulted in state time.[42]

Prisoners must be granted hearings within 72 hours of arrest.[43] However, this is not always practiced. The law that mandated the death penalty for the murder of a policeman or a prison guard was ruled unconstitutional.[44] Now, offenders who kill a policeman or a prison guard cannot be put to death.

Hispanics receive harsher sentences than whites or blacks and are more likely to be sent to prison.[45] However, the literature on ethnicity and sentencing is mixed, with some studies concluding that ethnicity is important and others concluding the opposite.

Very often judges hand down illegal sentences. In the early seventies, 30 convicted heroin dealers were given illegal sentences, either conditional or unconditional discharges for felony narcotics crimes, by judges even though the law specifically prohibits a judge from imposing such a light sentence.[46]

The rate of dismissals and acquittals for Mafiosa in New York City is five times higher than for other defendants. Judges are still largely immune from personal attack because of the traditional mystique of respect associated with judgeship. Some believe the practice of judge shopping should be abandoned.[47]

In the early seventies Judge Rinaldi let a heroin dealer go free; the dealer received a conditional discharge. A study revealed that in Brooklyn, in the early seventies, only 6 percent of Mafia narcotic dealers were sentenced to a year or more in prison. This figure compares with 31 percent in the Bronx and 28 percent in Queens. The same study revealed that 42 percent of felony narcotic cases in Brooklyn were dismissed compared with 15 percent in the Bronx. Judge Rinaldi was indicted on suspicion of perjury and fixing cases. Rinaldi imposed high bail and long sentences on blacks and Puerto Ricans, but gave defendants connected with organized crime families suspended sentences or fines instead of jail terms. Large-scale heroin dealers would receive very lenient sentences, even conditional discharges for class A narcotics felonies. Certain Brooklyn defense lawyers always won their cases when they appeared before Judge Rinaldi. Rinaldi admitted some of these corrupt practices.[48]

For years Brooklyn has been the most corrupt borough in the city. In the early seventies, during an 18-month period, five criminal indictments against Mafia members in Brooklyn were thrown out of court by the trial judge. Eventually all five were unanimously reinstated by the appellate division. All five dismissals were ordered by the same Brooklyn supreme court justice, Joseph Corso. Judge Corso's extraordinary permissiveness toward the Mafia was inconsistent with his treatment of other defendants and inconsistent with his record as an assemblyman.[49]

In New York City, for the period 1963 to 1973, 44.7 percent of indictments against organized crime figures were dismissed by state supreme court justices. In contrast, only 11.5 percent of the indictments against all other defendants were dismissed. A study showed that in 193 cases where Mafia members were actually convicted by a jury, the trial judge let the defendants off with no prison sentence 46 percent of the time. Another study revealed that judges in Brooklyn treated heroin dealers more leniently than the judges in any other part of the city.[50] Only 6 percent of the heroin dealers charged with a felony received more than one year in prison from Brooklyn judges. In contrast, 31.6 percent of the felony heroin defendants in the Bronx were sentenced to more than a year in prison. Brooklyn judges dismissed 42 percent of the felony cases against heroin dealers but Bronx judges dismissed only 15 percent of such cases.[51]

A study analyzed 62 felony narcotics arrests made between January, 1969, and October, 1971, in Bedford-Stuyvesant in Brooklyn. Of those arrested, 52 percent were dismissed, 7 percent were placed on probation, 3 percent were discharged, 7 percent jumped bail, 18 percent had not been sentenced, and 13 percent went to prison.[52]

The state legislature explored four felony narcotic cases in which the judge gave inexplicably permissive sentences to heroin dealers. Judge Culkin was found to have a history of leniency with Mafia members and police and politicians charged with corruption. Many of Judge Culkin's lenient sentences were later unanimously reversed by the appellate division.[53]

Three of Judge Koota's cases involving either narcotics or organized crime figures were under investigation because they were suspicious and because they were unsupported either by law or by logic. Koota's handling of several cases while he was Brooklyn D.A. still looks suspicious to law enforcement officials and to those concerned with a standard of equal justice. Koota's concern for the civil liberties of drug dealers and mobsters did not seem to extend to ordinary citizens. While he was an assistant district attorney, he insisted on widespread use of electronic eavesdropping.[54]

Sentence disparity is practiced in New York City. The *New York Times* reported that defendants who could not afford their own counsel were sentenced nearly twice as severely as defendants with private lawyers. Several Brooklyn judges have an unmistakable prejudice against blacks and Puerto Ricans and do not give minorities equal protection under the laws.[55]

In 1971, of 20,762 persons arrested for felony narcotic charges, only 2 percent were sentenced to more than one year in prison. In 1970, of 26,000 felon narcotic arrests, only 346, or about 1 percent, were sentenced to more than one year.[56]

Many judges were blatantly prejudiced against blacks and Puerto Ricans, calling defendants names like "scum" and "animal."[57] One judge sentenced a Puerto Rican to three years in prison for shoplifting some clothing, while another judge gave probation to a white defendant who wore a suit and had a private lawyer, even though he had been convicted of embezzling $150,000 from a bank.[58]

Prosecutors make sentencing recommendations to the judge, but judges sometimes reject prosecutorial recommendations because they are too severe.[59] A study done in the seventies found that judges usually accepted the deals negotiated between the prosecutor and the defense counsel, but in 79 percent of these cases the judges themselves took part in the negotiation process.[60]

In 1971, 52.2 percent of the defendants convicted in New York City were sentenced to state prison; this figure is more than twice the 24.4 percent of convicted upstate defendants who were sent to prison.[61]

Forty-one county and supreme court judges from all courts of New York state selected by a stratified random sample were asked to review eight actual presentence reports and to indicate the sentence that he or she would have imposed in the case. The judges were also asked to indicate the objective that the sentence was designed to serve—retribution, rehabilitation, deterrence, or incapacitation—and to state reasons for imposing the sentence. Judges presented with identical presentence reports differed substantially in both the type and length of sentence they imposed.[62]

Probation as a sentence is often treated as a catch-all disposition, handed to virtually every defendant deemed unsuitable for incarceration, without regard to actual need for supervision. Research has found that a prior criminal record is far from an infallible guide to future criminal conduct.[63]

According to a study released in 1982 the principal cause of New York state's growth in prison population was a series of public policy decisions made by the political leaders of the state during the 1970s. These decisions included reduction in funding for probation, a decline in the parole release rate, and especially the enactment of mandatory sentencing laws requiring prison terms for a broad range of offenses. As a consequence of these policies, the state has been sending more people to prison and has been keeping them there for longer periods of time. Of all the policies, mandatory prison sentences has been the principal factor driving prison populations up. With the support of Governor Nelson Rockefeller, the New York Drug Laws were enacted in 1973, instituting harsh prison sentences for a wide range of drug offenses. The punishments required by law for heroin, cocaine, and other drug offenses still rank among the most severe in the nation. In March, 1985, out of a New York State prison population of 34,317, 2,802 inmates, or 8 percent of the total, were under custody for Rockefeller drug offenses.[64]

The drug laws enacted under Rockefeller meant that drug dealers convicted of Class A felonies face a minimum sentence of one year to life and a maximum sentence of 15 years to life. The law was a reaction to the $6,000,000 Rockefeller drug rehabilitation program enacted in an election year. Because class A1 and A2 felonies could only be plea bargained down to class A3 felonies virtually every narcotic defendant went to trial. About 100 judgeships had to be created to handle the increased case load, at a cost of $100,000,000.[65]

The Second Felony Offender Law, which was enacted in 1973, required prison sentences for all repeat felons regardless of the nature of the offense or the background and motivation of the offender. Promoted by Governor Hugh Carey, the Violent Felony Offender Law was enacted in 1978; this law requires prison sentences for almost all first-time offenders convicted of crimes categorized by law as violent, such as robbery, assault, or burglary in the first or second degree. The case histories of offenders incarcerated under the Mandatory Sentencing Laws reveal that many offenders could have received either a shorter prison term or been sentenced to a less expensive or more suitable punishment. Many of the nearly 5,000 nonviolent second felony offenders currently in prison could have been handled in more appropriate ways. Many judges express frustration about the restraints imposed by mandatory sentencing laws and about the individual injustices that result from these laws.[66]

In one study a probability sample of 369 defendants arraigned on felony charges, whose cases were disposed of during the ten-month period from January, 1973, through October, 1973, was analyzed. Fifty-five percent of the defendants pleaded guilty; only 2 percent of all cases were disposed of through trial. Of the defendants who pleaded guilty, about half or 28 percent, obtained a fine, a conditional discharge, or probation. The other 27 percent of those convicted received incarceration. Of those incarcerated, 22 percent, the overwhelming majority, received sentences up to one year; 5 percent of all defendants arrested for a felony received prison for more than one year.[67]

In the overcrowded courts a good judge is one who gets rid of cases before the system drowns in them. Some cases are judged in five minutes, or even in 30 seconds.[68] The quality of judicial appointments is the cornerstone of an effective system for the administration of justice.[69]

Justices of the supreme court are elected by the voters of the various political districts for a period of 14 years.[70] Judges in criminal court are appointed for a period of ten years. However, politics is often involved in the appointment of both criminal court and supreme court judges.

A commission studying the court system revealed that the pressures of the court calendar were responsible for defendants receiving lighter sentences than they would receive if their individual cases were judged solely on their own merits. The commission found that sentencing was often inappropriate. Cases that were tried did not get to trial until a minimum of nine months after arrest. The commission also revealed that the probation department was not satisfying the judges who used their presentence reports. The clearance rate for warrants was relatively low; it was 57.1 percent in 1972; and it was 65.3 percent in 1973. The warrant squad is far too busy to process all warrants.[71]

Critics of disparity in sentencing fail to distinguish between sentencing disparities that grow out of differences in philosophy and bias from one judge to another, and disparities that reflect different attitudes about criminals and crimes—the different sentencing norms from one community to another. The latter is the most important cause of disparity because it cannot be changed by reform. There is no evidence that the courts have become more lenient.[72]

Extralegal variables enter into sentencing decisions; these reveal value assumptions about certain social groups. In a certain age group, 60 percent of Hispanics received prison sentences while only 15 percent of the non–Hispanics had been incarcerated. There is a greater proportion of Hispanics on probation than the proportion arrested, indicating a greater number of prosecutions. Hispanics also have a greater proportion incarcerated than on probation; the non–Hispanics have a greater proportion on probation than incarcerated.[73] A study for the Federal Bureau of Prisons revealed that the average prison sentence for whites was 42.9 months; this compares with an average sentence of 57.5 months for blacks and Puerto Ricans.[74]

Referring to the blackout in New York City in 1977, researchers found that 1,220 defendants pled guilty. Seventy-nine percent were sentenced. There were 2,677 arraignments. Only 27 percent of the blackout defendants walked in and out of court free, compared with 70 percent of the normal arrest group. About 428 blackout victims on their first court appearance were remanded, but 62 were dismissed and 93 were released on their own recognizance. Of the 79 percent sentenced, 427 received time served, 266 received conditional discharges, 190 received time plus a fine, 69 received probation, 3 received a fine, and 8 received an unconditional discharge. Of the 262 who received additional jail terms, about half were sentenced to 30 days; only 14 received a year or more. A large number had received punishment before trial in the form of excessive bail. Out of 1,742 sentences, 57 percent received jail time, and 75 percent received an additional penalty before their dispositions. A total of 988 received some jail time.[75]

Reforms

The Executive Advisory Committee was established by Governor Hugh L. Carey in December, 1977, to analyze felony sentencing in New York state. The committee concluded that sentencing in New York state was erratic and unpredictable; there was widespread sentencing disparity; similar offenders committing similar crimes often received substantially dissimilar sentences.

The committee recommended that for sentencing to achieve justice, laws must be fair, consistent, and uniformly applied to similar cases. For consistency in sentencing there must be a graduated system of penalties proportionate to the harm committed by criminal conduct. Judicial discretion must be retained to tailor penal sanctions to the unusual case, and to meet unforeseen combinations and circumstances, but this discretion should be structured and subject to meaningful review.

The committee revealed that the goals of sentencing could not be accomplished within the confines of the indeterminate sentence. They recommended that determinate sentencing models that have been proposed or adopted in other jurisdictions be adopted in New York state. The judge would impose a sentence within the range prescribed by the sentencing guidelines unless the court finds that specific aggravating or mitigating circumstances exist that are not reflected in the guidelines or that justify a different sentence.

The committee also recommended that parole release should be abolished for individuals subject to determinate sentencing. Parole release should be used only for individuals sentenced to indeterminate prison terms. Parole would continue to play a role in supervising a released offender. The committee also recommended that the presentence investigation function in the probation department should be removed and performed by an arm of the court; the sole business of probation should be the supervision of probationers.

The committee recommended that because plea bargaining plays a central role in our criminal justice system, steps should be taken to increase the public accountability of prosecutors; there must be plea-bargaining guidelines in relation to a sentencing guideline system. The committee indicated that mediation and arbitration programs on an entirely voluntary basis should be made available for cases that are susceptible to a solution outside the confines of the criminal court.

The committee believed that our present sentencing system places a veil of secrecy over sentencing, concealing from the public precisely who is making sentencing decisions, what these decisions are, and when they are made. They indicated that rehabilitation, a prime justification for the indeterminate sentence, should not be the basis for imposing a sentence of incarceration.[76]

Another study argued that for fairness and common sense to be restored to the criminal justice system, the mandatory sentencing laws enacted during the 1970s should be abolished. This study also argued that judicial discretion should be returned to the judge. The study indicated that prison has more and more become the dumping grounds for social problems, such as child abuse, joblessness, mental disability, and drug and alcohol dependency; these problems would be better handled through community-based programs.[77]

A study was conducted to analyze the criminal court of Manhattan in the five months from February, 1971 to June, 1971. Analyses of court records, observation, interviews, and questionnaires were all employed in the study. The principal focus was the MAP, or Master Calendar Part, and the other all-purpose parts of the courtroom. The study found that after reform the average number of appearances per case after arraignment was reduced from 3.0 to 2.5; the average time for appearance was reduced from 9.1 weeks to 4.9 weeks; and the average length of time between appearances was reduced from 3.3 weeks to 2.2 weeks. The reasons cited for these appearances were continuity of representation by the Legal Aid Society; reduced workloads for Legal Aid representatives; instituting the practice of giving a defendant who was to be represented by a Legal Aid attorney a slip of paper with the attorney's name; the use of a reminder slip for court dates; and the use of a check-in table where defendants might receive directions.

Another innovation instituted by the court was the practice of conducting conferences among judges, prosecutors, and legal defense attorneys away from the bench in the courtroom; this may have saved as much as one hour of the judges' time per day.

The rate of bail jumping and parole jumping was found to be lower in the MAP, 9.3 percent, than in all-purpose parts, 13.8 percent. Some explanations for the lower jump-rate in the MAP complex were the greater continuity of Legal Aid representatives and the adjournment reminder slips given to defendants.

Adjournments were lower in the Master Calendar Part, MAP, than in the all-purpose parts, resulting in a greater number of calendared cases disposed of. In addition to the continuity of Legal Aid, adjournment slips and check-in tables, other reforms initiated in MAP were adjournment by mail or telephone, and the splitting of the calendar into morning and afternoon segments. The cases in MAP were disposed of in a smaller number of appearances than in the all-purpose parts.

Other improvements recommended by the study were the elimination of noise in the courtrooms and in the MAP complex, or both.

Other recommendations included the strengthening of the flow of cases ready for hearings and trials in the various parts, and the transferring of administrative and clerical duties from the MAP calendar and backup parts to administrative and clerical personnel. Also recommended was the policy of lessening the absence of police officers and defense counsel in court and the imposition of sanctions for failure of officers and attorneys to appear in court.

The study also revealed that sentencing was lighter and that guilty pleas were more common in the MAP complex than in the all-purpose parts.

A second phase of the study was conducted in the first five months of 1972. This second study revealed that the MAP complex was not performing as effectively as the all-purpose parts system, and authorities shifted the resources which had been devoted to the MAP complex into the all-purpose parts. Although the number of dispositions per attorney per day had been 22 percent less for Legal Aid in MAP than in the all-purpose parts and 31 percent less for district attorneys in MAP than in the all-purpose parts, as revealed in the first phase of the study, it was also revealed that the cost per case per day was significantly larger in MAP than in the all-purpose parts.

It was also found that the reduction in case-loads in MAP indicated the possibility of insufficient judicial review. In addition, the second phase of the study revealed that although the MAP parts had been operating under an extremely pressured atmosphere for longer hours than the all-purpose parts, and with a great deal of noise, there was a low level of satisfaction for court officers and district attorneys, and a substantial loss of dignity and decorum; in addition, not enough cases were given to the all-purpose parts.

The study also revealed that the scheduled jury trials in the MAP complex had tied up Legal Aid lawyers frequently with the result that they had not made adequate arrangements for their other cases or had neglected their other cases. It was also found that the accelerated adjournment office, the check-in table, and the split calendars in MAP had minimal impact. However, the heavier staffing in MAP had resulted in legal aid attorneys and district attorneys devoting more time to each case.

The all-purpose parts were shown to have had an advantage in light of seven measures. There was more attention devoted to each case; more active hours in the backup parts; lower costs; higher job satisfaction, dignity and decorum; and more dispositions per judge per day and per attorney per day. However, there was a higher rate of dismissals and guilty pleas in the MAP complex.

The study revealed that the MAP failed to outperform the all-purpose parts in spite of the substantial amount of funds devoted to it, and it failed to prove or disprove the validity of a number of the central concepts because of ineffective implementation of these concepts.

The study concluded that the all-purpose parts of a complex should be located in close physical proximity. A second recommendation was to calendar cases for different times of the day. The possibility of extra hours in the court should be explored. The precalendar conferences in MAP were found to be successful. The screening of cases before these cases were called by a judge could save considerable time. The elimination in daily workload and courtroom congestion could also improve conditions. There has been a trend toward smaller calendars in the MAP complex in the second phase of the study. This has been the result of heavier staffing of district attorneys and Legal Aid attorneys in the MAP complex. The time spent per case per judge was found to be important.

In spite of the reforms, the study concluded that the comparison of the MAP complex with the all-purpose parts revealed that the differences between the two parts were not significant. The number of appearances per case had remained unchanged in 1972 from 1971, except for a slight increase for misdemeanors in the MAP complex. There was a significant improvement in felony appearances in the MAP complex and the all-purpose parts. However, the MAP complex disposed of misdemeanors more quickly in 1971 and 1972 than the other parts.

Many district attorneys were calling for a termination of the continuity of service, with a return to the system of each attorney representing any defendant. However, the Legal Aid attorneys were quite pleased with the continuity of service system.

In effect, the saving of courtroom time in MAP was no more than 15 minutes per day. However, as the calendar size increased, less and less time could be devoted to each case. Judges either granted adjournments or transferred more cases to other parts.

Because staffing was heavier in the MAP complex, the actual disposition of cases per attorney was smaller in MAP than in the all-purpose parts. However, staffing meant heavier costs. There were significant differences between the MAP and the all-purpose parts in respect to warrants issued and executed. The study also revealed that the absence of legal actors resulted in 26 percent of all adjournments.[78]

More Hispanics are needed in criminal justice.[79] A commission studying criminal justice in New York City recommended all courts in New York City be integrated into a single state court system and be financed by the state.[80]

The justice system is treated as a loosely related group of parts and is not seen as a total process; there is a general inability to identify weak spots and bottlenecks in the system, an inability to effectively evaluate day-to-day operations as well as special programs, and an inability to make the optimal use of available resources, including legal, custodial, and alternate programs.[81]

Empirical Studies

In this section I will review some empirical studies that I have done since 1981 in reference to the courts of New York City. These studies pertain to prosecuting, legal defense, and sentencing.

Prosecution

I analyzed 55 felony cases and 82 misdemeanor cases, a total of 137 cases, for the year 1982, for Brooklyn Supreme Court and Criminal Court. Both quantitative and qualitative methods were used to analyze the data. Quantitative methods consisted of log-linear methods, and qualitative methods consisted of an analysis of case records and observation.

My general conclusions were that the final charges made by prosecutors did not differ much from the arrest charges. Changes were minor; only 36 out of 137 cases, or 26 percent, involved some change in the charge. Prosecutors' recommendations for sentencing were not rigid; about 26 percent of the cases involved a change of recommendation from severe to a more lenient recommendation. This was sometimes due to the fact that the defendant refused the first offer of the charge. The results also indicated that the strength of the case was important. The strength of the case involved legal evidence, a credible witness or witnesses, or a confession by the defendant. The prior record of the defendant was also important. The results also showed that judges and defense attorneys participate in plea bargaining. Prosecutors appeared to try to individualize each case.

Log-linear methods revealed that the strength of the case and the prior record of the defendant were important for charging, and prior record and the charge were important for the prosecutors' recommendations. The offender-victim category of a black or Puerto Rican defendant versus a white victim, or an organization, had some effect on the charge. Also important for the charge was the relationship between the defendant and the victim, that is a stranger or an intimate. However, the offender-victim category and the relationship between the defendant and the victim were not important for recommendations of prosecutors.

I concluded that although several factors were important for prosecution, there were many chance factors involved, such as the personality of the prosecutor or defendant's appearance, etc.[82]

In another study, I analyzed 459 closed probation cases in Brooklyn for the years 1974 and 1976. Selected randomly, the cases included both felonies and misdemeanors. Multiple regression in stages and discriminant-analysis were the statistical methods used to analyze the data. The two dependent variables were seriousness of final charge and charge reduction. Thirty-two independent variables were analyzed.

The results showed that the more serious the original charge, the more serious the final charge. The stronger the evidence against the defendant, the less the charges were reduced. If a crime involved a victim, the more serious the final charge. If the defendant was accused of a burglary or a robbery, their charges were more likely to be reduced, possibly because these burglary and robbery are serious charges involving heavy sentences.

Extralegal factors had less impact on the seriousness of the original charge or charge reduction; however, the younger the defendant, the more the charges were reduced. The offender-victim category and the relationship between the offender and victim had no significant effect on the dependent variables.

The R^2, or proportion of variance explained, was no higher than .13, indicating that much discretion or perhaps other unexplained or omitted variables entered into prosecutorial charging.[83]

Legal Defense

In 1983 I interviewed 35 defendants and 34 of the lawyers assigned to the defendants' cases in Brooklyn Criminal Court, a lower criminal court. Only seven defendants were represented by a private attorney; the remainder were assigned either a Legal Aid lawyer or an 18-B lawyer, a private attorney paid by the court. The interviews were supplemented by observation in the courtroom.

The results showed that the mean number of visits by the lawyers to the defendants was 3.9, with a range of 19. All defendants except five were satisfied with the number of lawyers' visits. Twenty-four defendants liked their lawyers, and nine disliked them. The reasons for liking them included change of pretrial status from remand to bail, reduction in sentence, or a promise of a lenient disposition, and the honesty and availability of the lawyer. All those who had a private attorney were satisfied with their lawyers.

Many defendants revealed their lawyers told them to plead guilty, and tried to obtain the best offer for them, implying that only a plea would result in the best offer. Most of the lawyers were concerned with sentencing outcomes.

I concluded that the most important function of the defense attorney was to influence the defendant to plead guilty and to try to negotiate for the most favorable outcome of the case. I also concluded that the defense role is influenced by the prosecutor and judge. Defense attorneys seem to individualize each case. The private attorneys seemed more concerned with defendants than did the public defenders. I also concluded that the lawyers' role is constrained by the sociological situation of the courtroom, and is, therefore, sometimes influenced by chance factors.[84]

Sentencing

I analyzed three separate random samples of misdemeanor cases for the years 1972 through 1976 for Brooklyn Criminal Court. Sample 1 consisted of 983 cases in which defendants were sentenced with a probation report; sample 2 consisted of 836 cases in which defendants were sentenced without a probation report; and sample 3 consisted of 100 cases in which the defendants were mainly in jail and a short probation report, called a pro forma, was prepared without a recommendation. The quantitative methods employed were path analysis and discriminant analysis.

Probation officers' recommendations have a strong influence on judges' decisions. A number of legal variables also contribute to a judge's decisions. Pretrial status, for example, is important for judges' decisions, and the seriousness of the charge is important for defendants sentenced without a probation report.

The results also showed the number of prior arrests, adjustment in a prior correctional program, and pretrial status were the strongest factors affecting probation officers' recommendations. Some legal and, to a lesser extent, some extralegal factors had a small impact on probation officers' recommendations.

The results demonstrated that judges and probation officers were consistent in their sentencing; they both arrived at similar dispositions for similar cases. Defendants received a lot of individual attention in the processing of their cases. The sentence a defendant received depended to a large extent upon the particular judge and probation officer assigned to the case. The probation officer was very influential in sentencing outcomes. There was no evidence of racial discrimination in the sentencing process.[85]

In another study, I analyzed a random sample of 463 closed probation cases and the corresponding court papers pertaining to these cases for the years 1977, 1978, and 1979 for Brooklyn Criminal Court, a misdemeanor court. Twenty-five variables, including three dependent variables—prosecutors' promises, probation officers' recommendations, and judges' dispositions— were included in the analyses. Path analysis was the statistical method employed.

The results showed that prosecutors were influenced by the pretrial status of the defendants to a great extent and by the prior record to a lesser extent. Probation officers seemed to be influenced by the prior record, pretrial status, adjustment in a prior correctional program, and employment status of the defendant. Probation officers did not seem to be influenced by prosecutors' promises to a great extent. Judges were influenced by recommendations of probation officers, especially for the dispositions of conditional and unconditional discharge and fine, and to a lesser extent the disposition of jail. Judges were influenced by promises of jail recommended by prosecutors. Judges were influenced by pretrial status and disposition of prior convictions. Judges were not influenced by either a promise or a recommendation of probation.

I concluded that pretrial status was influential in sentencing. Although promises of prosecutors and recommendations of probation officers were both influential in sentencing, probation officers' recommendations were more influential because prosecutors' promises were not made in every case and were loosely constructed. The results showed no evidence of racial discrimination.[86]

In another study I analyzed a systematic sample of 420 closed probation cases for the years 1980, 1981, and 1982 for Brooklyn Criminal Court, a misdemeanor court. There were ten independent variables, and two dependent variables, prosecutors' promises and sentence length imposed by the judge. Path analysis using a recursive model was the statistical method used in the analysis.

The results showed that prosecutors' recommendations for sentence length correlated with judges' dispositions for sentence length; the longer the sentence recommended by the prosecutor, the longer the jail sentence imposed by the judge.

The prosecutors' recommendations depended upon dispositions of prior arrests, whether or not a defendant was in a prior correctional program, and the offender-victim category. However, the proportion of variance explained, or R^2, for the model with prosecutors' recommendations was only .06 and statistically nonsignificant. However, for the model with dispositions of judges the R^2 was .40. Several indirect factors, including the dispositions of prior arrests, prior correctional programs, the offender-victim category, and sex, affected the dispositions of judges.

The results showed that judges followed prosecutors' recommendations about 66 percent of the time. The judges were more punitive than prosecutors about 84 percent of the time, and more lenient than prosecutors about 16 percent of the time. Prosecutors only made recommendations in about three-quarters of the cases. There was no evidence of racial discrimination. This study did reveal, however, the importance of prosecutors' recommendations in sentence length in misdemeanor court.[87]

In another study, I analyzed 504 closed probation misdemeanor cases in the Bronx Probation Department for the years 1981 and 1982. The cases were selected randomly, and path analysis, using a recursive model, and discriminant analysis, were the statistical methods employed. There were 28 variables in the analysis including three dependent variables: recommendation of prosecutor, recommendation of probation officer, and disposition of the judge.

The results showed that the number of charges, age, and adjustment on prior probation and parole were important for promises of prosecutors; legal variables had an indirect effect. However, the model fitted the data poorly, explaining only about 2 percent of the variance. Prior arrests, pretrial status, and promises of prosecutors influenced probation officers' recommendations directly and legal variables affected their recommendations indirectly. The R^2, or proportion of variance explained for the probation officers, was .25. Judges considered promises of prosecutors, the recommendations of probation officers, and pretrial status, and to a lesser extent legal variables in sentencing dispositions. The R^2 for judges was .39.[88]

Summary

We see that many practices in the court system have been in operation since the turn of the century. Plea bargaining, legal representation, disparity in sentencing, etc. have been in practice since at least about 1900. Some discrimination in sentencing exists; more lenient sentences are given to certain groups of people such as offenders who commit crimes against intimate victims, organized crime figures, and members of the Mafia. However, there is some evidence that this situation is changing. More organized crime figures are now being prosecuted. Public opinion is important.

We see that the court system is influenced by various laws. The Second Felony Offender Law, the Mandatory Sentencing Law, and the harsh drug laws are responsible for today's higher rate of incarceration.

The courts have received much criticism and many suggestions for reform. Some people believe that sentences are too harsh and some believe that sentences are too lenient.

It appears that prosecutors, probation officers, and judges, and, to a lesser extent, lawyers are instrumental in the sentencing process. Some of the above legal actors are influential at one time and some at other times. The most important factors used in making decisions are prior record, pretrial status, recommendations of prosecutors and probation officers, adjustment in prior correctional programs, seriousness of charge, and sometimes employment. Prosecutors are concerned with the strength of the evidence, prior record, and the relationship between the offender and the victim. It is debatable whether ethnicity is influential in sentencing.

It also appears from the empirical studies that very often chance factors, such as the particular legal actor or actors assigned to a case, caseload pressures, etc., enter into sentencing decisions; a defendant's fate depends to a certain extent on these chance factors.

CORRECTIONS IN
NEW YORK CITY

History of Corrections

The jails and prisons in New York City are run by the New York City Department of Correction. Many city detainees, when sentenced, are sent to upstate prisons, such as Attica, Sing Sing, Bedford Hills, and Downstate. Many of this city's jails and prisons are at Riker's Island, located at Hazen Street, East Elmhurst, New York. Each of the five boroughs also has its own jails.

The history of corrections in New York City mainly centers around the politics and construction of women's facilities in New York City. The literature on the history of corrections in New York City is rather sparse.[1]

In city jails, bread and water diets, and "the hole," an isolation cell, were forms of punishment for some recalcitrant inmates; these forms of punishment were finally eliminated in the 1960s.[2] Work release, a program in which inmates work during the day and return to prison at night, began in Wisconsin in 1917, but was introduced in New York only in 1968.[3]

Women over the age of 16 who are convicted of felonies and sentenced to a period of imprisonment are confined to Bedford Hills, a women's prison located in upstate New York, which opened in the early 1900s.[4]

During the Colonial period, from 1650 to the 1750s, women were figures of unquestioned worth and importance, partners with their husbands in the economy of the farm.[5] However, after this period, women were discriminated against in social and economic relations. This was also true of female inmates and personnel in correction facilities.

The first jail and prison nicknamed the Tombs opened in 1838. All the jails in New York County at that time were known as "Tombs." The Tombs in those days were cold, dirty, vermin-ridden places, where the wealthy could

91

still procure the privileges always attendant on money, while the poor suffered even more indignities because of their lack of money.[6] Prior to 1832, execution of state prisoners was performed in public, presumably to deter others from following their example. The demand for admission to the prison yard of the Tombs to watch an execution was very great, and hundreds had to be refused.[7] The capacity of the Tombs was about 200; however, during the 1870s, there were as many as 500 prisoners in the Tombs, necessitating two or three men in a cell. The prison for males was wholly separated from the females, and contained about 150 cells, arranged in four tiers.[8]

In upstate New York, at Sing Sing prison, some inmates were shown preferential treatment. For example, Charles Huntingdon, a Wall Street banker, was shown every indulgence; he wore a white shirt, kept his side whiskers, and was permitted to walk all over the prison grounds with a spaniel following him. He was also permitted to lodge in the hospital and to take his meals there.[9]

Reformers became involved in the correctional arena at the time of the social welfare era, the 1800s, when this arena was populated not with professionals, but with the wealthy.[10]

In the early 1900s reports indicated that not all keepers or guards were brutal. The majority of the officials were described as honorable, kindly men. Convicts had underground means of communication of which the officials did not always know.[11]

Female Inmates, Jails, and Prisons

Prior to 1932 women felons in New York City were sent to Auburn or Sing Sing prison in upstate New York, two experimental prisons in the penitentiary system. Although the women at Auburn chose their own work, they never received instruction, exercise, or recreation. They were left alone all day and had few restraints placed on their talking and behavior. However, they were subjected to physical punishment despite a state law that forbade flogging or clubbing of women, for any reason. Rachael Welsh, an inmate who was pregnant, died because of a flogging. Despite public outcry and an investigation of her death, flogging continued. Judges supported the practice on the grounds that felons were not ordinary people and that physical force was needed to keep order.

Some women were confined at Bellevue Hospital jail in New York City. In 1833 inspectors reported that 36 women were confined to one room. Because building a separate female facility would be costly, female prisoners were sent to Auburn and Sing Sing. Although a separate female unit was built in 1839, health and hospital care were poor, especially for pregnant women and babies, and infant mortality was high. Conditions were crowded and unhealthy.

Despite these problems, the legislature would not authorize the building of a separate institution for women. As late as 1928, four years before the House of Detention for Women was completed, women were still being incarcerated at Bellevue Hospital.

In 1844 Mrs. Elizabeth Farnham was appointed matron at Sing Sing. She believed that environmental conditions, not inheritance, caused criminal behavior. She believed that education instead of harsh treatment and punishment was needed at Sing Sing.

From 1790 to 1870 the treatment of women in prison was generally primitive and punitive, with overcrowded conditions, poor food and medical care, little or no education or vocational training, and small hope of employment upon discharge. However, the need for separate quarters to incarcerate females supervised by matrons became well established during that period.

In New York State the Magdalen Home and the House of Refuge were two examples of reform-sponsored quasi-penal institutions that provided separate quarters for women under female supervision. Most inmates were black or foreign. Although matrons were employed in most private and many government penal institutions, the overall supervision and control of women prisoners were usually in the hands of male administrators. Thus, the women in the reform movement of that era advocated separate female penal institutions where women would teach female inmates to be proper women through love, religion, education, and work.

On April 15, 1887, the House of Refuge at Hudson opened for 250 female misdemeanants 16 to 30 years of age who had committed minor offenses and had a background of sexual immorality. Because of the success at Hudson and the need for space, a second institution for women called the Western House of Refuge for Women at Auburn was opened on December 8, 1893. It housed 234 misdemeanants and first-time felons from age 16 to 30 years old. The first real reformatory for women, called Bedford Hills, opened in 1901 at Bedford Hills, New York. Considered the most innovative institution in America, it was outstanding for its medical treatment. In 1904 the House of Refuge became the New York State Training School for Girls, and housed girls from 12 to 15 years of age.

Before 1932 most women were incarcerated in a wing of the New York Workhouse on Blackwell's Island (in 1921 Blackwell Island was renamed Welfare Island). On Welfare Island, in 1929, social service was introduced when social workers were appointed on an experimental basis to serve female first offenders who were not real criminals. Social workers were also appointed to the Second Prison District. Also, before 1932, the Jefferson Market Prison, an institution primarily for men, had set aside 60 cells for women but did not provide enough custodial personnel to supervise them. Unless there was a serious medical problem, ill women remained in their cells, unattended, until they recovered. By 1920 conditions in the Jefferson Market Prison were so wretched that Joseph Kennedy, the state prison commissioner, declared it "unsanitary and ridden with crime." Finally, in July, 1921, the Jefferson Market Prison was closed and women thereafter were incarcerated in the south wing of the Workhouse on Welfare Island. Some attempt at classification of the women prisoners was instituted.

In 1914 Mary Harris was appointed superintendent of the Workhouse. Harris introduced many worthwhile changes in an effort to make life tolerable for the inmates. Prior to 1914 women were never allowed outside during the entire period of their incarceration. Under Harris medical care improved and additional personnel were appointed. For the first time, alcoholics, narcotics addicts, and those suffering from venereal disease were treated by female physicians.

Workhouse sentences varied from one day to two years, but most of the women were sentenced from 60 to 90 days. Because of an absence of rehabilitation programs, the recidivism rate was high. Boredom and idleness characterized life at the Workhouse.

The Jefferson Market Prison was renovated and reopened in 1923. In January, 1924, the Women's Farm Colony at Greycourt in Orange County, New York, opened. Meanwhile, many organizations continued their pressure on city officials for a separate women's facility for incarcerated female inmates.

Females were housed in Brooklyn, Queens, and the Fifth District Prison at 170 East 125th Street, Manhattan, pending construction of a new female facility, the House of Detention for Women.

To summarize, prior to 1933 women inmates were housed in crowded, unsanitary conditions without adequate medical care, education, recreation, and vocational training. Unsentenced women were housed in local station houses and in specific areas set aside for them in male institutions.

The House of Detention for Women

The House of Detention for Women (HDW) was officially opened on March 29, 1932. It was located at 10 Greenwich Avenue, New York City. It opened as an example of the world's model correctional facility for women, but it closed (in 1971) as an example of much that was wrong in penal practices. All inmates at first were housed together in a common cell, and it was not unusual to have mothers with babies in their arms. The women slept on wooden benches in unsanitary vermin-infested surroundings.

Superintendent Collins of HDW encouraged poetry classes, music appreciation, and choir lessons. She also believed that a program of sports, work, and good medical care was beneficial. Attempts at rehabilitation were made. The women were examined for illness and a hospital with 28 beds served the sick and kept them separated from the general population. The original plan was to prevent any contact between old and youthful offenders, the sick and the healthy, first offenders and experienced women criminals, felons and misdemeanants, and material witnesses, drug addicts, and mentally ill and the general population.

The press described the HDW as a "luxury jail" more like a "hotel and a hospital" than a prison. The women were described as "inmates" and not "prisoners."

HDW was considered the epitome of penal design and treatment. It was equipped with the most modern electrical plumbing and refrigeration machinery, and it provided medical, recreational, religious, and social services. It started as an example of what a penal institution should be. It had space for 401 women, so that crowding was not a problem. However, this utopian situation lasted for less than two years.

It must be emphasized that the HDW was built in 1932, during some of the most desperate days of the Great Depression. New York City was trying to reduce expenditures. The Department of Correction was preparing to close other institutions housing females and transfer them to the HDW. The Women's Farm Colony at Greycourt was closed on April 24, 1931. The 100-year-old Correction Hospital was closed in 1934.

Thus, as early as 1935 overcrowding became evident at HDW. In that year the number of inmates reached 500, 99 more than the capacity of 401. HDW contained both adolescents from 16 to 21 and adults. It housed all types of offenders: detainees, sentenced inmates, state parole violators, minors, runaways from the state training schools, and federal inmates who were sentenced to less than a year and a day.

High expectations for improved care and services for incarcerated women failed to be realized. In addition, the original design for HDW did not provide facilities for education, training, and recreation. It was not equipped with a school, a library, or areas for outdoor recreation or training programs. There was inadequate space and equipment for rehabilitation programming for sentenced offenders.

HDW reached a capacity of 568 in 1935, 627 in 1936, and 688 in 1938. Women were doubled up in cells designed for one inmate. Insufficient supplies made it difficult to maintain sanitary standards. Adequate medical services, special services, education, training, and recreation were lacking. The result was boredom and subsequent disciplinary problems.

Since there was no other penal institution for females in New York City, all types of inmates were held at HDW, including adults and adolescents, civil cases, material witnesses, parole violators, federal inmates, prostitutes, the mentally ill, drug addicts, alcoholics, and venereal disease cases.

New York City was the only city in New York state that housed inmates sentenced for more than one year. Other cities sent their inmates to upstate prisons.

The depression in the 1930s prevented construction of a new women's facility or improvement at HDW. As women found employment in war industries in the 1940s, the population at HDW declined to a low of 324 on May 17, 1944, and 267 on March 3, 1949. However, in the 1950s the prison population at HDW began to rise, and from that time until its closing in 1971 overcrowding constituted the major problem at HDW.

Commissioner of Correction Kross, a female, was a firm believer in rehabilitation. She tried to solve existing problems at HDW, and also tried to convince city officials of the need for another institution to house female offenders. In spite of her efforts, a riot broke out at HDW on September 24, 1954; this riot brought the issue of HDW to the public's attention.

The staff at HDW was insufficient and inexperienced; it lacked a knowledge of basic penological concepts. Supervision was poor. The city moved slowly through the process of selecting a new site for a new female correction facility. Meanwhile, the situation at HDW deteriorated and more riots occurred. The press protested; community organizations expressed concern; investigations were conducted; and the state government finally intervened.

A riot occurred at HDW on April 29, 1958, and three correctional officers were hurt. Adverse publicity resulted. The custodial staff at HDW became tense and angry with Kross because they resented her concern for the inmates and her disregard for the custodial staff.

Finally, in 1961, the New York State Correctional Commission approved Riker's Island as the site for a new women's correctional facility. The census at HDW in 1962 was 720, although HDW was designed for a capacity of 401. The Correctional Association of New York could not wait for a new women's prison to be built.

Beginning on May 4, 1965, grand jury hearings were held in the supreme court of the state of New York concerning conditions at HDW. During 28 sessions 89 witnesses testified, including nine women who had made charges against the HDW, public officials who had conducted an investigation of HDW, the superintendent, civilian and associate personnel at HDW, members of the New York City Department of Correction and the New York State Commission of Correction, and members of the Bureau of Prisons of the United States Department of Correction. At the close of the hearings in December, 1965, the grand jury concluded that allegations against the HDW were unfounded, but it gave specific recommendations for improvement.

In November, 1965, John V. Lindsay was elected mayor of New York City, and, influenced by the grand jury findings, accorded top priority for the construction of a new prison for women.

Ana M. Kross held the office of commissioner of correction of New York City from 1954 to 1966. In 1964 Kross received an award from the Women's National Press Club for her dedication and work in penal reform and rehabilitation. Kross led a campaign for a new female penal institution, but her goal was not realized until after she had left office. Kross stressed education, rehabilitation — both vocational and academic — scientific diagnosis, classification, and assignment, adequate medical care and meaningful psychotherapeutic treatment, religious counseling and observance, constructive recreational activities, prerelease guidance, and the necessity for adequate aftercare. She also was responsible for the improved training of personnel, the organization of the board of corrections, and the involvement of volunteer organizations in prison work and rehabilitation.

Kross laid the groundwork for the conversion from custody to rehabilitation, and she appointed a sociologist from City College of New York, Professor Harry M. Schulman, as first deputy commissioner. With his help she began to develop a modern penal administration and a comprehensive program for inmate treatment and rehabilitation. The major problem that Kross faced in her efforts to implement rehabilitation programs was that corrections was the stepchild of city planning and budgeting.

The Kross administration increased civilian professional and nonprofessional staff; provided space for a school, library, and training programs; organized and coordinated community resources and services; and allocated money to establish and conduct many other programs. Religious services, the commissary, and recreation underwent changes in structure, and social services and mental health services were expanded in staff and scope. All the innovations initiated by Kross were extended to the new women's facility that opened in 1971.

Kross expanded the role of chaplains so that they could serve more efficiently as an integral part of the department's social service programs. She encouraged the chaplains to include psychiatric and psychological counseling in their programs.

In 1933 an education program was developed at HDW, designed to offer the inmates practical knowledge they could use constructively after discharge. Kross authorized the conversion of the superintendent's apartment into a school and library area, and the use of other available space for classrooms and vocational training. From 1960 to 1965, 26 women who had completed the 1,000 hours of training to qualify for a license graduated from HDW's Beauty School. They passed the New York State Cosmetology Examination and received their state certificates. As of 1975 not one of these graduates had returned to prison. The music and art course was started at HDW in 1957.

In 1964 the court mandated that a law library be opened under the supervision of the New York City Department of Correction.

Prior to 1950, in HDW, black officers and inmates were assigned to housing areas called "black corridors." This showed that discrimination existed to some extent at the HDW in its early days.[12]

Although relatively little material has been presented here on men's prisons, it appears that conditions in men's prisons in the early days were probably as bad or even worse than female prisons.

Juvenile Institutions

Spofford Youth Center is populated by 15-year-old career criminals ranging from thieves to killers. It is described as a "hell hole."[13] Spofford has been described as a "fortress," like a maximum security detention center. The boys are not permitted to keep any personal belongings in their rooms, not even photographs or clothing. Every morning each boy is given a shirt and pants for the day. They are not permitted to keep a radio in their rooms. These measures are for security.[14]

Spofford House for 7- to 16-year-olds is in the South Bronx. It has long been known for brutality, sadism, forced homosexuality, overcrowding, and corruption. A few improvements have been made. The overcrowding has ended, and there is a new infirmary. There are no rehabilitation services there. There were complaints of beatings. Nothing was going on in the classrooms. Although the legal limit for detention at Spofford is supposed to be 45 days, some inmates have been detained there for six or more months.[15]

In New York City, Euphrasian Residence is an alternative to detention. It gives compassionate care to troubled adolescents in a short period of time, even in a locked facility. In addition to psychological testing and social work, interviews, and counseling, Euphrasian Residence has made its school an integral part of its program.[16]

It is difficult to evaluate conditions at Spofford or other juvenile institutions; it is difficult to ascertain if change, and how much change, has taken place since the early review of the literature. Now juveniles can be committed to the Department of Youth. Judges sometimes send juveniles to juvenile institutions when sentenced; however, now judges can sentence some older juveniles to adult institutions under law. However, Spofford continues to be the only city detention facility for boys. There are some upstate facilities, however.

Jails and Prisons

As mentioned, city jails are located in all the boroughs of New York City. Sentenced inmates are generally housed in city jails if the sentences are one year or less. Offenders sentenced in New York City for periods over one year are generally sent to institutions upstate.

New York State Prisons

In 1966 pressures from the New York City Correctional Administration and the office of the mayor mandated legislative changes that forced McGinnis, the state commissioner of corrections, to accept some city prisoners. McGinnis did not want New York City inmates, even though the state prison system was underpopulated at that time.[17]

A comparison of the committed percentages of New York City Puerto Ricans to state prisons with the incarceration of Puerto Ricans in New York state as a whole revealed that the Puerto Rican proportion of new inmates from New York City is greater than the Puerto Rican proportion of new inmates from the state as a whole. The percentage of Puerto Rican males from New York City newly admitted to the prison population of New York state was more than twice as high as the estimated percentage of the Puerto Ricans in the city's male population. In 1971, 21.1 percent of New York City's male residents admitted to state prisons were Puerto Rican, while the 1970 census data revealed that Puerto Ricans accounted for 7.3 percent of New York City's male population. In 1977, 1,610 out of a total of 5,406, or 29.7 percent, of the newly committed New York City's male residents to state prison were Puerto Rican, compared with the 21.4 percent Puerto Rican share of the commitment on the statewide level. In addition, the number of all new admissions from the city increased by 70.4 percent between 1971 and 1977, but in the same period the number of Puerto Rican males newly admitted from New York City increased by 152 percent.[18]

Between 1971 and 1977, among the new female admissions to prison from New York City, the percentage of black women decreased while the percentage of Puerto Rican women rose from 18.1 percent to 28.6 percent. Women comprised only 2.9 percent of the state prison population in 1984.[19]

At the end of March, 1979, 19.8 percent of the 20,122 prisoners of both sexes in New York State correctional facilities were Puerto Rican; and 19.9 percent of the 19,565 male inmates were identified as Puerto Rican.[20]

Part of the overrepresentation of Puerto Rican inmates from New York City and from New York state as a whole is almost certainly due to the young age structure of the Puerto Rican male population. However, the large percentage of increase of the Puerto Rican inmates from New York City is due to a shift in the ethnic balance of the correctional population in the state.[21]

From 1973 to 1979 there was a gradual increase in the percentage of Puerto Rican inmates in New York state prisons, while the proportion of white inmates remained relatively stable and the proportion of black inmates decreased slightly. Between 1971 and 1977 the absolute number of Puerto Ricans being admitted to New York state prisons increased by more than 144 percent, and the percentage of Puerto Ricans in the total inmate population also increased. Black inmates currently account for the largest percentage of new admissions, white males are next, with Puerto Ricans accounting for the smallest percentage of the three groups. But if commitment rates continue at the rate described above, Puerto Ricans will soon outnumber whites and perhaps will become the second largest group of inmates in state facilities.[22]

Puerto Rican admissions in 1976 and in 1977 were considerably higher than Puerto Rican releases. Thirty-eight percent of white inmates and 26.6 percent of black inmates completed high school compared with 13.6 percent of Puerto Ricans. About 40 percent of Puerto Ricans did not proceed beyond elementary school compared with 19.2 percent of blacks and 22.1 percent of whites.[23]

Clinton Prison is considered one of the most brutal prisons in upstate New York. While most of the prison functions normally, almost 50 men are locked in solitary confinement, in filthy $5' \times 7'$ cages, some for as long as 11 months, without notice, without a hearing, without hope that the warden, the legislature, the governor, or the superintendent will intervene. Very often prisoners suspected of being militant or political are placed in solitary confinement.[24]

Over two-thirds of New York state prisoners come from New York City. Inmates in state prisons are classified before being sent to prisons. The prior record and the length of the inmate's sentence largely determines how a person is classified. Not only do prisons teach inmates the wrong skills, but there is little effort made to help inmates find jobs in the community in the field in which they have been trained. Women in prison are taught to serve, cook, clean, become waitresses, typists, homemakers and mothers.[25]

On March 14, 1985, out of a New York state prison population of 34,317, 2,802 inmates, or 8 percent of the total, were under custody for the Rockefeller drug offenses. Case studies of prisoners demonstrate that mandatory sentencing has caused surges in state prison populations, and that many offenders could have received shorter prison terms or could have been sentenced to less expensive and more suitable alternative punishments. Many of the nearly 5,000 nonviolent second felony offenders currently in prison could have been handled in other, more appropriate ways.[26]

In the early eighties, New York City alone accounted for 58 percent of the arrests and 55 percent of the indictments filed in the state courts. Sixty-seven percent of the inmates in the state prison system came from New York City.[27]

However, the state prison population was declining from the late 1960s to the early 1970s.[28]

Of a random sample of felons sentenced to a state prison in 1973, two-thirds of them for a violent crime, 58.3 percent were black and 15.3 percent were Puerto Rican; relative to the population, three times as many were black.[29]

In 1984, in New York state, there were 13 maximum security facilities, 22 medium security facilities, and 16 minimum security facilities.[30]

Some believe that prison deters married men more than single men. The crime rate inside prison is at least as high as it is outside prison. Intra-inmate violence has increased dramatically in recent years. Although studies are contradictory, inmates serve shorter sentences than formerly.[31]

Population of Jails and Prisons

There are various statistics in New York City on the number of inmates in city jails for various years; some of these statistics are contradictory. It is difficult to obtain a clear picture of the inmate population because of the disparate sources of statistics. In addition, the statistics of the inmate population do not always differentiate between sentenced and pretrial inmates.

In the mid–1970s, Riker's Island's 18 facilities housed about 60,000 men and women annually. On any one day, they held about 7,000 prisoners, of which 5,000 were awaiting trial.[32] In the early 1970s, in one week, more than 8,000 inmates were in jails awaiting trials.[33]

In 1969 jails and prisons in New York City had a detention or inmate population of 12,560; in 1970 the population was 13,084; and in 1971, 12,350. Sixty percent of those in custody were trial defendants. However, in 1973–74, the percentage of trial defendants had risen to 70 percent; this might have been the result of the drug legislation enacted at that time. In 1964 the daily sentenced population in New York City jails was 6,955 compared with 3,986 in 1972; in 1964, detention cases were 3,893 compared with 7,596 in 1972. In 1973 the daily sentenced population was less than 3,000 men and women. In recent years defendants have been obliged to remain longer in detention because of overcrowded courts and because defense attorneys believe that the longer the trial can be delayed, the greater the favorable chances for the defendants.[34]

On February 3, 1972, the city's correctional institutions held 11,425 prisoners, 134 percent of capacity. On January 4, 1973, the census was 9,990, 116 percent of capacity. This decrease in prison population was the result of a reduction in the numbers of short-term sentenced prisoners committed by the courts, possibly because drug addicts at that time were sent to methadone maintenance programs instead of jails or prisons.[35]

The actual prison population in contrast to the detention population in

1970 numbered more than 2,000 inmates; in the early 1970s, this population had decreased to about 900 men.[36]

There are 1,523 sentenced inmates in our system at any one time who have been convicted of property crimes. In 1977 the average length of detention was 26 days. In 1981 the average stay increased to 49 days. During the first ten months of 1982 the average stay decreased to 44 days—this was the first decrease in the six years prior to 1982. In 1983 the average length of stay was again 26 days. In 1982 the detention population was 2,870.[37]

In the early 1970s over 60 percent of the prison population was in detention awaiting a chance to establish their guilt or innocence.[38] The average daily jail population increased from 7,101 in 1977 to 9,973 in 1983, an increase of 2,872, or 40 percent. On November 26, 1984, the total jail population was 10,700. The size of the sentenced population in New York City jails and prisons has been fairly constant during recent years; however, the average daily detainee population rose from 4,410 to 7,087, an increase of 2,677, or 61 percent. The proportion of the detainee population in New York City jails far exceeds the sentenced population; this situation is also true of most other jails nationwide. However, even though the number of arrests in New York City practically doubled between 1968 and 1977, the percentage of defendants kept in pretrial detention fell by almost 60 percent.[39]

In New York City the amount of money that a defendant must raise to be released before sentencing is about 50 percent of the total bail. About 40 percent of the defendants appearing before judges are allowed to meet alternatives to bail, and about 60 percent of those defendants make bail compared with 35 percent of those who do not have this option.[40] In 1984 there were 6,700 detainees in New York City jails.[41]

A study was conducted in the late 1970s on the inmates of New York City's jails. A systematic sample of 1,367 incarcerations that terminated between April 11, 1978, and March 31, 1979, was studied. Female inmates were excluded. The results showed that the presence of warrants and the number of court-ordered psychiatric exams were positively related to the length of detention. Demographic variables were not related to the length of detention. About two-thirds, or 66.2 percent, of the incoming population stayed in detention no more than eight days. The mean length of detention was 35.2 days, and the median was 4.9 days. Of the incoming detainees, 85 percent were either black or Hispanic.

More than half of those remanded had only a misdemeanor or violation charge at admission. The mean length of time between admission and sentence for this group was 2.3 days. The other remand group consisted of those with felony charges on admission. Their mean length of time between admission and sentence was 20.1 days.

Smaller and more specialized groups in the detention population included visiting state prisoners and parole violators.

Approximately three out of four detainees, or 76.6 percent, were incarcerated following criminal court arraignment. The majority of detainees had committed crimes in their county of residence.

The mean age of detainees was 26, and the medium was 24. Whites comprised 14.9 percent of the total, blacks 60 percent, and Hispanics about 23.7 percent. The percentage of high school graduates was no lower than the percentage in the city population after controlling for race and family income. About 19.2 percent of the sample was employed as laborers or as transportation workers. About one-third of the adults, 32.5 percent, claimed to be unemployed or without any occupation. About 15.3 percent claimed to be addicts; many addicts had been remanded to jails because of the closing of state drug facilities. A majority of the detainees, about 66.7 percent, were single. A disproportionate share of detainees, 30.6 percent, had relatively minor misdemeanor charges. Defendants facing more serious charges, A or B felonies, received higher bails than others, although there were some exceptions. The large majority of city prisoners were black and Puerto Rican.

City-sentenced inmates spent one to three days in detention after being sentenced, while state-sentenced inmates spent many months in detention before transfer to state prisons. Court processing took longer for felons because they had to go to grand jury and supreme court in addition to criminal court.[42]

During 1983 the New York City Department of Correction's jails housed a daily average population of 9,973. A sample of 137 sentenced inmates statistically selected from the 20,135 sentenced inmates released from Riker's Island during the period from January 1 through December 9, 1983, was studied. The results of the study showed that errors in bookkeeping affected as many as 3,040 of the released sentenced inmates, and 50 percent of the currently pretrial inmates. These errors were caused by both under- and overstays among the inmates. One of the contributing factors to the late release of inmates was the failure to locate inmate records, files, and documents on time. The study revealed that between 1,120 and 3,282 sentenced inmates were discharged later and between 282 and 1,792 inmates were discharged earlier than required. The overstays cost about $293,000, reduced by understays, and added to already overcrowded conditions.[43]

Conditions in City Jails and Prisons

Information about conditions in city jails and prisons comes from disparate sources, mainly reports from about 1970 to the early 1980s. It is difficult to determine if some of these conditions have changed, although there probably has been some change for the better from the earlier years to the latter years, possibly due to court intervention into prisons.

In the Kew Garden jail in Queens, in the early 1970s, about one-half of the inmate population was awaiting trial. Most inmates had been awaiting trial for more than four months. They were locked in their cells for 21 hours a day. They had no recreation facilities or radio; they had no games. There was no methadone withdrawal treatment for narcotic addicts, although about 60 percent of all inmates were addicts. Only a part-time psychiatrist was on duty nine hours a week; he was expected to service all 530 inmates. Although Kew Gardens was considered the most modern of all city jails, it had neither dormitories nor hospital facilities.[44]

In the early 1970s, 17 suicides occurred in New York City jails and prisons in a two-year period. New York City experienced far more deaths per 1,000 inmates than any other major city in the country.[45] From 1970 to 1974, 43 inmates took their own lives while in pretrial custody; 8 suicides occurred in 1970; 11 in 1971; 11 in 1972; and 13 in 1973. Even though by 1973 more correction personnel were available, there were improvements in medical services, and classification programs were functioning, still the suicide rate was high.[46]

In city jails health care was almost nonexistent. Often inmates were diagnosed incorrectly, given the wrong medicine, or told that they were faking if they complained of sickness. Another defect in jails was the absence of rehabilitative programs. Commissioner McGrath, head of the Department of Correction, New York City, during the early 1970s, was described as not caring about corrections. He was described as only wanting to keep the "lid on," ignoring problems, taking the guards' word about everything, and not bothering the mayor so the mayor would not notice him.[47]

In March, 1971, when the Rankin Report was publicized, it named 18 guards guilty of using excessive force against inmates at the Queens jail. Commissioner McGrath refused to suspend the guards. However, in December, 1971, McGrath was finally asked to resign.[48]

In 1981, 5,300 disciplinary proceedings were heard; in the first ten months of 1983, 7,000 disciplinary proceedings were heard. Inmate grievances, which totaled 7,200 in 1980, escalated to 1,000 a month in 1983.[49]

In the early 1970s one of the loudest complaints echoed by thousands of inmates was that of badly prepared food and cold plates. In that same year there was no means of voicing inmate grievances. Poor inmates could not purchase commissary items. Spanish-speaking inmates had a difficult time communicating. Entertainment and reading-matter were scarce. The indigent inmate was not given free toiletries upon admission. Adequate bedding and other essential housekeeping supplies were not always available. Many defendants appeared in court unshaven and unbathed. In the Manhattan House of Detention detainees were locked inside their cells 16 hours a day. There was a high proportion of addicts attempting suicide.[50]

In the early 1970s in city jails, many inmates had a variety of medical problems, including pulmonary, cardiac, and kidney disease and injuries that needed attention. Many suffered from the shakes, asthma, epilepsy, breathing difficulties, high blood pressure, hernia, chest pains, ulcers, T.B., and a variety of mental health problems.[51]

The inmates in the early 1970s were better educated, younger, and more vocal than the inmates of the 1950s or earlier. The inmates in the 1970s were worried that their constitutional rights were being violated. The admission procedures into prison horrified, degraded, humiliated, depersonalized, secluded, contaminated, and dispossessed the inmate in order to feed him into the administration machinery of the establishment.[52]

With the appointment of Commissioner Malcolm in January, 1972, the Department of Correction tried to resolve inmate grievances that related to prisons and the immediate circumstances of inmate confinement. A prison council program was initiated, which tried to look at differences between detained and sentenced inmates. The council consisted of the warden, his representatives, a representative of corrections and superior officers, a representative of the Board of Corrections, a chaplain, a Health Services Administration representative, and several representatives of the prisoners.[53]

A nonrandom sample of 70 male inmates at Riker's Island in 1973 was given the MMPI (Minnesota Multiphasic Personality Inventory). Thirty-eight were black, 19 were Puerto Rican, and 13 were white. About 25 subjects asked to be excused during the test. The results showed that this group was characterized by individuals lacking social conformity, self-control, displaying psychological deviance, hypomaniacal impulsivity, and schizoid behavior. The researchers in this study believed that serious psychopathology in the sample of 70 inmates suggested a potential for violence and self-mutilation. However, the researchers also believed that the study neither confirmed nor failed to confirm the validity of the MMPI in prison settings; in addition, it failed to support the use of the MMPI as an instrument that can differentiate subgroups.

The researchers also found that the inmate group was impulsive, distractable, rebellious, and nonconforming. They found avoidance of close personal ties, dissatisfaction with family and social life, and superficial gaiety and gregariousness. The younger inmates were found to be more depressed and schizoid than the older ones. Single inmates showed more questionable profiles than older men.

The researchers concluded that the MMPI is not a valuable instrument in a prison setting since its predicted capacity is limited and its descriptive use adds little to our understanding.[54]

A study was conducted of 17,252 infracting events which occurred in the Department of Correction prison facilities between October 1, 1977, and March 31, 1979. The results showed that within the detained category the adolescent infraction rate was more than 50 percent higher than the rate for adults. When only serious events were considered, detainees had a higher rate than the convicted. Sentenced inmates with one exception had higher rates than detainees for crimes that did not involve interpersonal violence. The results also showed that the lowest infraction rates occurred on weekends. Detainees were likely to use more force than the sentenced inmates. Within the detainee group, infracting adults were more likely to use force than adolescents. Adolescents were more likely to be accused of misbehavior and violent misbehavior.

The results also showed that findings of guilt were made for one or more offenses in 81.8 percent of the cases. Sentenced inmates were somewhat more likely to be found guilty than detainees. Loss of good time was the most frequent punishment for sentenced inmates and punitive segregation was the most frequent punishment for detainees; punitive segregation was the second most frequent punishment for the convicted. Less than 1 percent were arrested for a penal law crime.[55]

A study of infractions occurring between October 1, 1977, and March 31, 1978, in male pretrial detention facilities, was conducted. The data were restricted to incarcerations ending between April 1, 1978, and March 31, 1979. A total of 44,906 cases and a sample of about 5,000 infractions were studied. The sample was stratified and multivariate analysis was performed on the data.

The results showed that detainees 25 years old or younger were much more likely to infract than the older detainees. The taller the detainee, the less likelihood of infractions. The Hispanics were more likely to infract than the blacks, whites, or Orientals. The higher the education, the less likelihood of infracting. The detainees who were unemployed at the time of the infraction were more likely to infract than the employed. Drug users were less likely to infract than non–drug users.

The results also showed that those charged with serious felonies were more likely to infract than those charged with misdemeanors. Those who infracted had a longer detention period than noninfractors.

In addition, the results showed that 7.1 percent of the inmate population infracted and that 1.3 percent of the population infracted more than once. Almost 70 percent of those with a court order for a psychiatric examination committed multiple infractions. About 18 percent of the detainees committed serious infractions which included infractions involving harm or threat of harm to self or others. Those committing serious infractions were likely to be older than noninfractors or nonserious infractors and to have a nonserious admission charge. These infractors were evenly distributed among the ethnic groups. The absence of a named contact was the strongest predictor of the group of violent infractors.[56]

Another study of infractions was made among inmates in detention who were discharged from the facilities of the New York City Department of Correction between April 1, 1978, and March 31, 1979. Only the infractions occurring between October 1, 1977, and March 31, 1979, were studied. The study involved more than 6,100 infractions.

Of the 44,906 incarcerations studied, only 3,245, or 7.23 percent, contained an infraction of any kind, and less than 2 percent contained a serious infraction; very few contained a violent infraction. Approximately 5 percent of the first infractions and serious infractions had occurred by the third day. This suggests that the first days of incarceration are particularly dangerous. However, many infractions occurred in later time periods. About one-fourth of those who committed a serious infraction committed another infraction, suggesting that the act of committing a serious infraction was a predictor of future infractive behavior.[57]

It appeared that 15 years after the Attica Riot, the correction system seemed dedicated to a return of the internally direct secure custodial administration facilitated by an outsider hands-off policy.[58] It appeared that there was no fundamental change in the fall in 1974, four years after the riots. There has been no fundamental change in New York City's penal system; there have only been superficial changes.[59]

Prison libraries, like prisons, generally have been used as dumping places for rejected materials and supplies that cannot be handled easily elsewhere. However, five newspapers and 53 periodicals are now delivered in substantial volumes on a regular basis to the Department of Correction for distribution throughout the prison system. The Adolescent Remand Shelter in 1971 was considered the worst prison in the city. It was a maximum security facility. A new facility opened in 1972.[60]

For several years, the roof of the Tombs, which was the only available area within the prison for fresh air and recreation, was unused because of lack of funds for repairs. The necessary $12,000 was found, the repair work was completed, and the roof was opened for extensive use for the prisoners.[61]

A federal court order resulted in the release of 611 pretrial inmates during the first two weeks of November, 1984. New York City lags behind other systems in the country in the use of work-release programs in jails.[62]

Centron, an inmate of Brooklyn House of Detention, was said by Commissioner George McGrath to have attacked two guards with a knife and as a result died when the guards disarmed him. However, Eugene Gold, the district attorney for Brooklyn, said that the truth was that Centron did not carry a knife and that he did not attack the guards. Gold stated that Centron had died as a result of a "homicidal assault" by four correction officers.[63]

Women's Jail and Prisons

In the early 1970s the Women's Prison at Riker's Island was described as "nothing works." Most of the rehabilitative programs were not in operation because of a shortage of correction officers. The prison population was 40 over capacity. The classroom, the gym, the library, the outdoor recreation areas, the sewing rooms, and the beauty shop were all partially idle and empty. The health system was considered a horror. The commissary was badly stocked and overpriced. The prison itself was run on a strict military regimentation. The physicians were worse. Some of the "Dracula-like" doctors were removed from the prison. These physicians were replaced by younger, more humane medical personnel, and a contract was negotiated with Montefiore Hospital in the Bronx to provide improved health care for the women.[64]

The New York City Correctional Institution for Women (NYCCIFW) opened in 1971 on Riker's Island, East Elmhurst, Queens. The facility could house 679 inmates (300 detainees, 320 sentenced inmates, and 59 in the infirmary). There were 55 acres of land for outdoor recreation.

The average length of stay at NYCCIFW was two weeks. The leadership of both HDW (House of Detention for Women) and NYCCIFW was always in the hands of educated, dedicated women who believed in rehabilitating the inmates rather than operating solely in a custodial role.

The routine at NYCCIFW was the same as that at HDW, but more services were available at the former, due to the design and availability of space. At NYCCIFW, detainees and sentenced women were housed separately, and adolescents between 16 and 21 were separated from adults.

The women at NYCCIFW took part in the decision-making process concerning their activities while they were incarcerated. The women were treated with respect and the dehumanizing aspects of institutionalization were kept to a minimum.

At NYCCIFW, in cases of infractions, the women were punished by denying them privileges, by locking them in their cells, or by placing them in solitary confinement. However, because women were disciplined after receiving an infraction, many correctional officers developed personal methods of dealing with inmates so that they rarely wrote up an infraction. However, except for an assault on an officer, punishment was mild.

Between 1970 and 1975 there was neither censorship nor a limit to the number of items mailed out, and incoming mail was checked only for contraband or money.

By the end of 1975 the census at NYCCIFW averaged 350 with a capacity of 679.

In 1971, after the Attica riots, the inmates at NYCCIFW complained of inadequate medical and mental health care, and public interest in conditions in prisons increased. However, after Attica, a major reorganization of health services occurred at NYCCIFW. Two positive changes at the NYCCIFW were the establishment of the inmate council and the furlough system. A total of 126 women received furloughs between 1972 and 1975. Only six women absconded and all except one were apprehended. Work-release was introduced.

There were many training opportunities available for women at NYCCIFW between 1971 and 1975. However, women had difficulty in mastering skills either because they did not wish to enter a "man's field" or because of limited educational achievement. In 1975 no aftercare existed for most female ex-offenders. Few women were employed after discharge from prison. Part of the problem was that most female offenders received short sentences. The average stay for women was two weeks, and few stayed longer than 60 days. Although resident training programs were available in the community, the number of female offenders eligible and interested in them was small.[65]

In NYCCIFW in 1976 the staff was over 90 percent black and the inmates about 85 percent black.[66]

In December, 1979, Bayview Correctional Facility, located at 550 West 20th Street in Manhattan, became a women's prison. A study of the Bayview Correctional Facility was conducted. The study covered the period from October, 1983, to October, 1984; observation was used as a method of analysis. The results showed a large number of male guards compared with female guards. On November 28, 1983, and in January, 1984, six male prison guards and a sergeant were suspended without pay from the Department of Correction for improper and unauthorized relationships with inmates, including sexual activities.

Prior to May, 1984, delays in obtaining outside medical care ranged anywhere from one to six months. Mental health services were practically nonexistent at Bayview. The academic programs were insufficient to meet the needs of the prison population. The general library was virtually nonexistent. There were unsanitary and health-threatening conditions in the kitchen. The complaints voiced by inmates concerned the small portions of food, nonnutritionally balanced meals, and infrequent servings of fresh vegetables and fruits. Several areas, including the visiting room and the cafeteria, required innovation and expansion even for short-term use.[67]

Riots in New York City Jails and Prisons

In August, 1970, more than 1,000 inmates took control of sections of the Manhattan House of Detention for men and held eight correction officers as hostage. Later, in October, 1970, riots broke out in all five of the city's detention facilities.[68]

A riot erupted in the Long Island City jail in Queens. The correction officers began to systematically club the prisoners who had participated in the riots in the courtyard of the jail with ax-handles, baseball bats, and riot clubs. The guards were exonerated despite photographic evidence of their guilt.

Another riot broke out in the jail in Kew Gardens in October, 1970. The rioters surrendered after receiving a promise of no reprisals, but many were beaten secretly behind closed doors after the trouble was over. As a result of conditions in Kew Gardens, a class action in behalf of 800 inmates was submitted to the Eastern Court against Mayor Lindsay, Commissioner McGrath, Warden John Kennedy, and Deputy Warden Albert Ossakow. Shorty, a black inmate at Kew Gardens was killed. Although the guards said he had died of an overdose, his head was split open and his sheet contained large blood stains.

After the riot in Kew Gardens, inmate wounds were left untreated; inmates were warned not to talk to Legal Aid lawyers; inmate letters, pictures, and lawbooks were confiscated; many inmates were confined for days without toilet paper, blankets, or solid food; and many inmates were subjected to sadistic beatings.

In July, 1971, United States Magistrate Vincent Catogio dismissed the class action lawsuit initiated by the 800 inmates, concluding that the inmate charges of brutality were a gigantic fraud. The Rankin Report accused Warden Ossakow and ten correction officers of using unnecessary and excessive force on inmates. Warden Ossakow was permitted to plead guilty at a departmental trial and to retire, allowing him to keep his pension. He was fined $600.[69]

A black inmate at the Tombs struck a correction officer and was quickly removed from the floor. Other black inmates felt that the black inmate was being abused, and, in their frustration, seized ten white inmates and beat them. Peace was restored when the black inmate was returned, unchained, to his floor. On August 11, 1970, at breakfast, five officials were taken hostage by inmates, who voiced their grievances to the press and to representatives of the mayor's office. They listed ten grievances including overcrowding, lack of proper medical care, guard brutality, prolonged trials, and excessive bail. The Tombs, built to house 900 inmates, was averaging 1,900, and had 1,991 at the time of the riots. Some cells held three inmates, with at least one sleeping on the floor. Three other officers were taken captive and 800 inmates were involved in the riots. They set fires, smashed windows, and went on a seven-hour rampage. Furniture, mattresses, plumbing, and much else was destroyed.[70]

In October, 1970, 1,450 men were jammed into 875 cells at the Tombs. On October 1, 1970, a riot exploded and ended on October 5, 1970. In January, 1971, Beyden, an inmate, and six other inmates, were indicted on 50 separate counts of first degree kidnapping for taking hostages. Although none of the hostages was hurt, although none disputed the legitimacy of the inmates' demands, and although no beatings occurred during the riots, these inmates were still indicted. In Brooklyn, District Attorney Gold dropped or plea bargained all charges against 35 inmates indicted on charges during the riots, similar to the charges of the seven inmates in the Tombs.[71]

In October, 1970, riots broke out in five of the city's detention facilities. The inmates in the 1970 riots viewed the media as crucial to publicizing their demands so as to gain the support of the mass public predisposed to minority rights, and to mobilizing the blacks and the Puerto Ricans in the larger society outside of prisons.[72] From October 1 to October 5, rebellious inmates in the major detention centers in New York City held 28 people hostage. When the October riots erupted, the Department of Correction had a capacity for only 7,993 single cell occupancy, but the occupancy rate throughout New York City was 147 percent above capacity, with 11,809 inmates housed in these cells.[73]

In late August, 1970, 84 inmates from Manhattan and Queens refused to make court appearances. This form of protest was repeated many times. On October 1, 1970, during the lunch hour, inmates of the Branch Queens House of Detention surprised seven officers by taking control of the detention center. Negotiations between the inmates and the city correctional commissioner followed. The commissioner promised no reprisals if the guards were released. The inmates demanded an immediate bail review for 47 inmates. The bail was reviewed but the inmates reneged on their promise to release the hostages. In the Tombs, in August, 1970, during a movie in the auditorium, 220 inmates seized control of the 11th floor. Fifteen hostages were taken.[74]

On Friday, October 2, 1970, about 9 P.M., a riot erupted at the Queens House of Detention for Men at Kew Gardens. Two more riots broke out on Saturday. On Saturday, October 3, at Brooklyn House of Detention for Men, the most overcrowded facility in the city's correctional system, inmates grabbed four hostages, smashed windows, and burned bedding. A riot broke out at the Adolescent Remand Shelter at Riker's Island. In the Brooklyn riot 200 inmates and 12 guards were hurt.[75]

The class action brought to court by inmates on October 26, 1970, during the riots, resulted in a landmark decision handed down by United States District Judge Morris E. Lasker on January 7, 1974. Specifically, it was charged that unconvicted detainees suffered numerous physical conditions depriving them of their rights under the First, Fifth, Sixth, Eighth, and Fourteenth Amendments with reference to overcrowding, unsanitary conditions, lack of light and air, excessive noise, mistreatment by guards, arbitrary discipline, inadequate medical care, lack of recreation, and restrictions on visiting and mail. New York City had subjected them to degrading and punitive conditions inconsistent with their status as pretrial inmates who were presumed innocent, and had violated their rights to due process of law, to equal protection of the laws, and to be free from cruel and unusual punishment.[76]

Riots occurred in prison throughout the United States during this period. The riots in New York City and elsewhere, and research by government in criminal justice, resulted in national interest in the crime problem.[77]

In the institutions in which riots occurred in the 1970s, prisoners were locked into their cells continuously for several months.[78]

Probation, Parole, Other Alternatives

Probation

Probation is given as a sentence in lieu of jail or prison if a defendant's criminal record is not too serious. Under probation supervision, a defendant or probationer is under legal contract to obey the orders of probation that he and the judge sign. Such orders pertain to rearrests, reporting, drug, alcohol, and psychiatric problems, keeping hours, leaving the city or state, restitution, fines, etc. If a probationer does not meet these conditions, he can be returned to court for resentencing if the probation officer decides to violate the probationer's supervision. However, there is a great deal of flexibility in both the interpretation of the conditions of probation and the rules for violating probation. Probation in New York City is administered by the County of New York City but is indirectly supervised by New York State.

In 1977 there were approximately 55,000 offenders under the supervision of local probation departments in the state, almost three times the number incarcerated in New York's prisons.[79]

Although probation often amounts to little more than a suspended sentence, it has nonetheless proven to be at least as effective as incarceration in preventing recidivism, at a fraction of the cost. Supervision sometimes entails nothing more than an occasional office visit, and the provision of meaningful service to the probationer is rare. In addition, the selection of probationers is haphazard, and generally unrelated to the defendants' needs or suitability for probation supervision. Reports of probation agencies in counties out of New York City have stressed the pro forma quality of supervision, the lack of coordination with community resources, and the inadequacy of supervision plans and service delivery. Probation is often treated as a catch-all disposition, handed to virtually every defendant felt unsuitable for incarceration without regard to actual need for supervision.[80]

A study of the violation practices of probation officers was done in New York City in the mid–1970s. A 33-item questionnaire, employed in previous studies, was sent to all probation officers of misdemeanants in New York City County during the period from July, 1973, to June, 1974. About 5.3 percent, or 41 probation officers, responded.

The results showed that 44 percent were highly client-service oriented; 37 percent were moderately so; 12 percent were undecided; and 7 percent were control-oriented. The results were not significantly related to the level of education, experience, or age of the probation officers, although these had some effect. The more highly service-oriented the probation officer, the lower the number of violations issued. However, no relationship was found between the probation officers' orientation and the kind of violation issued. For example, failure to report and absconding were used three times as often as failure to obtain treatment.[81]

In early 1979 an Intensive Supervision Program (I.S.P.) was established in the New York Division of Probation, and was put into operation in a number of locations throughout the state on an experimental basis. The premise was that by placing into limited caseloads those probationers considered to be at the highest risk of rearrest, the probation officers involved would be able to work more closely, more intensively, with these persons. Each probation officer had a maximum of 25 cases with a minimum of eight personal and collateral contacts per month.

An evaluation of I.S.P. at the end of two years revealed that recidivism had been dramatically reduced, that adjustment into the community was positive, and that there was a much higher rate of follow-through in program referrals.

The typical I.S.P. probationer is accepted into the program based on a numerical score obtained from an assessment instrument completed by the probation officer. It is not clear whether I.S.P. probationers are people who could otherwise have been placed on regular probation or would have gone to jail. However, I.S.P. probation is less costly than jail.[82]

Although drugs are a big problem in probation, there are no probation officers who specialize in this area of supervision.[83]

At the end of this chapter, empirical studies on probation will be analyzed.

Parole

Parole is supervision of defendants after the latter have served part of a prison sentence. Parolees are supervised by parole officers. Parole is administered by the state of New York.

In New York State, in the 1970s, the New York State Parole Board released seven inmates out of ten at their first appearance before the board.[84] The determination of a three-member panel of the parole board is not final, but is subject to "appellate review" by a full board of parole.[85]

Parole is aimed more at surveillance than assistance. Since the parole officer is armed with the power to return the offender to prison for violation of rules governing his or her conduct during the supervision process, the parole officer is more apt to assume the role of policeman rather than a social worker.[86]

There is no effective job placement program for parolees. Legally, before an inmate can be released on parole, he must have a job or the reasonable assurance of a job. But little is done to help an inmate find a job while he is still in prison. Approximately 44.6 percent of all parolees do not have jobs upon release, but only an assurance of work. Of those who do have jobs upon release, only 5.1 percent have obtained them through the assistance of the parole officials; about 25.5 percent have found them through their own efforts.[87] Parolees can not be discriminated against by employers and state licensing agencies, unless the parolee's conviction is reasonably related to the job or license sought.[88]

An inmate released on parole has approximately a one-in-three chance of returning to prison to serve all or part of his or her remaining sentence.[89]

The parole board should have written guidelines for its use. During the year 1979 the average number of interviews conducted by each board member was 1,275; in 1980, it was 1,198. In 1979, the overall parole rate for incarcerated inmates of state facilities was 55 percent; it was 52 percent in 1980. In cases of offenses involving physical violence, the parole board seems to weigh prior criminal history more heavily in its decision to release an offender than in cases in which there is little or no physical violence to a victim.[90]

The proportion of Puerto Ricans released on parole may be disproportionately small.[91]

Other Alternatives

Eighteen projects involving 2,860 men and boys in rehabilitation in New York City were evaluated. The major conclusion of the study was that in reference to the amounts and types of crime committed, the costs to the victim were so high that the rehabilitation services of the 18 projects failed as approaches to the prevention and control of particularly violent crimes. The failure was unrelated to the differences among the projects or to environmental factors, such as unemployment. The rehabilitative services in the 18 projects involved remedial education, job referrals, training and placement, counseling, legal aid, and drug addiction treatment.

Study results indicated that 20 percent of those reported to be nonrecidivists actually committed unapprehended crimes after project entrance.

A respondent in the evaluation had to be in the program at least 12 months to be included in the evaluation. More than 90 percent of the clients in the projects had been arrested at least once before entering the projects, and most of the remainder had other types of police records before project entry.

A step-wise linear regression was used to analyze the data. The number of arrests before project entry, and the stage of project entry, with interaction, were the independent variables. However, only about 15 percent of the variance was explained by all the independent variables together.

Other nonparametric tests revealed that the relationship between prior criminal history and recidivism was not linear. Of the 2,860 clients, ranging in age from 7 to 71, 1,182, or 41 percent, were arrested a total of 2,072 times during the 12 months after project entry. Of those arrests, however, 605, or 29 percent, were arrested for violent crimes. When violent crime was used as the dependent variable, the amount of variance explained was only 8 percent for all age groups.

Seriousness of offense and the total number of arrests before entry were used as independent variables. A regression analysis was used for each of nine age groups. The results showed findings similar to those previously concluded. There was no improvement in recidivism rates. However, there was a relationship between severity of criminal history and recidivism for the age groups 13–18 and to some extent for those over 19.

The author concluded that in general, the proportion of recidivists increased as the level of severity increased.[92]

Because the public was concerned with the increasing crime rate associated with drug addiction, Governor Rockefeller, in the early 1970s, inaugurated state treatment programs under the Narcotic Addiction Control Commission. Rockefeller poured more money and effort into the treatment of illegal drug users in New York than any other jurisdiction in the country.[93] However, all these drug facilities are now permanently closed.

The Vera Institute of Justice now operates community service sentencing projects in the Bronx, Brooklyn, and Manhattan. Six hundred defendants were sentenced to 70 hours of service each in 1982. Estimates revealed that about 40 percent of these defendants would receive jail sentences averaging 100 days each. Nearly 90 percent of the participants completed their sentence; the remaining 10 percent were referred back to the court for resentencing. The results showed that individuals sentenced to community service did not commit crimes after the six-month period from sentencing at a greater rate than those with identical charges and prior criminal history who were incarcerated at Riker's Island for part of that period.[94]

A sample of 676 men strictly supervised in labor crews, each required to perform 70 hours of community service, sponsored by the Vera Institute of

Justice, was studied. The defendants were nonviolent criminals. Three boroughs, the Bronx, Brooklyn, and Manhattan, were involved. More than 80 offenders in the program were interviewed; a comparable group of inmates who received jail sentences was also analyzed. The inmates were chosen both randomly and nonrandomly. Participants were given close supervision and praised for their services. A good proportion of the sample would have gone to jail for periods up to several months. Most of the participants were black or Hispanic, with prior records of between 5 and 13 arrests.

Results showed that many participants believed that they had broken the law; 20 percent believed that the victim was other than themselves; 16 percent believed that they were the victims; a third believed that their community work was punishment. During a six-month period, 43 percent of the participants were rearrested for minor crimes.

The author concluded that about 33 percent of the participants' rearrests would have been averted for a one-year period if the participants had been given jail sentences rather than community participation. He also concluded that about 15 arrests per 100 participants would have been averted if the participants were sent to jail. The author concludes that although community service is not a panacea, it is worthwhile because of the pride the participants have in working and because of the lesser strain and costs in incarceration.[95]

Suggested Reforms

It has been said that Rockefeller was not interested in correctional reform. As late as October, 1969, reform groups were still urging a state takeover of all sentenced prisoners in local institutions to relieve inhumane overcrowding, and to provide for rehabilitative programming not fiscally viable in local institutions. One of the measures supported by the reformers was work-release programs, which was eventually enacted into law.

The Department of Parole and the Department of Correction were amalgamated into the Department of Correctional Services in 1970 under the former head of parole, G. Oswald. In the 1960s, the penal system of New York state was not subject to review by any outside power source. However, in the 1970s, the courts became involved in the problem of state penal conditions, reversing their historical position of noninterference in state penal matters. When the federal courts became involved in penal conditions, the New York State Correctional bureaucracy and administration viewed the federal court decisions as extraordinarily threatening to their control of the institutions. The correctional administration perceived that their control was being eroded by the courts.

Oswald tried to change the department from its custodial orientation to one emphasizing rehabilitation. Oswald stated that in all his reforms he had received little assistance from the traditional religious and social reformers, and had incurred the hostility of the correctional officers who were fearful of inmates out of their cells. It is interesting to note that after the Auburn and Attica riots, correction officers' demands included prison reform proposals identical with those of the inmates. One of the reasons Oswald did not get money for programs even after the Attica riot was because of a polarization in the legislature between the pro-inmate interests and the custodial interests.

In November, 1983, Judge Morris Lasker of the Federal District Court ordered New York City to comply with a limit he had placed on the number of inmates housed in the House of Detention for Men at Riker's Island. This order resulted in the release of some 600 prisoners to the streets of New York City.

However, as mentioned previously, it appears that 15 years after Attica the correctional system seemed destined to a return to the internally custodial administration facilitated by an outsider hands-off policy which had characterized the 1950s.[96]

The period of the early and mid-1960s was characterized by a continuation of the status quo and support of custodial interests. An examination of Governor Rockefeller's actions in the 1970s in reference to the law and order problem shows that they were in harmony with the interests of the correctional bureaucracy and the law enforcement community. This, however, does not imply that Rockefeller responded solely to law-enforcement interests. In the absence of effective lobbying by reformers for institutional change, the correctional bureaucracy remained more or less secure in the maintenance of the status quo.[97]

As the free labor market outside the prison expanded, labor interests began to exert political pressures on the state legislature to restrict the use of prison labor and thereby eliminate their competition.[98]

When furloughs for women's prisons were introduced into the correctional system, the response from the community was positive.[99]

In spite of the prison riots of the early 1970s, there has been no "fundamental changes" in New York City's penal system; there have only been "superficial changes" of one kind or another.[100]

A committee to suggest reform for jail overcrowding met six times between December 1, 1982, and January 27, 1983, at John Jay College of Criminal Justice. One suggestion was that defendants who have bail of $2,500 or less be permitted to post 10 percent cash as security. Credit cards and personal checks should be accepted for posting bonds. An immediate credit checking system should be instituted. It was estimated that posting bond would save as many as 1,200 beds in jails, and that immediate credit checking would save as many as 100 beds in jails.

Another suggestion was to increase Criminal Justice Agency services for more reliable notification to defendants for the expedition of bail, for better information at first adjournment, and for more services. With an expenditure of $300,000, as many as 300 correction beds each day could be saved at a savings of $3,285,000.

Another recommendation was aimed toward decreasing presentence detention. For each day of decrease, 169 beds would be saved.

Another suggestion specified that defendants sentenced to an indeterminate term would be housed in other than secure facilities and would report only in the daytime and not on weekends. The Department of Correction should specify the duration, place, and time of confinement. This would save 25 to 45 beds each weekend.

The committee suggested that if 90 percent of all defendants with $1,000 or less bail would post their 10 percent down, the average daily detainee population would be reduced by 930. If 25 percent of the defendants with $1,000 to $2,500 could post 10 percent down, the average daily population in jail would be reduced by 300. If defendants with $1,000 or less bail would obtain only one less day of jail, then almost 100 beds in jail would be saved daily.

The committee recommended use of community service in lieu of jail or prison. If 100 defendants were sentenced to community service in lieu of jail, then an estimate of 4,000 bed days would be saved in jail for this period.

The committee recommended the use of restitution in lieu of jail. If only about 1 percent of all defendants convicted of property crime were sentenced to restitution in lieu of jail, 5,560 bed days annually would be saved, 15.2 beds each day.

The committee indicated that some defendants were incarcerated before sentencing because judges did not believe that they would return to court. If just ten defendants under this category were released, $109,500 would be saved.

The committee also believed that reinterviewing and updating information by the Criminal Justice Agency would result in releasing many defendants or detainees.

The committee concluded that expediting cases through the criminal courts is the key to relieving jail overcrowding. To accomplish this goal, the committee suggested that each and every department in the process must cooperate and coordinate their efforts. The committee also concluded that if 50 percent of the intermittent prisoners were sentenced to either a jail location outside of a jail facility or for limited hours, 25–45 beds per weekend would be saved.[101]

In 1970 members of the New York State Board of Corrections made hundreds of visits to New York City jails under the jurisdiction of the New York City Department of Correction.[102]

In the early 1970s a state commission recommended that the Board of Corrections act in an ombudsman capacity to handle grievances from both employees and inmates of jails and prisons. The commission also recommended that funding for the city correctional institutions should be assumed by New York state.[103] Others have suggested that the state should assume the costs for local correctional activities provided certain conditions are met that ensure the quality of inmate service.[104]

The Executive Advisory Committee on Sentencing recommended that the sole business of the probation department should be the supervision of probationers, and that presentence investigations should be removed from the department and prepared by an arm of the court. The quality of supervision should be upgraded and should be given the resources to do the job. The committee also suggested determinate sentencing, and this could mean that the parole board would perform a discretionary release function only for inmates who had been sentenced under the prior indeterminate system. Parole release would be abolished because it could serve no legitimate function under a sentencing guidelines system.[105]

A committee recommended state takeover of probation functions. State takeover of probation has been suggested in a number of comprehensive reports since the mid–1960s. However, state takeover of the correctional services would not ensure a higher quality of inmate services.[106]

Empirical Studies

Jails

During the spring of 1981 I interviewed 68 inmates and ex-inmates who had served time at either Riker's Island or Brooklyn House of Detention. I also interviewed some relatives of the inmates or ex-inmates. My sample was selected nonrandomly. A standardized questionnaire of 19 questions was used as an interview guide. My object was to ascertain the respondents' attitudes toward their jail experiences in New York City. However, not all the inmates answered all the questions.

The results showed that 33 of the inmates were working while in remand. Twenty-four of the 33 liked their work and 24 chose to work voluntarily. Fourteen inmates wanted to work, but could not find work. Only 15 of the inmates attended educational programs; 13 of the 15 attended them voluntarily; only five liked the programs. However, 15 inmates wanted to attend, if they could.

Thirty-seven believed that they had enough leisure time to do what they wanted. Forty-five made negative remarks about the food. Twenty-eight had been in one or more fights. Five had been assaulted sexually. About half described the other inmates in favorable terms. Forty-eight had at least some friends; only 12 described themselves as leaders.

Only 14 had either attended or knew of the existence of an inmate-council meeting. Eighteen out of 50 inmates had some grievances. Only 18, or half of those who responded, were satisfied with the attention they received for their problems. Forty-seven believed that guards had yelled and 45 believed that guards had hit inmates. Sixteen of the inmates had been personally hit by a correction officer. Thirty-nine stated that correction officers showed favoritism. Some believed that correction officers hit prisoners for no apparent reason.

Only 18 had something positive to say about their jail experiences; some had both positive and negative comments.

Thirty-three respondents were victims of a crime on the street; 18 respondents experienced burglaries in their homes; 40 had been in one or more fights on the street; 20 had lived on the street; 19 had to worry about their next meal.

It appeared that inmates who were housed in Brooklyn had a more favorable attitude toward jail than those housed in Riker's Island. Many believed that friends were necessary for protection in jail. Many saw friends from the neighborhood in jail.

I concluded that inmates have both positive and negative experiences toward jail. Jail life is an extension of life in the street. There is no typical inmate. Jail is not a place where everyone is fighting all the time. There are a great variety of human responses to imprisonment. Jail may not be a deterrent for everyone.[107]

In another study I interviewed 80 remand defendants in the spring of 1983. This was a nonprobability sample; all defendants were charged with a misdemeanor. An open-ended questionnaire consisting of four main questions was administered to the respondents to determine jail discipline.

The results showed that only ten defendants had been disciplined at their present jail. Several had been "written up" for a disturbance. One had been beaten by a correctional officer. Nineteen defendants had been yelled at by correctional officers. Forty defendants had witnessed other inmates disciplined and beaten; 48 had witnessed correction officers yelling at other inmates. Some of the reasons for the discipline were talking, stepping out of line, making extra phone calls, possessing extra food, hitting a correction officer, answering a correction officer, refusing to take a shower, etc. Many defendants stated that correction officers had taken inmates out of sight for beatings. However, many defendants believed the same correctional officers were nice.

The results also showed that 41 defendants believed that the discipline was "tight" where they were. Some defendants differentiated among the jails and prisons in reference to discipline.

I concluded that some inmates are disciplined for both minor and major disturbances. However, not all inmates are disciplined. Much depends on the individual correction officer. Prison discipline is related to the particular jail or prison in which a defendant is housed.[108]

Probation

I analyzed a systematic sample of 450 misdemeanor cases for the years 1977 and 1978 for Brooklyn. Path analysis and discriminant analysis were used as statistical procedures. A content analysis was made of the reasons stated in probation reports for termination of probation; this content analysis was considered like a pilot study. The results of the content analysis revealed that the number of arrests, failure to keep appointments, and cooperation were the most important reasons in rank order given by probation officers for termination of probation. Sixteen variables, including disposition of judge and recommendation of probation officer as dependent variables, and two interaction terms, were analyzed. One variable was eliminated due to multicollinearity. An analysis of recommendations and dispositions revealed that judges followed recommendations about 54 percent of the time. About 51 percent of the probationers received a favorable termination, 33 percent received termination without comment or termination due to maximum expiration, and 15 percent received an unfavorable termination.

The characteristics of the sample revealed that the mean number of arrests before probation was 2.48 and while on probation was .636. The most frequent number of arrests before and during probation was zero, indicating perhaps that a selective population was being placed on probation.

The results of path analysis and discriminant analysis revealed that the more the probationer was in jail on another case, the less he or she cooperated, the more severe the recommendation. The more he or she was employed, the more lenient was the recommendation. Judges seemed to follow the recommendations of probation officers to a great extent. For judges, the more the probationer was in jail while on probation, the more severe the disposition; the more he or she cooperated or was employed, the more lenient the disposition. Discriminant analysis showed the importance of prior record for probation officers and judges.

I concluded that prior record was not influential in probation termination. Even if an arrest occurred while on probation, this did not necessarily mean an unfavorable termination. Failure to keep appointments while on probation was not significantly related to termination. Cooperation was found to be important. The fact that probation officers influenced judges' decisions in termination give a lot of power to probation officers. Therefore, perhaps probation officers should be the ones who terminate a case instead of judges.[109]

I analyzed by regression analysis 400 closed probation cases for the years 1978 and 1979 for the Bronx. Nine independent variables were used in the analysis; termination of probation was the dependent variable. The sample was a nonprobability sample or could be considered a population, since all cases for these years were analyzed. In addition, I conducted interviews with 13 probation officers, chosen nonrandomly, to determine factors probation officers used in termination of probation.

The interviews with the probation officers revealed that the number of arrests while on supervision was the most important factor in termination of probation. Failure to report and employment were considered less important.

Only seven of the 400 cases were felonies; the rest were misdemeanors. The mean number of arrests prior to being placed on probation was 1.735. The mean number of arrests while on probation was .745, or less than one arrest. Two hundred and forty of the probationers had no arrest while on probation. The mean number of failures to report was 2.7; 187 out of 400 probationers reported without any failure. One hundred and sixty-nine probationers had no prior arrests before being placed on probation. Of the 400 cases, 132 were terminated unfavorably, 160 by statute of limitation or no comment, and 118 were terminated favorably. It appeared that the probationers were not a particularly criminal group; those placed on probation seemed to have a relatively light record and did not get arrested while on probation.

The results of the regression analysis revealed in rank order from the highest to lowest effect that the more the probationer cooperated during supervision—for example, entered drug therapy if needed—the more favorable the termination of probation; the more the probationer was employed, the more favorable the termination; the less serious the crime during supervision, the more favorable the termination; and the less severe the disposition of offenses committed during supervision, the more favorable the termination. The R^2, or the proportion of variance explained, was .59, and highly significant.

I concluded that probation officers valued cooperation as the most important factor in termination of probation, possibly because cooperation is correlated with the probation officers' authority and power. If a probationer was arrested during supervision, this did not mean that he or she would be terminated unfavorably; it depended on the seriousness and disposition of the offense. Failure to report did not necessarily mean an unfavorable termination, perhaps because failure to report is normative to probationers or because it is difficult to terminate or violate a probationer's case on failure to report alone.

I also concluded that all probation cases could be classified as "easy" and "difficult" cases, and that probation officers must decide how to terminate these difficult cases, which could be a subjective process. An unfavorable termination did not necessarily mean a jail sentence or even that a probationer would have to go to court. It might simply mean that the probation officer could not do any more for the probationer. I also concluded that probation officers might not be completely cognizant of the rank order in importance of the factors affecting termination of probation.[110]

An analysis of variance using a completely randomized factorial design with two treatments was performed on 48 probationers' cases for the Bronx in 1986. One treatment consisted of four levels based on the number of telephone calls, letters, and field visits to the home. One level was 0–5 telephone calls and/or letters; a second level was 0–5 letters and/or telephone calls with a field visit; a third level was 6–10 telephone calls and/or letters; and a fourth level was the same as the third level with the addition of a field trip.

The second treatment consisted of two levels. One level was biweekly reporting, and the second level was monthly reporting. The criterion or dependent variable was the number of failures to report for the first year of probation. All the assumptions of the F test and the model were met except random assignment to treatment groups; however, the F test is sometimes open to slight departures from the assumptions.

The results of the analysis of variance revealed that the number of letters and/or telephone calls with or without field visits was significantly related to failure to report. Biweekly or monthly reporting alone was not significantly related to failure to report; however, there was significant interaction between the number of calls and letters with or without a field visit and biweekly or monthly reporting.

Interviews with several probation officers revealed that they varied on the time they would wait before initiating a violation of probation, or how many letters or telephone calls they would make or send to a probationer who did not report. However, all stated that they would give a probationer a chance to report by telephone, letter, or field visit before initiating a violation of probation.

I concluded that telephone calls and/or letters and/or field trips and failure to report is a two-way causation; failure to report can initiate action for the probation officers in the use of sending letters and making calls and field visits; and sending letters and making calls and field visits can initiate failure to report. I also concluded that more research, particularly using controlled experiments, were needed to analyze the importance of "failure to report" in probation supervision.[111]

Summary

We see that history repeats itself. Some of the criticism directed at jails and prisons today was heard during the nineteenth century: overcrowded conditions, lack of facilities, inhuman conditions, and protest, especially from female inmates. Although a cyclical pattern is evident, some conditions are more severe in certain periods than in others. For example, overcrowding in detention seems to be a pressing problem today. The North Facility in Riker's Island and the Brooklyn Correctional Facility in Brooklyn are the latest penal institutions opened to handle the overcrowding. Recently prison ships have been contemplated by the Correction Department to end prison overcrowding.

It can be seen that the detainee population surpasses the sentenced population by thousands. Much of the protest in prisons and jails of New York City involves being remanded before sentencing. Suggested reforms include shortening the detention period by providing alternative bail conditions and the use of such options as community service, restitution, intermittent incarceration, and state takeover of city jails.

We see that two philosophies, rehabilitation and custody, dominate correctional thought and actions. Reformers and liberals in state legislatures or in corrections, like Kross and Katherine Davis, have exerted great efforts at rehabilitation. Some of the reformers, like Kross, were instrumental in initiating reforms. For example, Kross succeeded in initiating the building of a new facility at Riker's Island for women, the NYCCIFW. She also was instrumental in initiating reform at the institution. Various women reformers were instrumental in gaining reforms for women way back in the 19th century.

The courts were also active in penal institutions. However, it is difficult to ascertain the effect the courts have had upon jails and prisons. Although some institutions are more open today, much of what takes place behind prison and jail walls remains hidden. Many conditions described in the literature probably still take place, including inmate beatings, poor food, poor medical attention, fights, stabbings, inadequate services, etc.

Relatively little literature exists on probation, parole, and other alternatives in New York City compared with the literature on jails and prisons. However, suggested reforms in these areas are state takeover of probation and parole, guidelines for parole, more determinate sentencing with the reduction of parole service, selection in probation supervision, and the elimination of the presentence function in probation. Community service is suggested as an alternative to probation. The coordination of various parts of the criminal justice system is recommended.

6

CONCLUSIONS

New York City is the largest city in the country. It stretches for miles. Its heterogeneous population of over eight million is so diverse, consisting of so many cultural and ethnic groups, that it is as large as many a small nation.

Many subjective elements enter into the criminal justice system. Critics of the justice system and those who attempt to run the various components of the justice system are often in conflict. Even within the system, judges, defense attorneys, prosecutors, probation officers, parole officers, counselors, and others are often in conflict about what is right and what is wrong with the justice system.

Take sentencing, for example. Many factors enter into sentencing. Long fixed sentences anger defense attorneys who constantly seek ways to secure lighter sentences for the clients. An indeterminate sentence might ease this problem because defense and prosecution might find agreement easier with a range of sentence time, a minimum and a maximum, then with a fixed sentence without hope of parole. But then many prosecutors believe that open ended sentences are not harsh enough. The judge's discretion, one day off of jail time for every three days served, parole, work-release, etc., – all are elements in the system that serve to mitigate sentencing and to appease certain groups.

Many critics believe that probation is a "slap on the wrist." Some critics state that probation is often little more than a superficial visit, and that the true activities of probationers are unknown to probation officers. Many probation cases are terminated because probation officers decide that they cannot work with their probationers any longer. Probationers can abscond and never be found. All these complaints have merit. However, supporters of probation claim that probation has great potential and that improvements in the supervision process can have beneficial effects. This certainly is true also. This same analysis applies to parole.

Most policemen are critical of the criminal justice system. They are the ones who make the arrests, and they constantly face danger and death. Every arrest is a cause for danger. But the police bring their own flaws into the system. In this analysis we found that some police are brutal and sadistic; many policemen are corrupt; many are not trained properly for some of the jobs they do; many white officers are bigots and most minority officers suffer the ongoing effects of discrimination; tension exists between the administrative bureaucracy and the street policemen. It is to be expected that many policemen will have different opinions how to handle different types of arrests.[1]

The public is divided on punishment. The layman does not really know the inside working of the criminal justice system. Surveys reveal that a certain percentage of the public is for this or that sentence, but this is a matter of degree. Some opt for severe penalties, while others support more lenient sentences; a sentence of 10 years is too soft to some but too harsh to others.[2]

The point is that opinion is varied. Opinions are not necessarily either or. Opinion on actions vary by degrees. This is especially true of criminal justice. Opinion among professionals varies on who is a criminal. Is a criminal one who is convicted? Is a criminal one who gets arrested regardless of conviction? Is a criminal anyone who commits a crime although he or she is never apprehended? This latter definition might include the majority of the population.

Values also enter into opinions in the criminal justice system. Some members of high socioeconomic classes find all types of criminality repugnant. Some crimes are committed by all socioeconomic classes. Street-crimes are committed by the lower socioeconomic classes. Homicide takes place more frequently among certain cultures in New York City because theoretically there exists a "subculture of violence" that condones certain types of violence. The members of the culture of violence do not necessarily consider violence "criminal," and they are willing to take the risk of punishment for their crimes. What is considered criminal to the larger society may not be considered criminal to members of this "subculture of violence." Some homicides on the street and in prison are examples of this type of violence.[3]

There is a diversity of values among critics of the criminal justice system. We found that reformers of prisons who opted for rehabilitation in prisons had a difficult fight on their hands. Reformers wanted improvements in prison, but these reformers fought for years and usually met with negative results for their efforts. For example, Kross, the commissioner of correction, fought for a new women's facility for years, beginning in the 1950s, but a new women's facility was not built until 1971. We also found that in spite of Attica and major riots in prisons in New York City in 1970, the custodial forces were stronger than the rehabilitative forces within the prisons hierarchy. In spite of interference by the courts, inmates are still subject to inhumane conditions in jails and prisons. What takes place in prisons, although more open, is still secretive, not revealed to the public.

Values will always enter into any criminal justice system. When higher, middle-class values are threatened, all potential resources are mobilized. This was true of some outstanding cases in New York City. This was true of the Bernhard Goetz case, concerning the white gunman who shot four black youths in the subway in December, 1984. The youths were trying to rob him, but Goetz shot without warning, and seriously paralyzed one youth and wounded three others.

This case resulted in nationwide opinion on the subject. The public was divided between those who thought Goetz was justified because he was a victim, and those who thought that he should be punished. The major point in this case was whether Goetz had a right to take the law into his own hands. Although Goetz was sentenced to six months in jail, five years probation with psychological counseling, community service, and a fine, the issue is still unsettled, and the public is still divided on the results of this case. When Goetz spent all his resources on legal fees, public donations poured in to help him. Many blacks were resentful of the outcome of the case. The victims are now suing Goetz for millions of dollars.[4]

Robert Chambers, a 19-year-old, upper-class, white offender, was accused of murdering Jennifer Levin, a 19-year-old waitress whom Chambers met in a bar. The couple apparently had sex in Central Park, where Levin's body was found the next day near the Metropolitan Museum of Art at 80th Street and 5th Avenue. Chambers served some remand time, but his family, who was well off, was able to bail him out after a couple of months. Letters addressed to the judge from the cardinal of the New York diocese and from other prominent people, asked that the court "go easy" on Chambers because of his impeccable character. Meanwhile, this district attorney uncovered the fact that Chambers was a suspect in some prior burglaries. On March 25, 1988, Chambers received 5 to 15 years prison.

Three black men were attacked by a gang of white youths in Howard Beach, Queens, a predominantly white area, on December 20, 1986. This incident took place in a pizza shop at 12 P.M. on a Saturday night. The blacks were threatened with bats and clubs, and one black man, Michael Griffith, ran out into the street and was killed by a passing automobile. The black lawyer, Mason, who represented the black men, was vociferous in yelling discrimination, and demanded a special prosecutor, a request which was granted. On January 21, 1988, one defendant received 10 to 30 years in prison; on February 5, 1988, a second defendant received 6 to 18 years in prison; on February 11, 1988, a third defendant received 5 to 15 years in prison; a fourth defendant was acquitted. At least eight others faced sentencing on lesser charges, and some did receive lesser sentences. There were many racial demonstrations prior to the sentencing of the youths.

Another example of a prominent case in New York City that also attracted national attention involved Bess Myerson, the former Miss America of 1945, who was head of the Cultural Affairs Department in New York City. She was accused of influencing a 74-year-old female judge to lower alimony payments for her racketeer boyfriend, who is now serving a prison sentence, and accused of obtaining a job for this judge's daughter as a reward for reducing alimony. Myerson, the female judge, and the boyfriend were all acquitted on the charges.

Mario Biaggi, a Bronx congressman, and Meade Esposito, an important political figure, were accused of bribery and other infamous acts while performing their duties. Some of the charges were reduced or dismissed, but Biaggi was sentenced to 30 months in jail and a $500,000 fine and Esposito was sentenced to two years probation and a $500,000 fine for accepting unlawful gratuities.

Certain Mafia members are always in the news but some manage to evade prison. If Mafia members are imprisoned, they seem to be able to take their time.[5]

Sometimes in prominent cases a lifetime of resources are expended to fight cases. Many street offenders do not have the resources to fight their cases. Many lower-class offenders obtain the services of Legal Aid defenders because they are unemployed and receive welfare. Practically all plead guilty in order to reduce their sentences. Defense attorneys very often serve the function of influencing these offenders to plead guilty whether or not they are guilty.[6]

These different actions by different classes of offenders involve different value systems. The Howard Beach Incident and the Bernhard Goetz case demonstrate that when racial issues are involved, total resources are mobilized to support certain value systems. The Bess Myerson and the Esposito and Biaggi cases involved white-collar crime, and the Robert Chambers case was a crime with a higher socioeconomic class offender. Other offenders, primarily from lower socioeconomic background, although they face years in prison, cannot fight their cases in that way, possibly due to the lack of resources and possibly due to the fact that they accept punishment as part of the price of committing a crime. An offender who commits serious assault under the rules of a subculture of violence knows that he might be punished for such a crime.[7] Again, values and subjective criteria enter into the criminal justice system.[8]

Criminal Justice in New York City

I have emphasized some important facets of the criminal justice system of New York City. Historical material on the police, the courts, and corrections has been presented. We see from this analysis that many of the problems that take place in criminal justice today are really old problems that have bothered critics for at least a hundred years or more. The police in New York City have always had to contend with a high amount of crime. Discrimination between white and black officers has always existed in the police force. Prosecutors always had to deal with high caseloads, and many decisions, particularly in misdemeanor offenses, were settled with assemblyline dispositions. Jails and prisons have always been crowded. Critics of punishment have always been divided between harsh and lenient punishment, with others in the middle. Punishment is not an either or phenomenon; it is more like a continuum, with various options open to the criminal justice agents.

There have always been defective practices in the criminal justice system of New York City. Corruption has always existed among the police of New York City. In spite of the Rankin Report and a campaign against police corruption in New York City in the 1970s, corruption among some police still exists today in New York City. There are all kinds of police. No one who is arrested knows what treatment to expect from the arresting police officer.

However, as pointed out, many officers risk their lives to help people. The same is true of correction officers. My empirical studies of inmate attitudes have demonstrated that some correction officers are humane and tolerant, and others are authoritarian and brutal. Therefore, the treatment an offender receives in jail and prison depends largely on the correction officer assigned to duty on the floor. This is also true of probation officers and parole officers. It is also true of prosecutors and judges. Many subjective elements enter into decisions made in criminal justice.

I have tried to demonstrate that reforms in criminal justice have been ongoing, with fits and starts, throughout New York City's history. For years, starting in the late 1800s, reformers have tried to mobilize political forces to improve conditions for female inmates. Females, as we have seen, have been treated inhumanely or harshly by male correction officers. For years, critics have fought for a new women's facility, and their wishes were finally met in 1932 and again in 1971. However, although there have been some improvements, critics demand more reforms. This was particularly true for the House of Detention for Women in Greenwich Village. Although not advertised in the media, the New York City Correctional Institution for Women at Riker's Island probably needs many improvements.

When the New York City Police Administration found that corruption was rampant among New York City police, an anticorruption campaign was immediately launched. Some police acted as informants on other police and serious corruption was eradicated. Many policemen were tried and convicted, and new rules were set forth to mitigate or eliminate corruption. Now supervisors in precincts have to be responsible for preventing corrupt practices among individual officers. Although all corruption has not been eliminated, officers are now more cautious and know that they can be brought up for charges for serious types of corruption.

The courts of New York City have always been a subject of reform. Politics and efficiency of operations have always been problems in the courts. Discrimination in sentencing has always been a problem. I have demonstrated how the MAP, the Master Calendar Project, was an attempt to reform the Manhattan Criminal Court in the early 1970s. MAP reforms reduced caseloads, saved court time, and expedited the flow of cases through the courts.

Policies to remove discrimination in hiring are considered reforms. The influx of minorities, women, blacks, and Hispanics have the function of reducing racial tensions in the city because now minorities have a chance to hold power. Female and black correction officers have taken their place in the prison system. This can have the effect of easing tensions in these institutions. Although there are still some problems between black and white officers within the police, this can be mitigated with the passing of time as more people begin to accept the value systems of minorities.[9]

The criminal justice system tries to remove deviant police officers. The mass media are quick to respond to incidents of unfair treatment. As we have already seen, there is a connection between the police and the mass media. When a white police officer shoots and kills a minority suspect, the media publicize this action and the public takes sides. The police administration is sensitive to public opinion. Many police officers are brought up on charges for these killings, even when they kill in the line of duty. Many minority groups demonstrate. No one knows for certain what took place. Although we saw that some police officers were exonerated of these charges, the suffering, the waiting, and the temporary suspension from the force of these officers are all forms of punishment.

Judges, prosecutors, and defense lawyers are subject to review by public opinion. We saw how many judges in the 1970s, particularly in Brooklyn, were indicted for showing favoritism to certain Mafia figures in sentencing. In the Larry Davis incident, concerning a black male who shot and injured several policemen and was a suspect in the murder of several drug dealers, the judge, who gave Davis probation for one of his prior offenses, resigned under the pressure of criticism about her choice of sentence. A judge in Brooklyn in the early 1980s resigned under pressure for imposing a lenient sentence on a female offender whom he had taken home with him because she had no place to go. Judges and prosecutors today must be very conscious not only of their colleagues, peers, and supervisors, but also of public opinion. This is not easy because public opinion is divided.[10]

Suggestions have been made for reform in the courts, probation, parole, sentencing, jails and prisons. For example, reformers want the state to take over probation and corrections. Critics have argued for the speedier disposition of cases because of the crowded conditions in jails and prisons. We saw that the greater proportion of inmates in jails are detainees. Mayor Koch has responded by building new facilities and by promising even more new facilities. Koch has also initiated a Civilian Review Board that now includes civilians as well as police officials to review civilian complaints against the police.

Certain individuals were also instrumental in initiating reforms. Police Commissioner Murphy was an example. Catherine Davis and Kross were other examples. Mayor Lindsay was conscious of police corruption and was partially responsible for the campaign against corruption. Other examples abound.

The point is that in spite of all the defects in the criminal justice system in New York City, the system still survives. Public opinion and periodic reform continue to improve the criminal justice system.

Although many critics talk of a "breakdown" in criminal justice, no one has really defined what is meant by a breakdown. Is a breakdown the heavy processing of cases? Is a breakdown the lenient sentences for serious offenses? Is a breakdown the large number of criminal justice warrants? Is a breakdown associated with the inefficiency of the courts?

I define a breakdown in criminal justice as the cessation of functions or structures of one of the components of criminal justice. For example, if prosecutors do not process all defendants because of a lack of time or resources, this is a breakdown. If judges do not sentence everyone, for the same reasons, this is a breakdown. The fact that warrants are not processed is not a breakdown. If warrant officers make an attempt to trace warrants even when defendants get rearrested, this is not a breakdown because some attempt to clear warrants has been made. Very often defendants who get rearrested have one or more outstanding warrants.[11] It might not be worthwhile to spend time on warrants.

The cessation of structures can or cannot be considered a breakdown, depending upon whether or not the elimination of the structure would ensure more efficient operation in the system. For example, there is talk of eliminating arraignment and trial by jury for some offenses. Some critics believe that arraignment and the jury are unnecessary because other parts can take over these structures. Some talk about the elimination of parole. However, if one or more of these structures are unnecessary and they do not interfere with the operation of the courts, this should not be considered a breakdown; however, if they cease to function when needed, because of lack of resources, and if they interfere with our principles in criminal justice, then there is a breakdown.

The criminal justice system in New York City is functioning, in spite of its many defects. There has not been any cessation of structures or function

However, it may take great analytical ability to determine when the system breaks down. It must be reemphasized, as we have seen in this book, that the courts are considered a loose conglomeration of separate functioning parts that are informally held together by flexible norms and values. This might be another reason why the system does not break down.

Punishment of Offenders

Many critics believe that offenders generally are unpunished in New York City. They believe that probation is a "slap on the wrist." I believe that critics, laymen in particular, do not really understand the concept of punishment when they talk in this way.

Punishment really starts at the time that the offender is arrested. First, the way the police officer handles the situation can have punitive effects on the offender. Some policemen, as we discovered, are inhumane and use force when making an arrest. If an offender does not expect an arrest, this can affect them psychologically and possibly physically. Then there is the degrading process of "booking" in which an offender must go to the police station and answer all kinds of questions and be interrogated, sometimes in a nonroutine way. Very often an offender stays in the precinct all night before going to court. If the offender goes to court, he is again subject to the degrading process of appearing before a judge. If the offender is poor, as many are, he is assigned a Legal Aid lawyer or an 18-B lawyer.

The judge often determines what, if any, bail is imposed. If an offender cannot make bail, he is incarcerated at Riker's Island or in another detention facility until the next court date.

Often the offender has no time to tell relatives that he has been arrested.[12] Then there is the question of whether or not the offender receives the proper warnings under the Miranda Decision, that anything he says at the initial arrest will be used as evidence against him. Once an offender is incarcerated, it is difficult for the offender to obtain release.

We have seen that decisions depend a lot on which legal actors are assigned to a particular case. No offender knows at first which lawyer, prosecutor, or judge will be defending, prosecuting, or disposing of their case. Of course, in the case of a private attorney, the offender knows who their lawyer or defense attorney is, but even here the offender does not know exactly how their case will be defended.

Legal actors are often changed without notice. This is true of prosecutors, defense attorneys, and judges. This can have consequences for any particular case.

Before sentencing a probation officer will often interview an offender in remand or in the office if the offender is at liberty. The offender is then subjected to a variety of questions by the probation officer. We found that the probation officer has a lot of power in sentencing. The offender must make a favorable impression before their probation officer. We also discovered that the outcome of a probation interview depends a great deal upon which probation officer is assigned to the case.[13]

In court, the offender suffers impositions of other types. If he is in remand, he is brought into court in handcuffs by the court officer. He very often is not informed of what to say. This is true even if an offender is at liberty. There is often a language barrier between Spanish-speaking offenders and legal actors. Attorneys very often do not have the time to instruct offenders of the proper procedure in court. Defense attorneys often try to persuade the offender to plead guilty in order to avoid trial and to mitigate punishment through a reduction of charges. If an offender decides to plead not guilty, he incurs the chance of staying in remand a long time, sometimes a year or more.

If an offender is remanded, he suffers the consequences of all the impositions of a jail term. We saw that correction officers vary in the treatment of inmates. We saw how overcrowded conditions prevail in jail. We saw that sometimes offenders overstay in jail because of adjourned dates in court. We also saw that sometimes conditions in jails are inhumane and horrible, with improper medical help and food. There is also a chance that an offender can be an object of an assault or rape in jail. We also saw the danger of riots in jail or prison.

At sentencing, an offender has to face a particular judge. Very often an offender knows what to expect at sentencing because the prosecutor makes a sentencing recommendation which both the defense attorney and probation officer reiterate to the offender. The judge is bound to keep to the promised sentence recommended by the prosecutor because very often the judge confers with the prosecutor and defense attorney on the type of sentence. It is primarily when prosecutors do not make a sentencing recommendation or when their sentencing recommendations are loosely constructed that the probation officer's recommendation has a lot of weight; this is when the offender is more uncertain of the sentence.

If an offender is placed on probation, in lieu of jail, or on parole, after serving part of his sentence, his fate often depends on the particular probation and parole officer assigned to the case. The conditions of probation and parole are like a legal contract, and a probation or parole officer can violate the offender's supervision for various reasons, including failure to report a new arrest and lack of cooperation. We found that probation officers have a lot of power in the revocation process. This is also true of parole officers.

The point of this discussion is that the whole criminal justice system is pervaded with impositions. According to the labeling theory, an offender labeled "a criminal" will sometimes engage in criminal or deviant behavior because of the label of "criminal" imposed by the system. He is called an "offender," a "convict," a "criminal," and "dangerous," etc. Sometimes this label itself can cause the offender to think of himself as a criminal and can cause him to engage in criminal behavior. There is also the stigma of the label of a criminal, and sometimes this label is imposed for life. The offender sometimes suffers from discrimination in employment because of his criminal record.[14]

Although certain actions in criminal justice are predictable in a general way, nothing can be predicted with certainty in criminal justice. We know that certain serious offenders will be sentenced to prison because the law requires it, as in the case of murder, but even here there is uncertainty. Many murder charges are reduced to justifiable homicide or manslaughter or even assault, and often the offender receives probation instead of prison.

Nonserious offenders and misdemeanants generally receive probation. However, there is always uncertainty on things not going according to precedent or informal rules, and mistakes are sometimes made that have dire consequences for the offender. Offenders placed on probation have a lot of freedom to interpret the rules of probation, but no offender knows exactly when his or her supervision will be violated because of the whims of a particular probation officer.

We really do not know exactly how much an offender suffers when he or she goes through the system. The offender does not always show overt signs of suffering. The suffering can be internal. For some offenders jail and prison is an extension of life on the streets. Some offenders can definitely take jail and prison, but the effects on him or her can last for years. However, a white middle-class or upper-middle-class offender may have all kinds of physical and psychological problems in adjusting to jail or prison.

The courts, the jails, and the prisons are overwhelmingly busy. Most legal actors have too many cases. Very often offenders receive assembly-line justice in the disposition of their cases. Mistakes are made. Inexperienced personnel are now serving many offenders. It sometimes takes years to learn the job. The criminal population is not necessarily a statistically normal population, and often dispositions do not seem to make sense. For example, offenders with nonserious crimes are sometimes given long prison sentences because of complications no one really understands. However, it is possible for any type of sentence to be imposed. Appeals are infrequent and costly, and very few offenders appeal sentences. The results of sentencing appeals are usually disappointing to be offender.[15]

This does not mean that some offenders do not receive individual attention

in their cases. I have seen many probationers and offenders receive individual attention in the supervision process and in the presentencing process. A lot depends on the offender and the probation officer. The same is true of the individual attention given by defense attorneys, prosecutors, judges, and parole officers. There are certain Legal Aid lawyers, for example, who devote a lot of attention to each case.

Our criminal justice system is now overburdened. I believe that criminal justice jobs are more dangerous now than in the past. I believe that the introduction of crack in the last year is particularly responsible for this. Crack can make some people kill. Probationers, for example, seem more unruly and hostile than in the past. Due to excessive caseloads, it is difficult to find which district attorney or Legal Aid lawyer is assigned to a case. In the district attorneys' offices, numerous cases lie everywhere. Warrant squads have too many cases to process, and, therefore, many offenders slip by the system, although very often those who abscond get rearrested. Correction officers are so busy that visits by other legal actors are not serviced as well as expected. Very often legal actors shift responsibility to other legal actors, for example, judges to lawyers, lawyers to probation officers, etc. I believe that being a judge in criminal court is a very vulnerable position, and therefore, a judge earns the money he or she receives.[16] This is also true of other positions in the criminal justice system.

One of the assumptions of the criminal justice system is that the offender has free will in deciding his or her own fate. Offenders decide whether or not to commit crime. Offenders decide whether or not they will enter a drug program. Offenders decide to work or not work. Offenders decide to cooperate or not cooperate with their probation and parole officers.

But does an offender have free will to choose his sentencing disposition? Does he have free will to work when he has no job skills? This is a philosophical question but it is also an unsettled question.

The prior record and seriousness of offense are powerful predictors of an offender's fate. Offenders are given chances to negate a life of crime. Generally, first offenders with relatively nonserious crimes are given probation or even less as a sentence. It is expected that this type of offender will try to cooperate with the probation officer assigned to the case and do what he can to rehabilitate himself or herself. We saw that not all arrests while on probation result in a violation of probation. Therefore, a second offense, as long as it does not come under the Second Felony Offender Law, or is not a very serious felony, can mean that the offender is sometimes given more than one chance to improve himself or herself.

Charge reduction is based to a certain extent on mitigation of punishment. Offenders who return on a warrant sometimes, but not always, are not punished

for their warrants. This is another example of getting a second chance. Adjournments and jury trials are other mechanisms built into the criminal justice system to distribute justice to offenders; adjournments give offenders a chance to fight their cases, and jury trials can be favorable to the offender.[17] Indeterminate sentencing is based on individual treatment of offenders.

The fear that police are less responsive to crime in ghetto areas also holds no truth. I have seen police frequently in the Bronx, where I work. Hardly a few minutes pass by without seeing or hearing a police car. When residents of the Bronx and other black and Hispanic neighborhoods call the police, the police do respond, although they might take longer than the residents desire. Some residents, as we have seen, are satisfied with police services; others are not. Not seeing many police in areas can mean either that police are avoiding the area, or that crime is so minimal that police are not so necessary in these areas.

The fear that courts are more lenient to blacks and Hispanics who commit crimes against other blacks or Hispanics compared with blacks and Hispanics who commit crimes against whites bears no truth. Throughout the years I have seen black and Hispanic offenders who commit crimes against other blacks or Hispanics receive severe punishment. No empirical evidence proves that intraracial crime is taken less seriously than interracial crime. Intraracial crime is punished heavily in New York City, not because this type of crime receives attention, but because ethnicity is not an important factor at this time in New York City in criminal justice outcomes.[18]

The point of this whole discussion on punishment is that offenders run the risk of punishment from many different sources. It is rare that an offender will escape any form of punishment. It must be reemphasized that the labeling process itself is punitive.

One final word must be said about jails and prisons. Although many different types of reforms have been suggested and implemented in jails and prisons, I believe that critics of prisons have failed to take the criminal into consideration. Some of the most beautiful prisons have the worst prison systems. The physical structure as well as social and psychological improvements have an effect on prison, but the prison population itself is also important. We know that some criminal behavior is learned in prison and much criminal behavior follows the inmate from the outside. Prison will always be bad and somewhat inhumane because of the prison population itself.

Moreover, prisons must necessarily be cold, inhumane, and unsafe places. They always were. Very often, some prisoners received favorable treatment in prison, particularly if he paid for his keep, but prisons necessarily have negative aspects. Prison itself connotes punishment; there must be some punitive aspects to prison. A luxurious life in prison may not act as a deterrent.

Another point is that if jails or prisons were built on a hospital model, the criminal would have to be considered sick, and the medical model does not really apply to most inmates. This does not mean that the prison cannot change; change is always possible. But there must be some punitive or negative aspects of prison if it is to survive as a system of punishment through incapacitation.[19]

Crime in New York City

It has already been mentioned that New York City does not have the highest crime rate in the nation. However, what about the safety of New Yorkers in respect to crime? Truthfully, criminals are living among New Yorkers all the time. There are probably criminals of all types on the subways. But many, if not most, of these offenders are not particularly dangerous.

Dangerousness cannot be predicted one hundred percent. Many offenders who are paroled commit serious crimes, much to the surprise of the parole board and the parole officer. This happened recently when an offender was released from parole, stole a young female's car in New Jersey, murdered the young female, and drove the car to Florida.[20] However, a case such as this is unusual.

It must also be emphasized that there is a debate in the literature about whether or not crime is planned or occurs on the spur of the moment. For example, murders are classified into two types: one type is premeditated and planned in advance, for example, when the Mafia hire hitmen to kill an enemy; the other type is unplanned and occurs suddenly, as for example, when an offender and his victim are drinking and have a violent fight, or when the offender suffers a psychotic breakdown. However, some might question whether or not crimes of theft or robbery are planned in advance or occur suddenly when circumstances are right for it.

For example, let us take the case of Bernhard Goetz. Four black youths confronted Goetz on a subway one Sunday night about 7 P.M. in Manhattan. They were planning to rob him and Goetz shot them. However, did they plan to rob someone that night or did they just happen to decide this when the opportunity presented itself?[21] Some offenders, it is said, can unconsciously plan their crimes without being aware of it. Therefore, some say that offenders do not know when they will commit more crimes or get rearrested.

Economic theory can also apply to offenders. Some believe that offenders calculate the risks of committing criminal acts before engaging in crime. They take their chances when committing crimes. If they believe that the chances of getting arrested are minimal, then they commit their crimes. Sometimes the odds are unfavorable for them because the element of luck or surprise works against their chances of success.

The question of who is a criminal must be considered. It is said that almost everyone is a criminal to a certain extent. It is said that we all have done things which, if known to the legal authorities, could be considered criminal. Even self-reporting surveys among high school students reveal that almost everyone from all socioeconomic classes and from all ethnic groups have committed nonserious minor offenses as a youth for which they were not apprehended, usually shoplifting or petty theft. Most workers steal items from the work place, if only pencils, paper, stamps, etc., and many travelers steal towels from hotels. This analysis applies not only to New York City but throughout the nation.

Closing Remarks

In summary, several facts are worthy of emphasizing about criminal justice in New York City. First, after years of experience dealing with offenders, I believe that most or almost all offenders in New York City are not really dangerous. Take drugs, for example. Many offenders buy and sell drugs in their neighborhoods. Many areas in the Bronx are hangouts for drug sellers and users. A great many cases in our courts involve routine arrests over drugs. An offender sells drugs to a plainclothesman. The officer immediately gets a back-up team and arrests one or two offenders. The offender hardly resists and is arrested. If this is a second felony arrest for the offender, he or she is sentenced under the Second Felony Law of New York State to about two to four years prison. The offender generally is not dangerous to others.[22] Of course, if the drug offender robs other people to support his or her habit, this can be dangerous. Generally the chances are that this type of crime, namely, drug activities, is confined to the neighborhood where the drug activities are centered and usually is restricted there to the offender or to the addicts who purchase drugs. In my opinion, most offenders who engage in drug sales are eventually caught.[23]

It must be emphasized that the drug problem, especially among our youth, is a serious social problem. Although individual treatment works to some extent, some major social changes must be imposed in our society to affect change. Perhaps a campaign for jobs for drug users may be worthwhile. Perhaps a crackdown on drug hangouts and the elimination of these hangouts is necessary. Perhaps officials must apprehend drug addicts, users, and sellers and place them in special facilities. Perhaps the courts should not sentence drug users so harshly because many of these users might be more psychologically ill than suspected. Social changes must be implemented with individual treatment.

Or take welfare frauds. Many women commit this type of crime because they cannot make ends meet on welfare. They supplement their income while receiving welfare without reporting the extra income to the Welfare Department. However, they are not dangerous offenders.

Second, much crime in New York or elsewhere is intraracial. Many criminals commit crimes within their own neighborhoods. They assault their spouses or relatives; they steal from their own relatives or friends; they commit sexual offenses against their relatives and friends. This means that much crime is confined to certain neighborhoods, and if a New Yorker does not live or work in this particular neighborhood, he or she is safe to a certain extent.

Of course, this does not imply that this type of crime should be condoned. It simply means that crime is geographically concentrated. We saw that the police concentrate in certain areas where crime is rampant and the offenders are punished severely. We also discussed the subculture of violence where norms of criminal behavior are confined to certain cultural groups. Certainly the residents of these crime-infested neighborhoods deserve the fullest protection of the law; they very often are victims. The point is that crime is not geographically even in this city.

Third, generally I find that the subways are safe. I have no automobile and always ride the subways. First, policemen are on duty on subway cars from 8 P.M. Even in the daytime hours, transit police are nearby. This does not mean that subway crime does not exist; it does mean that subways are particularly effective in getting you where you want to go without being a victim of a crime.[24]

Fourth, offenders generally lead a crime-free life most of the time. This is generally true throughout our culture. If they commit one or two crimes—for example, drug sales or petty larceny—and are not caught, they generally lead a crime-free life the rest of the day. Of course, this situation only applies to some offenders; some are constantly engaged in crimes for which they are not apprehended. Sometimes relatives of offenders do not know about their criminal activities. The point is that even criminals do not engage in criminal activity constantly; much of their activities are crime-free.

Fifth, it appears that most New Yorkers are law-abiding citizens. We tend to emphasize criminals in certain neighborhoods, but we do not look at the thousands of citizens in certain ethnic neighborhoods who constantly work and lead law-abiding lives.[25] Many of these citizens live in bad neighborhoods because of their low socioeconomic status. They might live in a building that has drug sellers and buyers, but they themselves are model citizens.[26]

Sixth, it appears to me that the criminal justice system is operating in the best way it can. Although improvements can be made, and have been made, many criminals are apprehended, incapacitated, deterred, and rehabilitated. Some are not. In a city the size of New York, it is impossible to apprehend, punish, incapacitate, deter, and rehabilitate everyone. The police do the best they can. The citizens know the importance of the police in their neighborhood.[27] The courts and prisons seem to function in spite of defects.

To sum, in a city as large, populous, and diverse as New York City, there is bound to be some crime. However, many residents of New York City are affected psychologically by the news media when the media play up certain selected crimes. Very often citizens are frightened of the language and mannerisms of certain ethnic groups in public places. This does not mean that these groups are criminals.[28] On subways with law-abiding citizens there are probably some offenders who are wanted on a warrant or are on probation and parole or have served prison terms. However, they are not dangerous. This diversity is to be expected in a city like New York.

Seventh, I am impressed with the concern that citizens have with the crime problem and the institutions of our criminal justice system. Public opinion is important both in New York City and elsewhere in our society. The power of public opinion has not been researched thoroughly. This concern about crime can help to mitigate the effects of criminal activity.

NOTES

Chapter 1: New York City as a Case Study

1. David Neubauer, *Criminal Justice in Middle America* (Morristown, N.J.: General Learning Press, 1974).

2. Jonathan D. Casper, *American Criminal Justice: The Defendant's Perspective* (Englewood Cliffs, N.J.: Prentice-Hall, 1972).

3. James Eisenstein and Herbert Jacob, *Felony Justice: An Organizational Analysis of Criminal Courts* (Boston: Little, Brown, 1977).

4. Martin A. Levin, *Urban Politics and the Criminal Courts* (Chicago: University of Chicago Press, 1977).

5. Stuart Nagel, "Disparities in Criminal Procedures," *University of California Law Review* 14 (August 1964): 1271–1305.

6. James R. Davis, *The Science of Criminal Justice* (Jefferson, N.C.: McFarland, 1986).

7. I, of course, have not reviewed all the literature. However, based on my knowledge, I am unaware of an intensive study of the type done in this book.

8. Jails usually include offenders who are awaiting dispositions or short-term sentenced defendants (those sentenced to a maximum of one year). Prisons usually include defendants sentenced to long terms (over one year and up to life, including defendants waiting on death row). However, very often the terms are used interchangeably.

9. "Probation" is supervision in lieu of prison or jail; "parole" is supervision before the termination of a defendant's prison sentence.

10. Work-release programs in prison are those in which inmates are incarcerated at night and on weekends, but allowed to work outside of prison during the day under supervision of prison officials.

11. Kenneth Culp Davis, *Discretionary Justice: A Preliminary Inquiry* (Baton Rouge: Louisiana State University Press, 1969), 4.

12. Ibid., 5, 18.

13. See Arthur J. Rosett and Donald Cressey, *Justice by Consent* (Philadelphia: Lippincott, 1976).

14. See Abraham Blumberg, "The Practice of Law as a Confidence Game: Organizational Cooptation of a Profession," *Law and Society Review* 1 (June 1967): 15–39.

15. A "defendant" is one who has pleaded or has been found guilty, and an "offender" is one who may or may not be in the system but whose guilt has not been officially

141

established. These terms are used interchangeably in the literature, as they will be used
here.

16. Charles Silberman, *Criminal Violence, Criminal Justice* (New York: Random
House, 1978), 119.

17. Ibid., 120. Hispanics include Puerto Ricans and other Latin groups.

18. Robert Daley, *Target Blue: An Insider's View of the N.Y.P.D.* (New York: Delacorte
Press, 1971), 87.

19. Robert Fishman, *Criminal Recidivism in New York City: An Evaluation of the Impact of Rehabilitation and Diversion Services* (New York: Praeger, 1977), 2.

20. Peter L. Sissons, *The Hispanic Experience of Criminal Justice* (New York: Fordham
University Press, 1979), 32.

21. This might not be the complete story. It might be possible that the ethnic composition of offenders and victims is more equally distributed or even reversed for certain types
of crime — for example, prostitution, gambling, or organized crime. Perhaps there is ethnic
discrimination in criminal justice.

22. Fishman, *Criminal Recidivism*, 2.

23. Silberman, *Criminal Violence*, 120. The other percentages were combinations of
whites and other ethnic groups. Silberman does not give statistics on the white composition
of the prison population.

24. Sissons, *Hispanic Experience*, 20. However, as Sissons states, Puerto Ricans might
become the second largest group of new inmates in the near future.

25. William J. Vanden-Heuvel, "Crises in the Prisons: A Commitment to Change" (Annual report of the New York City Board of Corrections, 1971), 14; Patricia Zangrillo, "The
New York City Male Detention Population" (A report prepared by the New York City
Criminal Justice Agency, 1981), 3. I can verify this by my many years of experience with
inmates. This might also reflect the situation in a number of cities in the United States.

26. Daley, *Target Blue*, 88.

27. Hans Zeisel, *The Limits of Law Enforcement* (Chicago: University of Chicago Press,
1982), 15.

28. Daley, *Target Blue*, 446. It probably is still true today.

29. Ibid.

30. Ibid., 226.

31. Barbara Gelb, *Varnished Brass* (New York: G.P. Putnam, 1983), 202, 290.

32. Mark H. Moore, James Q. Wilson, and Ralph Gants, "Violent Attacks and Chronic
Offenders: A Proposal for Concentrating the Resources of New York's Criminal Justice
System on the 'Hard Core' of the Crime Problem" (A report prepared by the New York State
Commission on Management/Productivity in the Police Sector, February, 1978), 13. A
youthful offender in New York City is one who is between 16 and 19 years old at the time
of the crime who must also meet certain eligibility requirements. The conviction of a youthful
offender is expunged.

33. Barbara McEleney, *Correctional Reform in New York: The Rockefeller Years and
Beyond* (Lanham, Md.: University Press of America, 1985), 49.

34. Roy M. Goodman et al., "Recommendations: Criminal Justice" (A report prepared
by the New York State Charter Revision Commission, May 24, 1975), 3.

35. Dennis Jay Kenney, *Crime, Fear, and New York City's Subways: The Role of Citizen
Action* (New York: Praeger, 1987).

36. Silberman, *Criminal Violence*, 205.

37. Paul Chevigny, *Police Power: Police Abuses in New York City* (New York: Pantheon
Books, 1969), xi–xii.

38. Gelb, *Varnished Brass*, 92.

39. Ibid., 108.

40. Walter Arm, *The Policeman: An Inside Look at His Role in a Modern Society* (New York: E.P. Dutton, 1969), 42.

41. Gelb, *Varnished Brass*, 270.

42. Nicholas Alex, *New York Cops Talk Back: A Study of a Beleaguered Minority* (New York: Wiley, 1976), 39, 40, 43. The number of police who have a criminal record is probably very small.

43. Knapp Commission, *Report on Police Corruption* (New York: George Braziller, 1972), 209. Perhaps they were talking about anticorruption reforms.

44. Gelb, *Varnished Brass*, 14. It is possible to have contradictory statements about any structure of the criminal justice system.

45. Ibid., 26.

46. Ibid., 249.

47. William Fox and Noel Hynd, *The Cop and the Kid* (New York: Congdon and Weed, 1983), 109–110.

48. Gelb, *Varnished Brass*, 91.

49. Daley, *Target Blue*, 90. He means in restricting the use of force.

50. Gerard Astor, *The New York Cops: An Informal History* (New York: Charles Scribner, 1971), 224; Daley, *Target Blue*, 81.

51. Elizabeth Reuss-Ianni, *Two Cultures of Policemen: Street Cops and Management Cops* (New Brunswick, N.J.: Transaction Books, 1983), 32. It is a little difficult to verify the year as 1976; it could have been 1975.

52. Fox and Hynd, *The Cop and the Kid*, 86–87, 88–89. This might be the same incident referred to in fn. 51.

53. Alex, *New York Cops Talk Back*, 186–187; Daley, *Target Blue*, 71–72. Alex still does not state whether the 75 percent was city-wide or precinct-wide. It appears that it was city-wide.

54. George Rios, "Changes in the New York City House of Detention: Riots and Reactions, August-October, 1970–March, 1974" (Masters thesis, John Jay College of Criminal Justice, New York, June, 1974), 59.

55. Daley, *Target Blue*, 311. This number has probably increased today.

56. Ibid., 49.

57. Jack Newfield, *Cruel and Unusual Justice* (New York: Holt, Rinehart and Winston, 1974), 125; Zeisel, *The Limits of Law Enforcement*, 8, 97.

58. Fishman, *Criminal Recidivism*, 2.

59. Executive Advisory Committee on Sentencing, "Crime and Punishment in New York: An Inquiry into Sentencing and the Criminal Justice System" (A report prepared by the Executive Advisory Committee on Sentencing, New York, March 1979), 17.

60. Moore, Wilson, and Gants, "Violent Attacks," 9.

61. Howard T. Senzel, *Cases* (New York: Viking Press, 1982), 210.

62. Reuss-Ianni, *Two Cultures*, 93. Very often statistics on criminal justice inputs and outputs are contradictory and sometimes inaccurate.

63. Diane Steelman, "New York City Jail Crises: Causes, Costs, and Solutions" (A report prepared by the Correctional Association of New York, 1984), 10.

64. Arthur L. Liman, "Recommendations to the Governor Regarding the Administration of the Criminal Justice System" (A report prepared by the Executive Advisory Commission on the Administration of Justice, New York, 1982), 84.

65. Silberman, *Criminal Violence*, 219.

66. Herbert T. Klein, *The Police: Damned If They Do, Damned If They Don't* (New York: Crow, 1968), x.

67. Senzel, *Cases*, 121–122.

68. Gelb, *Varnished Brass*, 34.

69. Paul Hoffman, *Courthouse* (New York: Hawthorne Books, 1979), preface.

70. Ibid., 7. Each borough has its own criminal court. Courts must handle cases in the borough in which the crimes occur.

71. Ibid., 17.

72. James A. Harper, "The Controversy Underlying Prearraignment Processing in New York City" (Masters thesis, John Jay College of Criminal Justice, New York, September, 1980), 14. It is difficult to say if this is all of New York City. It probably is.

73. Rios, "Changes," 109. Again, it is difficult to say if this is Manhattan only, or all of New York City.

74. New York City Rand Corporation, "The Flow of Defendants through the New York City Criminal Courts in 1967" (A report prepared by the New York City Rand Institute, 1967), v. Again, it is difficult to say whether this is Manhattan only, or all five boroughs. It is probably all New York City.

75. Hoffman, *Courthouse*, 87.

76. Howard Shapiro et al., "The Criminal Justice System in the City of New York: An Overview" (A report prepared by the New York State Commission of Investigation, 1974), 3.

77. Ibid., 107; Hoffman, *Courthouse*, 34–35.

78. Silberman, *Criminal Violence*, 354.

79. Hoffman, *Courthouse*, 72. This figure might have increased in recent years. Also, many new facilities were opened during the last several years.

80. Newfield, *Cruel and Unusual Justice*, 25–26.

81. Ibid., 22.

82. Rios, "Changes," 96.

83. Vanden-Heuvel, "Crises in the Prisons," 10.

84. Newfield, *Cruel and Unusual Justice*, 125.

85. Vanden-Heuvel, "Crises in the Prisons," 41–42.

86. Zangrillo, "The New York City's Male Detention Population," 2, 3. However, many await longer periods. New York law requires a maximum of 90 days from arrest to sentencing.

87. Correctional Association of New York, "Do They Belong in Prison?: The Impact of New York's Mandatory Sentencing Laws" (A report prepared by the Correctional Association of New York, 1985), 13.

88. Liman, "Recommendations," 24; Executive Advisory Committee on Sentencing, "Crime and Punishment," 68.

89. Executive Advisory Committee on Sentencing, "Crime and Punishment," 191.

90. Ibid., 93. The number has probably increased over the 10-year period.

Chapter 2: Theoretical Perspectives

1. John Gage Allee, ed., *Webster's Dictionary* (Binghamton, N.Y.: Gould, 1972).

2. Jess Stein, *The Random House Dictionary* (New York: Ballantine, 1980).

3. Sometimes academics dispute what is or is not a theory. Very often critics claim that what scholars call theories are not really theories at all, since all the interrelations among variables have not been completely specified. I believe that the definition of a theory is somewhat subjective and, therefore, what constitutes a theory is somewhat subjective.

4. Sissons, *The Hispanic Experience*.

5. Marvin E. Wolfgang and Franco Ferracuti, *The Subculture of Violence: Toward an Integrated Theory in Criminology* (London: Tavistock, 1967).

6. James R. Davis, "Families of Probationers: How the Criminal Justice System Affects Families of Offenders Placed on Probation" (Paper presented at the fifty-fifth annual meeting of the Eastern Sociological Society, Philadelphia, 1985).

7. Silberman, *Criminal Violence*, 51.

8. Wolfgang and Ferracuti, *Subculture of Violence*, 189. However, as Wolfgang and Ferracuti point out, one study revealed that two-thirds of homicide offenders had prior police records and three-fourths of these offenders had prior records of aggravated assault. Perhaps they mean that these prior records were nonserious. As previously mentioned, criminal justice data are sometimes inconsistent.

9. Silberman, *Criminal Violence*, 75, 80, 81.

10. Correctional Association of New York, "Do They Belong in Prison?", 46.

11. Moore, Wilson, and Gants, "Violent Attacks," 21.

12. Chevigny, *Police Power*, 131, 132, 134, 137, 140, 150, 152. Chevigny was talking about the New York City police in the 1960s. It is difficult to say if this is true today or if this applies to jurisdictions outside of New York City. It was already mentioned that some believe that the police are less violent today than they were 20 or 30 years ago.

13. Silberman, *Criminal Violence*, 204.

14. Chevigny, *Police Power*, 279.

15. Gelb, *Varnished Brass*, 94.

16. Daley, *Target Blue*, 98.

17. Alex, *New York Cops Talk Back*, 205.

18. Ibid., 207. Alex is referring to changes in police use of firearms.

19. It is important to study police over time. I think that many people believe that the police have never changed, but this proposition has never been tested.

20. Silberman, *Criminal Violence*, 204, 245.

21. Ibid., 265.

22. Ibid., 266.

23. Ibid., 297.

24. Executive Advisory Committee on Sentencing, "Crime and Punishment," 166.

25. Ibid., 113; Chevigny, *Police Power*, 250.

26. Silberman, *Criminal Violence*, 237.

27. Ibid., 298.

28. Ibid., 311.

29. Daley, *Target Blue*, 27.

Chapter 3: The Police of New York City

1. Astor, *The New York Cops*.

2. Eric Fishman, "New York City Criminal Justice System: 1895–1932" (Ph.D. diss., Columbia University, New York City, 1980), 47.

3. Ibid., 102.

4. Ibid., 312.

5. Ibid., Abstract.

6. Astor, *The New York Cops*, 122.

7. Allan N. Kornblum, *The Moral Hazards: Police Strategy for Honesty and Ethical Behavior* (Lexington, Mass.: Lexington Books, 1976), xix.

8. Steven Leinen, *Black Police, White Society* (New York: New York University Press, 1984), 8, 10, 13, 14, 22, 29, 31, 32, 51.

9. James I. Alexander, *Blue Coats, Black Skin: The Black Experience in the New York City Police Department since 1894* (Hicksville, N.Y.: Exposition Press, 1978), xiii–xiv.

10. Ibid.

11. Clarice Feinman, *Women in the Criminal Justice System* (New York: Praeger, 1980), 67, 69, 70, 76, 77, 79.

12. Reuss-Ianni, *Two Cultures*.

13. Silberman, *Criminal Violence*, 243–244.

14. Gene Radano, *Walking the Beat: A New York Policeman Tells What It's Like on His Side of the Law* (New York: World, 1968), 123.

15. Gelb, *Varnished Brass*, 18–19.

16. Daley, *Target Blue*, 57.

17. Ibid., 68.

18. Astor, *The New York Cops*, 185, 187. Whether this was true or not is another matter. The point is that the police might have acted on rumor, whether true or not.

19. Silberman, *Criminal Violence*, 452.

20. Chevigny, *Police Power*, 24, 26, 29, 48, 61, 72, 92, 98, 99, 103, 114, 121, 141, 153, 183, 205, 208, 231, 246.

21. Gelb, *Varnished Brass*, 91, 92, 95–96.

22. Daley, *Target Blue*, 485, 491, 494, 524; Alex, *New York Cops Talk Back*, 68.

23. Leinen, *Black Police, White Society*, 237.

24. Fox and Hynd, *The Cop and the Kid*, 16.

25. Daley, *Target Blue*, 24.

26. Robert Curvin and Bruce Porter, *Blackout Looting: New York City, July 13, 1977* (New York: Gardner, 1979), 79.

27. Daley, *Target Blue*, 98.

28. Ibid., 99.

29. Reuss-Ianni, *Two Cultures*, 47, 48, 53.

30. Ibid., 75, 76, 87.

31. Harper, "The Controversy Underlying Prearraignment," 49.

32. Alex, *New York Cops Talk Back*, 179.

33. Senzel, *Cases*, 233. However, it is unknown if this is still true today.

34. Klein, *The Police: Damned If They Do, Damned If They Don't*, 191. It is unknown if this is still true today; probably it is.

35. Reuss-Ianni, *Two Cultures*, 87.

36. Gelb, *Varnished Brass*, 249. Some of these suspensions were for corruption.

37. Reuss-Ianni, *Two Cultures*, 96, 111.

38. Alex, *New York Cops Talk Back*, 14, 20, 26, 56, 206.

39. Ibid., 127–128, 129, 132.

40. Ibid., 169, 214.

41. Arm, *The Policeman*, 56, 64, 77.

42. Paul Chevigny, *Cops and Rebels: A Study of Provocation* (New York: Pantheon Books, 1972), 47.

43. Senzel, *Cases*, 233.

44. Klein, *The Police*, 54. Whether this is still true today is unknown.

45. Goodman et al., "Recommendations," 14, 15.

46. Gelb, *Varnished Brass*, 226.

47. Ibid., 200–201.

48. Daley, *Target Blue*, 93. This is in conflict with Gelb, who states that 10 police were killed in 1971; see note 47.

49. Alex, *New York Cops Talk Back*, 151.

50. Klein, *The Police*, ix.

51. Wolfgang and Ferracuti, *Subculture of Violence*, 302.

52. Chevigny, *Police Power*, 132.

53. Leinen, *Black Police, White Society*, 20–21.

54. Daley, *Target Blue*, 184.

55. Clarice Feinman, "A History of the Treatment of Women Incarcerated in New York City, 1932–1976" (Ph.D. diss., New York University, 1976), 151.

56. Kornblum, *Moral Hazards*, 128.

57. Reuss-Ianni, *Two Cultures*, 100, 101, 102.

58. Alex, *New York Cops Talk Back*, 117.

59. Arm, *The Policeman*, 154.

60. Goodman et al., "Recommendations," 14, 15.

61. Curvin and Porter, *Blackout Looting*, 112, 168; Reuss-Ianni, *Two Cultures*, 116–118.

62. Chevigny, *Police Power*, xviii, 115, 285, 287.

63. Gelb, *Varnished Brass*, 258–260. The case of Thomas Ryan is probably the same case that Reuss-Ianni talks about, but she names the police officer in question "Kelly," perhaps a nickname. See note 29.

64. Alex, *New York Cops Talk Back*, 79.

65. Klein, *The Police*, 207. This might not be true today. The literature states that some black policemen have a difficult time in black neighborhoods because blacks expect lenient treatment from black officers.

66. Arm, *The Policeman*, 128.

67. Algernon D. Black, *The People and the Police* (New York: McGraw Hill, 1968), v.

68. Chevigny, *Police Power*, 105, 106.

69. Alex, *New York Cops Talk Back*, 76.

70. Black, *The People and the Police*, 74, 94, 95, 100, 101, 109.

71. Reuss-Ianni, *Two Cultures*, 105.

72. Leinen, *Black Police, White Society*, 238.

73. Annual Report of the New York City Police Department, "Civilian Complaint Review Board," 1986. It is believed, however, that this legislation has passed.

74. Knapp Commission, *Report on Police Corruption*, Foreword, I, 1, 14–15, 35–36, 39.

75. Daley, *Target Blue*, 131, 322.

76. Kornblum, *Moral Hazards*, 8, 79, 109, 111.

77. Astor, *The New York Cops*, 162, 165.

78. Eric Fishman, "New York City Criminal Justice System," 63.

79. Daley, *Target Blue*, 336.

80. Knapp Commission, *Report on Police Corruption*, 2, 4, 65, 83, 133, 163, 166, 168, 170, 181, 184; Daley, *Target Blue*, 279.

81. Knapp Commission, *Report on Police Corruption*, 18, 147–148.

82. Daley, *Target Blue*, 30.

83. Knapp Commission, *Report on Police Corruption*, 3, 6, 9, 13, 42, 45, 47, 55, 59, 61.

84. Alex, *New York Cops Talk Back*, 89, 110, 115.

85. Knapp Commission, *Report on Police Corruption*, 76, 87, 107, 193–194, 195, 221, 230, 252.

86. Newfield, *Cruel and Unusual Justice*, 146; Kornblum, *Moral Hazards*, 1, 6, 118.

87. Kornblum, *Moral Hazards*, 125–126.

88. Daley, *Target Blue*, 336, 353.

89. Ibid., 161.

90. Reuss-Ianni, *Two Cultures*, 80–81, 85.

91. Knapp Commission, *Report on Police Corruption*, 20, 90, 114, 148, 150, 236, 239. It is unknown if these departmental regulations are still in effect, since they go back to the early 1970s.

92. Hoffman, *Courthouse*, 51. Of course, gambling is now legalized in New York to a certain extent.

93. Alex, *New York Cops Talk Back*, 104. There is some truth in this. Corruption was publicized and prosecuted in the mid–1980s in reference to the parking violations and in reference to other government agencies.

94. Annual Report of the New York City Police Department, 1.

95. Gelb, *Varnished Brass*, 302. Even today, there is some evidence of police corruption in narcotics, but this is rare.

96. Leinen, *Black Police, White Society*, 1, 2, 30, 33, 39, 51, 62, 68, 79, 81, 85, 91, 100, 110, 124, 127, 163, 167, 168, 169, 175, 183, 197, 212, 223, 233.

97. Reuss-Ianni, *Two Cultures*, 6.

98. Alex, *New York Cops Talk Back*, 1–2, 5, 6, 9, 31, 34, 150, 152, 154, 157, 159–160, 161, 164, 166, 167. This study was done in the 1970s; things might be different now.

99. Klein, *The Police*, 207. See note 65.

100. Gelb, *Varnished Brass*, 127.

101. See Davis, *The Science of Criminal Justice*, 28, 29, 30, 31; Arthur Niederhoffer, *Beyond the Shield: Police in Urban Society* (Garden City, N.Y.: Doubleday, 1967).

102. Davis, *The Science of Criminal Justice*, 31; John H. McNamara, "Uncertainties in Police Work: The Relevance of Police Recruits' Backgrounds and Training," in David Bordua, ed., *The Police: Six Sociological Essays* (New York: Wiley, 1967), 181–249.

103. Leinen, *Black Police, White Society*, 20.

104. Fox and Hynd, *The Cop and the Kid*, 44–45, 54.

105. Daley, *Target Blue*, 18.

106. Alex, *New York Cops Talk Back*, 20, 26, 40.

107. Bernard Cohen and Jan M. Chaiken, *Police Background Characteristics and Performance* (Lexington, Mass.: Lexington Press, 1973).

108. Ibid.

109. James R. Davis, "The Arrest Process: The Interaction of the Defendant, the Complainant, and the Police" (Paper presented at the fifty-third annual meeting of the Eastern Sociological Society, Baltimore, 1983).

110. James R. Davis, "A Comparison of Attitudes toward the New York City Police" (Paper presented at the thirty-eighth annual meeting of the American Society of Criminology, Atlanta, 1986).

111. The concept of rationalization is used in the Weberian sense.

Chapter 4: The Courts of New York City

1. Eisenstein and Jacob, *Felony Justice*, 9–10, 15–16, 28; Davis, *The Science of Criminal Justice*, 42–43.

2. Lawrence B. Mohr, "Organizations, Decisions, and Courts," *Law and Society Review* 10 (Summer 1976): 621–642; Davis, *The Science of Criminal Justice*, 43.

3. Joseph Hoane, "Strategems and Values: An Analysis of Plea Bargaining in an Urban Court" (Ph.D. diss., New York University, 1978); Davis, *The Science of Criminal Justice*, 43.

4. Roberta Rovner-Pieczenik, *The Criminal Court: How It Works* (Lexington, Mass.: Lexington Books, 1978), xiii, 2–4, and "Urban Justice: Understanding the Adjudication of Felony Cases in an Urban Court" (Ph.D. diss., New York University, 1974), 39–40, 202; Davis, *The Science of Criminal Justice*, 44.

5. Malcolm M. Feeley, *The Process Is the Punishment* (New York: Russell Sage Foundation, 1979), 16, 18; Davis, *The Science of Criminal Justice*, 44.

6. This is based on my perceptions; I have been in the court system as a probation officer and researcher for over 20 years.

7. Davis, *The Science of Criminal Justice*, 46–47, 52–67.

8. Eric Fishman, "New York City Criminal Justice System."

9. Executive Advisory Committee on Sentencing, "Crime and Punishment," 7.

10. McEleney, *Correctional Reform*, 9.

11. Silberman, *Criminal, Violence, Criminal Justice*, 348, 349, 353–354, 357.

12. Newfield, *Cruel and Unusual Justice*, 49. However, juveniles have certain rights to-day, e.g., legal counsel.

13. Silberman, *Criminal Violence, Criminal Justice*, 312, 326, 334, 345. Some of this might have changed in the last decade.

14. Hoffman, *Courthouse*, 7.

15. Ibid.

16. Harper, "The Controversy Underlying Pre-Arraignment Processing." It is still believed that prefelony screening takes place in New York City.

17. New York City Rand Institute, "Flow of Defendants," 2, 19–20.

18. Hoffman, *Courthouse*, 92.

19. Newfield, *Cruel and Unusual Justice*, 105–106.

20. Zeisel, *The Limits of Law Enforcement*, 49, 214.

21. S. Andrew Schaffer, *Bail and Parole Jumping in Manhattan* (New York: Vera Institute of Justice, August, 1970).

22. Senzel, *Cases*, 7, 17.

23. Chevigny, *Police Power*, 113.

24. Hoffman, *Courthouse*, 15. This probation officer, who works in the Bronx, notices that in some cases different prosecutors are assigned to the same case.

25. Executive Advisory Committee on Sentencing, "Crime and Punishment," 17, 166.

26. Hoffman, *Courthouse*, 117.

27. Zeisel, *The Limits of Law Enforcement*, 236.

28. Silberman, *Criminal Violence, Criminal Justice*, 265, 282.

29. Executive Advisory Committee on Sentencing, "Crime and Punishment," 29.

30. Ibid., 147.

31. Zeisel, *The Limits of Law Enforcement*, 120, 127.

32. Shapiro et al., "The Criminal Justice System," 44.

33. Harrison Tweed, *The Legal Aid Society, New York City: 1876–1951* (New York: The Legal Aid Society, 1954), 91.

34. Hoffman, *Courthouse*, 22.

35. Newfield, *Cruel and Unusual Justice*, 81.

36. Chevigny, *Police Power*, 252. Whether this is true today is uncertain.

37. James R. Davis, *The Sentencing Dispositions of New York City Lower Court Criminal Judges* (Washington, D.C.: University Press of America, 1982), 149, 152.

38. Robert Fishman, "New York City Criminal Justice System," 10.

39. Ibtihaj Arafat and Kathleen McCaherty, "The Relation between Lawyers and Their Clients," in Robert M. Rich, ed., *Essays in the Theory and Practice of Criminal Justice*, (Washington, D.C.: University Press of America, 1978), 194–214.

40. Silberman, *Criminal Violence, Criminal Justice*, 261, 291, 297.

41. Robert Fishman, *Criminal Recidivism*, 67.

42. Gelb, *Varnished Brass* 122.

43. Hoffman, *Courthouse*, 20.

44. Ibid., 87.

45. Sisenro, *The Hispanic Experience*, vii.

46. Newfield, *Cruel, and Unusual Justice*, xii–xiii.

47. Ibid., 83, 95. However, some members of the Mafiosa are incarcerated at greater rates and for longer periods today than in the past. Judges today receive a lot of negative feedback from the public.

48. Ibid., 98, 101–102, 105–106, 111.

49. Ibid., 112, 113, 115.

50. Ibid., 116.

51. Ibid.

52. Ibid., 133–134.

53. Ibid., 137, 138.

54. Ibid., 159, 160, 163–164.

55. Ibid., 164, 168. However, the literature pertaining to New York City is mixed concerning sentencing disparity for defendants represented by Legal Aid compared with defendants represented by private counsel.

56. Ibid., 178. This might have changed because of the new drug laws. However, this also reveals that the numbers in arrests are substantially reduced at the disposition stage.

57. Ibid., 180. This might be because judges are under great pressure. However, this does not condone the practice of name calling. This might have changed today.

58. Ibid., 180. The author does not mention controls for other variables in these examples.

59. Executive Advisory Committee on Sentencing, "Crime and Punishment in New York," 29.

60. Zeisel, The Limits of Law Enforcement, 134.

61. Executive Advisory Committee on Sentencing, "Crime and Punishment in New York," 43–44.

62. Ibid., 44–45.

63. Ibid., 100, 119.

64. Correctional Association of New York, "Do They Belong in Prison?", 7, 13.

65. Hoffman, Courthouse, 130.

66. Correctional Association of New York, "Do They Belong in Prison?", 34, 43.

67. Zeisel, The Limits of Law Enforcement, 19.

68. Senzel, Cases, 257.

69. Goodman et al., "Recommendations," 20.

70. Shapiro et al., "The Criminal Justice System in the City of New York," 3.

71. Ibid., 11, 44, 97, 107; Hoffman, Courthouse, 34–35.

72. Silberman, Criminal Violence, Criminal Justice, 261, 286.

73. Sissons, The Hispanic Experience, 10, 11, 14, 45, 47.

74. Newfield, Cruel and Unusual Justice, 164.

75. Curvin and Porter, Blackout Looting, 102, 106, 107, 108.

76. Executive Advisory Committee on Sentencing, "Crime and Punishment in New York," i, iv, viii, ix, xii, xiii, xvi, 3, 125.

77. Correctional Association of New York, "Do They Belong in Prison?", 43, 44, 45.

78. John B. Jennings, Evaluation of the Manhattan Criminal Courts: Master Calendar Project, Phase I, February–June 30, 1971 (New York: New York City Rand Institute, January, 1972), and Final Evaluation of the Manhattan Criminal Courts: Master Calendar Project (New York: New York City Rand Institute, November, 1973). These improvements are probably not in effect today.

79. Sissons, The Hispanic Experience, 10.

80. Goodman et al., "Recommendations," 23.

81. Liman, "Recommendations to the Governor," 16–17.

82. James R. Davis, "The Charging and Sentencing Dispositions of Prosecutors in New York City" (Paper presented at the thirty-fifth annual meeting of the American Society of Criminology, Denver, 1983).

83. James R. Davis, "The Charging Process, Felony or Misdemeanor?: An Analysis of Prosecutorial Discretion in New York City" (Paper presented at the twenty-ninth annual meeting of the New York State Sociological Association, Oswego, N.Y., 1981).

84. James R. Davis, "The Role of the Defense Attorney in a New York City Lower Criminal Court" (Unpublished paper, 1983).

85. Davis, *The Sentencing Dispositions of New York City Lower Court Criminal Judges*.

86. James R. Davis, "The Sentencing Dispositions of Prosecutors, Probation Officers, and Judges in a New York City Lower Criminal Court" (Paper presented at the seventy-fifth annual meeting of the American Sociological Association, New York, August, 1980).

87. James R. Davis, "Determinants of Length of Imprisonment in a New York City Lower Criminal Court" (Paper presented at the thirty-first annual meeting of the New York State Sociological Association, Potsdam, N.Y., 1983).

88. James R. Davis, "A Criminal Justice Model Using Multivariate Statistical Methods" (Paper presented at the eighty-second annual meeting of the American Sociological Association, Chicago, August, 1987).

Chapter 5: Corrections in New York City

1. The Municipal Library in downtown Manhattan probably has some documents that portray the history of corrections in New York City. However, I did not believe that the amount of time and work required to gather such information would be worthwhile, since the focus of this book is on contemporary analysis. Also, the results of such a search might have been disappointing. However, I did search the documents at the Municipal Library and did find and include some sources obtained there in this book.

2. Hoffman, *Courthouse*, 88. It must be re-emphasized that jails generally contain presentence inmates and prisons contain sentenced inmates; however, as pointed out in chapter 1, some sentenced inmates serving short-term sentences of up to one year can do their sentenced time in jails rather than in prisons.

3. McEleney, *Correctional Reform in New York*, 60, 62.

4. Bellinda Rodgers McCarthy, *Easy Time: Female Inmates in Temporary Release* (Lexington, Mass.: Lexington Books, 1979), 15.

5. Feinman, *Imprisoned Women*, 8.

6. Charles Sutton, *The New York Tombs* (Montclair, N.J.: Patterson-Smith, 1973), vi. It must be remembered that each borough in New York City was like a separate city until the consolidation of the five boroughs in the early 1900s.

7. Ibid., ix, 168.

8. Ibid., 50.

9. Ibid., 189.

10. McEleney, *Correctional Reform in New York*, 127.

11. Thomas Mott Osborne, *Within Prison Walls* (Montclair, N.J.: Patterson-Smith, 1969), 135, 144.

12. The history of women's prisons is taken from Feinman, *Imprisoned Women*, and from *Women in the Criminal Justice System*, 53.

13. Fox and Hynd, *The Cop and the Kid*, 157.

14. Silberman, *Criminal Violence, Criminal Justice*, 326. Whether this has changed or not is unknown.

15. Newfield, *Cruel and Unusual Justice*, 44, 45.

16. Silberman, *Criminal Violence, Criminal Justice*, 328.

17. McEleney, *Correctional Reform in New York*, 56. This could include both sentenced and unsentenced inmates.

18. Sissons, *The Hispanic Experience*, 20.

19. Ibid., 21; Cathy Potler, "Women Prisoners at Bayview: A Neglected Population" (A report prepared by the Correctional Association of New York, 1985), 1.

20. Sissons, *The Hispanic Experience*, 17.

21. Ibid., 21, 23.

22. Ibid., 17, 20.

23. Ibid., 24, 26–27.

24. Newfield, *Cruel and Unusual Justice*, 53–54, 60, Whether this is true today is speculative, since this was applicable to the early 1970s.

25. Executive Advisory Committee on Sentencing, "Crime and Punishment in New York," 68, 70, 75; Feinman, *Imprisoned Women*, 308.

26. Correctional Association of New York, "Do They Belong in Prison?", 13, 43.

27. Liman, "Recommendations to the Governor," 24.

28. McEleney, *Correctional Reform in New York*, 25.

29. Silberman, *Criminal Violence, Criminal Justice*, 120. This might contradict the statements made by Sissons that the Puerto Ricans are becoming the second most prevalent ethnic force in the New York state prisons.

30. McEleney, *Correctional Reform in New York*, 137.

31. Silberman, *Criminal Violence, Criminal Justice*, 67, 193, 377, 406.

32. Hoffman, *Courthouse*, 72. Trials can simply mean hearings, not necessarily jury trials.

33. Newfield, *Cruel and Unusual Justice*, 125.

34. Rios, "Changes in the New York City House of Detention," 8, 9. It is assumed that all rates are daily rates; Rios does not always specify.

35. Ibid., 35.

36. Ibid., 108.

37. Gerald N. Lynch et al., "A Report by the Committee on Jail Overcrowding" (New York: John Jay College of Criminal Justice, 1982), 15, 24.

38. Vander-Heuvel, "Crisis in the Prisons," 41–42.

39. Steelman, "New York City Jail Crisis," 1–2, 7, 10.

40. Ibid., 13.

41. Ibid., 21.

42. Zangrillo, "The New York City Male Detention Population;" Vanden-Heuvel, "Crisis in the Prisons," 14, 25.

43. Edward V. Regan, "New York City Department of Correction: Inmate Release Recordkeeping" (A report prepared by the Office of the State Controller, Albany, N.Y., 1984).

44. Newfield, *Cruel and Unusual Justice*, 18, 21.

45. Ibid., 22, 25–26.

46. Rios, "Changes in the New York City House of Detention," 96.

47. Newfield, *Cruel and Unusual Justice*, 25, 27, 28.

48. Ibid., 29, 30. This might refer to the guards who had beaten the inmates during the riots of the 1970s.

49. McEleney, *Correctional Reform in New York*, 143. These disciplinary proceedings include both state and city statistics, not just New York City statistics.

50. Rios, "Changes in the New York City House of Detention," 44, 45, 46.

51. Ibid., 46.

52. Ibid., 46, 47–48.

53. Ibid., 83.

54. Peter S. Williams, "A Profile of New York City Inmates Utilizing the Minnesota Multiphasic Personality Inventory" (Masters thesis, John Jay College of Criminal Justice, New York, September, 1976).

55. New York City Criminal Justice Agency, "Inmate Misbehavior: A Description of Events Reported in the Institutions of New York City Department of Correction, October 1,

1977 to March 31, 1979" (A report prepared by the New York City Criminal Justice Agency, February, 1980).

56. Jean Yaremchuk and Floyd Schwartz, "Predicting Infractions: Risk Screening for Classification, Final Report," New York City Department of Correction, 1984. This might be the same data and study explained in note 55.

57. Michael Young, "When Inmates Infract and When to Classify" (A report prepared by the Department of Correction, New York City, September, 1986). This might be the same data and study conducted by Yaremchuk and Schwartz; see note 56. However, different conclusions were reached. This might also be the same study and data explained in note 55.

58. McEleney, *Correctional Reform in New York City*, 144.

59. Rios, "Changes in the New York City House of Detention," Abstract, 144.

60. Vanden-Heuvel, "Crisis in the Prisons," 14, 15, 28.

61. Ibid., 31.

62. Steelman, "New York City Jail Crisis," 1, 19.

63. Newfield, *Cruel and Unusual Justice*, 24.

64. Ibid., 37, 40, 43.

65. Feinman, *Imprisoned Women*, 1–2, 146, 150, 154, 165, 166, 167, 172, 218, 222, 227, 251, 260, 283, 285, 289, 291–292. The Women's Facility at Rikers now houses some male inmates.

66. Feinman, *Women in the Criminal Justice System*, 51.

67. Potler, "Women's Prisoners at Bayview."

68. McEleney, *Correctional Reform in New York*, 80–81.

69. Newfield, *Cruel and Unusual Justice*, 3, 5, 6, 7, 10, 11, 14, 15.

70. Rios, "Changes in the New York City House of Detention," 49, 50.

71. Newfield, *Cruel and Unusual Justice*, 66, 67–68.

72. McEleney, *Correctional Reform in New York*, 80–81.

73. Rios, "Changes in the New York City House of Detention," 39, 43.

74. Ibid., 52, 54, 56.

75. Ibid., 57–58.

76. Ibid., 92–93.

77. Feinman, *Imprisoned Women*, 258.

78. Vanden-Heuvel, "Crisis in the Prisons," 31.

79. Executive Advisory Committee on Sentencing, "Crime and Punishment in New York," 93. This figure is probably much higher now.

80. Ibid., 93, 96, 99, 100.

81. Beatrice Burg, "A Study of Practice Orientation and Practice Behavior in the New York City Department of Probation" (Master's thesis, John Jay College of Criminal Justice, New York City, January, 1977).

82. Lynch et al., "Report by the Committee on Jail Overcrowding," 11, 12, 13. Now each probation officer in intensive supervision has 30 cases.

83. Shapiro et al., "The Criminal Justice System in the City of New York," 128.

84. Silberman, *Criminal Violence, Criminal Justice*, 296.

85. Executive Advisory Committee on Sentencing, "Crime and Punishment in New York," 58.

86. Ibid., 81.

87. Ibid., 83–84.

88. Ibid., 191.

89. Ibid., 89.

90. Walter Collier et al., "An Analysis of Parole Use by Decision-Making Guidelines in New York State" (A report prepared by the New York State Division of Parole, Albany, N.Y., March, 1982).

91. Sissons, *The Hispanic Experience*, 14. This, however, is subject to empirical proof.

92. Robert Fishman, *Criminal Recidivism*, xvi, 3, 11, 15, 20, 23–24, 27, 54–55, 151, 154, 157–158.

93. McEleney, *Correctional Reform in New York*, 49.

94. Lynch et al., "Report by the Committee on Jail Overcrowding," 13, 14.

95. Douglas Corry McDonald, *Punishment without Walls: Community Service Sentencing in New York City* (New Brunswick, N.J.: Rutgers University Press, 1986). This might be the same study discussed in note 94.

96. McEleney, *Correctional Reform in New York*, 34, 60, 75, 77, 91–92, 100, 103, 109, 126, 140–141.

97. Ibid., 46, 64.

98. Ibid., 124.

99. McCarthy, *Easy Time*, 64.

100. Rios, "Changes in the New York City House of Detention," 90.

101. Lynch et al. "Report by the Committee on Jail Overcrowding," 3, 4, 5–6, 7, 10, 13–14, 15, 17–18, 20, 26, 28. Today, there are some defendants who only serve weekends in jail. These defendants have relatively small sentences, e.g., 30 to 60 days.

102. Vanden-Heuvel, "Crisis in the Prisons," 23.

103. Goodman et al., "Recommendations," 30–38.

104. Denis V. Curtis et al., "State Assumption of Court, Probation, and Collection Services in New York" (A report prepared by the Temporary Commission on City Finances, January, 1976), summary.

105. Executive Advisory Committee on Sentencing, "Crime and Punishment in New York," xiii, xv.

106. Curtis et al., "State Assumption of Court Probation," summary, 25.

107. James R. Davis, "Inmate Attitudes toward Their New York City Jail Experiences" (Paper presented at the fifty-second annual meeting of the Eastern Sociological Society, Philadelphia, 1982).

108. James R. Davis, "Prison Discipline: An Exploratory Study" (Paper presented at the thirty-sixth annual meeting of the American Society of Criminology, Cincinnati, 1984).

109. James R. Davis, "Determinants of Probation Officers' Recommendations for Termination of Probation" (Paper presented at the thirty-fourth annual meeting of the American Society of Criminology, Toronto, 1982).

110. James R. Davis, "An Analysis of Probation Supervision in New York City" (Paper presented at the thirty-seventh annual meeting of the American Society of Criminology, San Diego, 1985).

111. James R. Davis, "The Importance of 'Failure to Report' in Probation Supervision" (Paper presented at the twenty-fourth annual meeting of the Academy of Criminal Justice Sciences, St. Louis, 1987).

Chapter 6: Conclusions

1. I find this to be true in probation. I sometimes vary my techniques to suit the probationer. Many other probation officers have also varied their techniques in supervising their probationers.

2. This difference was evident in the case of Bernhard Goetz, the subway gunman who shot four youths in the subway in December, 1984. When Goetz was sentenced to six months of jail and five years probation, with 1,000 hours of community service and a $5,000 fine in October, 1987, the public varied on the appropriateness of the sentence. Some suggested many different sentences. Even though the victims were black, many blacks thought

that Goetz should have been given a dismissal in the case. This was also true of the Howard Beach case, in which a black man was killed trying to escape an angry crowd of whites on December 20, 1986. Three whites were sentenced to prison, up to a maximum of 30 years for one, and a couple of defendants were acquitted. Several more whites were sentenced to less serious dispositions. Still, the public was divided on the appropriateness of the sentences.

3. I have had at least two probationers in my caseload who died as a result of a stabbing and beating. In addition, one probationer was shot in the spine and remains paralyzed and another was hit in the head with a hammer and has been suffering disabling effects for a number of years.

4. Goetz was sentenced in October, 1987, but his six-month sentence was scheduled for February, 1988. This postponement was to enable Goetz's lawyer to appeal the sentence. Goetz's lawyer was beaten by unidentified assailants in front of his offices in the summer of 1987. On June 28, 1988, the appellate court repealed the six-month jail term, and ordered a resentencing. Goetz finally received a one-year jail term.

5. This might be because sometimes Mafia figures are given special consideration in prison. However, lately many Mafia members are sent to prison for long terms.

6. This does not imply that some lower-class offenders do not mobilize resources to fight their cases. I have seen many offenders from lower-class backgrounds who have mobilized resources from families and friends to fight their cases.

7. This does not mean that such an offender would not try to mitigate the harshness of any possible sentence that might be imposed.

8. I have seen even indigent offenders mobilize resources among friends and relatives. Some of these offenders and their families have spent their last dollar for private attorneys, but my guess is that these offenders would have received the same punishment with Legal Aid as with private attorneys. Again, values enter into decisions.

9. I have found that some female officers in prisons seem to be more humane and kind than some male officers. In the women's cells, female officers seem to be more considerate of inmate needs compared with male officers. This is also true of female court officers. Of course, types vary between both sexes. Part of the explanation might be the socializing role of females and part of the explanation might be the smaller number of female offenders in prison, although both sexes deal with male offenders.

10. Larry Davis was supervised by a female probation officer in the Bronx where I work. The Larry Davis case was scrutinized by Central Office. I as well as other probation officers have had cases which scrutinized by Central Office. The point is that even probation officers must be sensitive to public opinion and to the administration, because any case can be scrutinized to see if the probation officer was acting in the best interest of the community and to see if probationers who committed serious crimes were given violations of probation.

11. I was guilty of not defining "breakdown" in my book, *The Science of Criminal Justice*. There I suggested that the criminal justice system will never break down because there are no right or wrong answers to criminal justice decisions and because criminal justice has existed since the beginning of civilization.

12. Very often, I receive calls from relatives of offenders wanting to know where their sons and daughers are. I suggest the possibility that their sons and daughters have been arrested.

13. Most cases do not require a probation report. However, certain criteria are mandatory for a presentence report, e.g., disposition of probation, prison over one year, felonies, etc. However, sometimes a judge will informally bypass these criteria in order to speed up the sentencing process.

14. Very often the offender is issued a certificate of relief of disability to expunge any prior offense from the record and to help the offender obtain employment more easily.

15. I had a case of an offender who had appealed a long prison sentence and had received a shorter prison sentence because of the appeal. However, this is unusual. The offender had already been in prison for several years when he appealed.

16. I have been a probation officer for 20 years, and in the last two years have had some threatening probationers. Not only are many probationers hostile, but occasionally someone comes back and wants to know why I placed him in jail or prison. Occasionally an offender returns with hostile remarks. Sometimes probationers' relatives call us because the probationer is acting inappropriately or is threatening in the house, or because they want to evict the probationer. Very often these relatives believe that we are responsible for helping them. One probationer once told me that he was homeless and ready to do something drastic to his mother-in-law because she prevented him from seeing his daughter. He demanded that we help him. Several mothers of probationers have threatened probation officers for not getting their drug addict probationer into a drug program, even though the probationers had dropped out of the program. The relatives threatened to report us. Many probationers insist on minority-group probation officers. The point is that every probation officer is vulnerable today and has a dangerous, threatening job.

17. Generally, if an offender pleads not guilty or goes to trial, the outcome is more unfavorable to him or her. Only a minority of offenders take their cases to trial; most offenders plead guilty to a less serious charge than the original charge.

18. This is not to say that ethnic factors play no part in decisions; however, there is no proof that they are the decisive factor.

19. This is only my opinion. Again, some critics may not agree with me.

20. The victim was Lisa Ana O'Boyle. Her body was found in New Jersey on October 13, 1987. The offender was captured and remanded. He received a life sentence.

21. Some of the victims admitted that they had planned to rob Goetz. However, the question is still unanswered as to when the idea had occurred to them.

22. However, cocaine or crack, which is associated with many drug arrests, can cause a person to kill. Recently, two youths under 16 set a man ablaze while the latter was in his truck. The victim died. I suspect drug use. Recently, a 46-year-old, middle-class, white lawyer and his common-law wife were implicated in the death of their six-year-old adopted daughter. The lawyer admitted drug use. A baby was riddled with bullets from a machine gun in Brooklyn. The offender admitted taking cocaine.

23. I do not have any empirical proof of this, but this is based on my experience as a probation officer.

24. I believe that one has more to fear from subway breakdowns than from criminals in the subway.

25. I see hundreds of citizens in Hispanic and black neighborhoods coming from work every day. They are generally not engaged in any crime.

26. I was told many times by model citizens that their building is full of drugs and that they had contacted the landlord and had circulated petitions among the residents to remove the drug addicts and pushers.

27. In certain neighborhoods police are rarely seen, but this can be because crime is low in certain neighborhoods and police do not want to waste resources in neighborhoods in which they are not needed.

28. Very often some blacks and Hispanics stare at whites in subways or act loud or boisterous. This does not mean that they are criminals; it is just their mannerisms or customs.

BIBLIOGRAPHY

Alex, Nicholas. *New York Cops Talk Back: A Study of a Beleaguered Minority.* New York: Wiley, 1976.

Alexander, James I. *Blue Coats, Black Skin: The Black Experience in the New York City Police Department since 1894.* Hicksville, N.Y.: Exposition Press, 1978.

Allee, John Gage. *Webster's Dictionary.* Binghamton, N.Y.: Gould, 1972.

Annual Report of the New York City Police Department. "Civilian Complaint Review Board." New York City: New York Police Department, 1986.

Arafat, Obtihaj, and Kathleen McCaherty. "The Relation Between Lawyers and Their Clients." In *Essays in Theory and Practice of Criminal Justice,* edited by Robert M. Rich. Washington, D.C.: University Press of America, 1978, 194–214.

Arm, Walter. *The Policeman: An Inside Look at His Role in a Modern Society.* New York: E.P. Dutton, 1969.

Astor, Gerard. *The New York Cops: An Informal History.* New York: Charles Scribner, 1971.

Black, Algernon D. *The People and the Police.* New York: McGraw-Hill, 1968.

Blumberg, Abraham. "The Practice of Law as a Confidence Game: Organizational Cooptation of a Profession." *Law and Society Review* 1 (June 1967) 15–39.

Bordua, David, ed. *The Police: Six Sociological Essays.* New York: Wiley, 1967.

Burg, Beatrice. "A Study of Practice Orientation and Practice Behavior in the New York City Department of Probation." Masters thesis, John Jay College of Criminal Justice, New York City, January, 1977.

Casper, Jonathan D. *American Criminal Justice: The Defendant's Perspective.* Englewood Cliffs, N.J.: Prentice-Hall, 1972.

Chevigny, Paul. *Cops and Rebels: A Study of Provocation.* New York: Pantheon Books, 1972.
_____. *Police Power: Police Abuses in New York City.* New York: Pantheon Books, 1969.

Cohen, Bernard, and Jan M. Chaiken. *Police Background Characteristics and Performance.* Lexington, Mass.: Lexington Press, 1973.

Collier, Walter, et al. "An Analysis of Parole Use by Decision-Making Guidelines in New York State." A report prepared by the New York State Division of Parole. Albany, N.Y., New York State Division of Parole, March, 1982.

Correctional Association of New York. "Do They Belong in Prison?: The Impact of New York's Mandatory Sentencing Laws in the Administration of Justice." A report prepared by the Correctional Association of New York. New York, 1985.

Curtis, Denis V., et al. "State Assumption of Court Probation, and Collection Services in New York." A report prepared by the Temporary Commission on City Finances, New York, January, 1976.

Curvin, Robert, and Bruce Porter. *Blackout Looting: New York City, July 13, 1977.* New York: Gardner, 1979.

Daley, Robert. *Target Blue: An Insider's View of the N.Y.P.D.* New York: Delacorte Press, 1971.

Davis, James R. "An Analysis of Probation Supervision in New York City." Paper presented at the thirty-seventh annual meeting of the American Society of Criminology, San Diego, 1985.

————. "The Arrest Process: The Interaction of the Defendant, the Complainant, and the Police." Paper presented at the fifty-third annual meeting of the Eastern Sociological Society, Baltimore, 1983.

————. "The Charging and Sentencing Dispositions of Prosecutors in New York City." Paper presented at the thirty-fifth annual meeting of the American Society of Criminology, Denver, 1983.

————. "The Charging Process, Felony or Misdemeanor?: An Analysis of Prosecutorial Discretion in New York City." Paper presented at the twenty-ninth annual meeting of the New York State Sociological Association, Oswego, N.Y., 1981.

————. "A Comparison of Attitudes toward the New York City Police." Paper presented at the thirty-eighth annual meeting of the American Society of Criminology, Atlanta, 1986.

————. "A Criminal Justice Model Using Multivariate Statistical Methods." Paper presented at the eighty-second annual meeting of the American Sociological Association, Chicago, 1987.

————. "Determinants of Length of Imprisonment in a New York City Lower Criminal Court." Paper presented at the thirty-first annual meeting of the New York State Sociological Association, Potsdam, N.Y., 1983.

————. "Determinants of Probation Officers' Recommendations for Termination of Probation." Paper presented at the thirty-fourth annual meeting of the American Society of Criminology, Toronto, 1982.

————. "Families of Probationers: How the Criminal Justice System Affects Families of Offenders Placed on Probation." Paper presented at the fifty-fifth annual meeting of the Eastern Sociological Society, Philadelphia, 1985.

————. "The Importance of 'Failure to Report' in Probation Supervision." Paper presented at the twenty-fourth annual meeting of the Academy of Criminal Justice Sciences, St. Louis, 1987.

————. "Inmate Attitudes toward Their New York City Jail Experiences." Paper presented at the fifty-second annual meeting of the Eastern Sociological Society, Philadelphia, 1982.

————. "Prison Discipline: An Exploratory Study." Paper presented at the thirty-sixth annual meeting of the American Society of Criminology, Cincinnati, 1984.

————. "The Role of the Defense Attorney in a New York City Lower Criminal Court." Unpublished paper, 1983.

————. *The Science of Criminal Justice.* Jefferson, N.C.: McFarland, 1986.

————. *The Sentencing Dispositions of New York City Lower Court Criminal Judges.* Washington, D.C.: University Press of America, 1982.

————. "The Sentencing Dispositions of Prosecutors, Probation Officers, and Judges in a New York City Lower Criminal Court." Paper presented at the seventy-fifth annual meeting of the American Sociological Association, New York, 1980.

Davis, Kenneth Culp. *Discretionary Justice: A Preliminary Inquiry.* Baton Rouge: Louisiana State University Press, 1969.

Eisenstein, James, and Herbert Jacob. *Felony Justice: An Organizational Analysis of Criminal Courts.* Boston: Little, Brown, 1977.

Executive Advisory Committee on Sentencing. "Crime and Punishment in New York: An Inquiry into Sentencing and the Criminal Justice System." A report prepared by the Executive Advisory Committee on Sentencing. New York, March, 1979.

Feeley, Malcolm M. *The Process Is the Punishment.* New York: Russell Sage Foundation, 1979.

Feinman, Clarice. "Imprisoned Women: A History of the Treatment of Women Incarcerated in New York City, 1932–1976." Ph.D. diss., New York University, 1976.

_____. *Women in the Criminal Justice System.* New York: Praeger, 1980.

Fishman, Eric. "New York City Criminal Justice System: 1895–1932." Ph.D. diss., Columbia University, New York City, 1980.

Fishman, Robert. *Criminal Recidivism in New York City: An Evaluation of the Impact of Rehabilitation and Diversion Services.* New York: Praeger, 1977.

Fox, William, and Noel Hynd. *The Cop and the Kid.* New York: Congdon and Weed, 1983.

Gelb, Barbara. *Varnished Brass.* New York: G.P. Putnam, 1983.

Goodman, Roy M., et al. "Recommendations: Criminal Justice." A report prepared by the New York State Charter Revision Commission. New York, May 24, 1975.

Harper, James A. "The Controversy Underlying Pre-Arraignment Processing in New York City." Master's thesis, John Jay College of Criminal Justice, New York, 1980.

Hoane, Joseph. "Strategems and Values: An Analysis of Plea Bargaining in an Urban Court." Ph.D. diss., New York University, 1978.

Hoffman, Paul. *Courthouse.* New York: Hawthorne Books, 1979.

Jennings, John B. *Evaluation of the Manhattan Criminal Courts: Master Calendar Project, Phase I, February 1–June 30, 1971.* New York: New York City Rand Institute, January, 1972.

_____. *Final Evaluation of the Manhattan Criminal Courts: Master Calendar Project.* New York: New York City Rand Institute, November, 1973.

Kenney, Dennis Jay. *Crime, Fear, and New York City's Subways: The Role of Citizen Action.* New York: Praeger, 1987.

Klein, Herbert T. *The Police: Damned If They Do, Damned If They Don't.* New York: Crow, 1968.

Knapp Commission. *Report on Police Corruption.* New York: George Braziller, 1972.

Kornblum, Allan N. *The Moral Hazards: Police Strategy for Honesty and Ethical Behavior.* Lexington, Mass.: Lexington Books, 1976.

Leinen, Steven. *Black Police, White Society.* New York: New York University Press, 1984.

Levin, Martin A. *Urban Politics and the Criminal Courts.* Chicago: University of Chicago Press, 1977.

Liman, Arthur L. "Recommendations to the Governor Regarding the Administration of the Criminal Justice System." A report prepared by the Executive Advisory Commission on the Administration of Justice. Albany, New York, 1982.

Lynch, Gerard N., et al. "Report by the Committee on Jail Overcrowding." New York: John Jay College of Criminal Justice, 1982.

McCarthy, Belinda Rogers. *Easy Time: Female Inmates in Temporary Release.* Lexington, Mass.: Lexington Books, 1979.

McDonald, Douglas Corry. *Punishment Without Walls: Community Service Sentencing in New York City.* New Brunswick, N.J.: Rutgers University Press, 1986.

McEleney, Barbara Lavin. *Correctional Reform in New York: The Rockefeller Years and Beyond.* Lanham, Md.: University Press of America, 1985.

McNamara, John H. "Uncertainties in Police Work: The Relevance of Police Recruits' Backgrounds and Training." In *The Police: Six Sociological Essays,* edited by David Bordua, 181–249. New York: Wiley, 1967.

Mohr, Laurence B. "Organizations, Decisions, and Courts." *Law and Society Review* 10 (Summer 1976): 621–642.

Moore, Mark H., James Q. Wilson, and Ralph Gants. "Violent Attacks and Chronic Offenders: A Proposal for Concentrating the Resources of New York's Criminal Justice System on the 'Hard Core' of the Crime Problem." A report prepared by the New York State Commission on Management/Productivity in the Public Sector. Albany, N.Y., February, 1978.

Nagel, Stuart. "Disparities in Criminal Procedures." *University of California Law Review* 14 (August 1964): 1271–1305.

Neubauer, David. *Criminal Justice in Middle America.* Morristown, N.J.: General Learning Press, 1974.

Newfield, Jack. *Cruel and Unusual Justice.* New York: Holt, Rinehart and Winston, 1974.

New York City Criminal Justice Agency. "Inmate Misbehavior: A Description of Events Reported in the Institutions of New York City Department of Correction, October 1, 1977 to March 31, 1979." A report prepared by the New York City Criminal Justice Agency. New York, February, 1980.

New York City Rand Corporation. "The Flow of Defendants through the New York City Criminal Courts in 1967." A report prepared by the New York City Rand Institute. New York, 1967.

Niederhoffer, Arthur. *Beyond the Shield: Police in Urban Society.* Garden City, N.Y.: Doubleday, 1967.

Osborne, Thomas Mott. *Within Prison Walls.* Montclair, N.J.: Patterson-Smith, 1969.

Potler, Cathy. "Women's Prisoners at Bayview: A Neglected Population." A report prepared by the Correctional Association of New York. New York, 1985.

Radano, Gene. *Walking the Beat: A New York Policeman Tells What It's Like on His Side of the Law.* New York: World, 1968.

Regan, Edward V. "New York City Department of Correction: Inmate Release Bookkeeping." A report prepared by the Office of the State Controller. Albany, N.Y., 1984.

Reuss-Ianni, Elizabeth. *Two Cultures of Policemen: Street Cops and Management Cops.* New Brunswick, N.J.: Transaction Books, 1983.

Rich, Robert M., ed. *Essays in Theory and Practice of Criminal Justice.* Washington, D.C.: University Press of America, 1978.

Rios, George. "Changes in the New York City House of Detention: Riots and Reactions, August–October, 1970–March, 1974." Masters thesis, John Jay College of Criminal Justice, New York, June, 1974.

Rosett, Arthur J., and Donald Cressey. *Justice by Consent.* Philadelphia: Lippincott, 1976.

Rovner-Pieczenik, Roberta. *The Criminal Court: How It Works.* Lexington, Mass.: Lexington Books, 1978.

————. "Urban Justice: Understanding the Adjudication of Felony Cases in an Urban Court." Ph.D. diss., New York University, 1974.

Schaffer, S. Andrew. *Bail and Parole Jumping in Manhattan.* New York: Vera Institute of Justice, August, 1970.

Senzel, Howard T. *Cases.* New York: Viking Press, 1982.

Shapiro, Howard, et al. "The Criminal Justice System in the City of New York: An Overview." A report prepared by the New York State Commission of Investigation. New York, 1974.

Silberman, Charles. *Criminal Violence, Criminal Justice.* New York: Random House, 1978.

Sissons, Peter L. *The Hispanic Experience of Criminal Justice.* New York: Fordham University Press, 1979.

Steelman, Diane. "New York City Jail Crises: Causes, Costs, and Sanctions." A report prepared by the Correctional Association of New York. New York, 1984.

Stein, Jess, ed. *The Random House Dictionary.* Revised Edition. New York: Ballantine, 1980.

Sutton, Charles. *The New York Tombs.* Montclair, N.J.: Patterson-Smith, 1973.

Tweed, Harrison. *The Legal Aid Society, New York City: 1876–1951.* New York: Legal Aid Society, 1954.

Vanden-Heuvel, William J. "Crisis in the Prisons: A Commitment to Change." Annual report of the New York City Board of Corrections. New York, 1971.

Williams, Peter S. "A Profile of New York City Inmates Utilizing the Minnesota Multiphasic Personality Inventory." Masters thesis, John Jay College of Criminal Justice, New York, September, 1976.

Wolfgang, Marvin E., and Franco Ferracuti. *The Subculture of Violence: Toward an Integrated Theory in Criminology.* London: Tavistock, 1967.

Yaremchuk, Jean, and Floyd Schwartz. "Predicting Infractions: Risk Screening for Classification, Final Report." New York: New York City Department of Correction, 1984.

Young, Michael. "When Inmates Infract and When to Classify." A report prepared by the Department of Correction. New York, September, 1986.

Zangrillo, Patricia. "The New York City Male Detention Population." A report prepared by the New York City Criminal Justice Agency. New York, 1981.

Zeisel, Hans. *The Limits of Law Enforcement.* Chicago: University of Chicago Press, 1982.

AUTHOR INDEX

163

SUBJECT INDEX

165

tion 97, 107, 117, 124, 126; Greycourt
94, 95; guards 92, 96, 98, 104, 107–
108, 109, 129, 130, 133; House of
Detention for Women 94–98; House of
Refuge at Hudson 93; infractions 106–
107, 120–121; Jefferson Market Prison
93, 94; length of stay 14, 94, 96, 102,
103, 109; numbers incarcerated 14,
95, 96, 100, 102, 108, 109, 110, 111,
124, 129, 131; reforms 92–98, 105,
109, 116–119, 124, 126, 130, 131, 136;
riots 96, 107, 109, 110–112, 117; Sing-
Sing Prison 92; Spofford 98; suicides
14, 104; the Tombs 91–92, 107, 110–
111; treatment of female inmates 92–
98, 100, 108–109, 129; treatment of
male inmates 103–105, 119–121; see
also Jails and prisons, infractions
Juveniles 29, 68, 69–70; see also Jails
and prisons, Spofford; Theoretical
perspectives, juveniles

Legal defense: attitudes toward 76, 87;
function of 65, 75, 87, 128, 133; importance of 75–76

Methodology, of books 2
Myerson, Bess 128

Parole 82, 113–114, 116, 119, 124, 131,
133, 137
Police: arrests 12–13, 27, 29, 30, 39,
40, 59–60, 61; assaults upon and killings of 13, 29, 41–42; attitudes of 23,
33–34, 39, 41, 42, 50, 56, 125–126;
blackout–1977 43–44; blacks and
Hispanics 28–29, 30–33, 45, 51,
53–55, 58–59, 126, 129, 130, 136;
characteristics of 55–57, 58–59;
Civilian Review Board 45–46, 50; corruption 28, 29, 30, 33, 40, 47–50,
51, 52–53, 61, 126, 129, 130; punishment for 28, 29, 47, 50–51, 53, 129;
discretion 37–38; force and brutality,

12, 23, 28, 34, 38, 39, 40, 44–45,
62; Knapp Commission 47, 48, 49,
50, 51, 52; other civilian complaints
44, 49, 53, 57–59, 60–61; police-
women 33, 55; reforms 42, 47, 52,
130; reputation of 11–12; requirements
for joining 108, 109, 110; role 23, 41,
43, 55–56, 60–61; solidarity 34, 39,
41, 54, 61, 126; street cops versus
management cops 34, 61; strikes 12;
training 42, 56, 57– 59, 126
Probation: intensive 113; nature of 112,
125, 129, 132, 133, 135; numbers on
14, 112; termination 121–123, 125;
violations 4, 113, 123; project evaluation 114–115; Prosecution: factors in
decisions 85–87, 90; functions of 74,
133; reform 74; see also Criminal
justice, actors, plea bargaining, punishment; Theoretical perspectives

Sentencing: disparities 64–65, 77–78,
81, 90, 130; dispositions 76–77, 78,
79, 80, 81, 87–90; ethnicity 65, 77,
78–79, 81, 88–90; growth in prison
sentences 79–80; illegal sentences 78;
probation 7, 79, 81, 82, 133, 134,
135; reforms 9, 81–82, 119, 124,
131

Theoretical perspectives: conflict in Hispanic culture 16; conflict theory 15, 65;
counseling 22–23; definition 15; double standard 15–16, 136; Hispanic civil
law versus common law 16–17; Hispanic culture and family 17, 21–22;
Hispanic inmates 18–19, 99–101, 103;
Hispanic violence 17; juveniles 25; law
and social control 25; offenders
22–23, 135, 137, 139; subculture of
violence 19–21, 126, 128; victims
23–24; see also Victims

Victims 59, 66, 67, 69, 71, 74, 90; see
also Theoretical perspectives

DATE DUE REMINDER

Please do not remove
this date due slip.